CONTEXTS

Series Editor:

Steven Matthews
Oxford Brookes University, UK

Other titles in the series

Romantic Literature Jennifer Breen, University of North London, UK
and Mary Noble, Princeton University, USA
Victorian Fiction Gail Marshall, University of Leeds, UK
Renaissance Drama Andrew McRae, University of Exeter, UK
Modernism Steven Matthews, Oxford Brookes University, UK
Postmodern Literature Ian Gregson, University of Wales, Bangor, UK

THE LONG 18th CENTURY

PAUL BAINES

Senior Lecturer in English Literature, University of Liverpool

ARNOLD

A member of the Hodder Headline Group
LONDON
Distributed in the United States of America by
Oxford University Press Inc., New York

First published in Great Britain in 2004 by
Arnold, a member of the Hodder Headline Group,
338 Euston Road, London NW1 3BH

http://www.arnoldpublishers.com

Distributed in the United States of America by
Oxford University Press Inc.,
198 Madison Avenue, New York, NY10016

British Library Cataloguing in Publication Data
A catalogue record for this book is available from the British Library

Library of Congress Cataloging-in-Publication Data
A catalog record for this book is available from the Library of Congress

ISBN 0 340 81372 5

1 2 3 4 5 6 7 8 9 10

Typeset in 10 on 13 pt Sabon by Phoenix Photosetting, Chatham, Kent
Printed and bound in Great Britain by CPI, Bath

Contents

Series editor's preface

The plural in the title of this series, *Contexts*, is intentional. Literature, while it emerges from, and responds to, historical, social and cultural moments, also to a large extent establishes its own contexts, through the particular inflection it puts upon its ostensible 'materials', themes and preoccupations. Therefore, rather than offering a traditional 'major works/ historical background/ parallel discussion, each *Contexts* volume takes its instigation from the ways in which literary texts have defined their areas of reference, and in which they are in active dialogue with key cultural ideas and events of their time. What aspects of a period most concerned writers? What effect upon literary form have various social and cultural trends had? How have different texts responded to single historical events? How do different texts, ultimately, 'speak back' to their period?

Historical background is made readily available in each volume, but is always closely integrated within discussion of literary texts. As such, the narrative woven around each literary historical period in the individual volumes follows no uniform pattern, but reflects their particular author's sense of the ways in which the contexts of their period establish themselves – generically, thematically, or involving debates about language, gender, religion or social change, for example. While each volume provides detailed discussion of its period's most studied literary works, it also asks informed questions about the canon and periodization itself. Each volume also contains a timeline, full bibliography, and several contemporary literary, cultural, or historical documents which provide material for further reflection and discussion.

Steven Matthews

Preface

The 'long eighteenth century' presents particular problems of definition and scope. The phrase suggests that certain key features of eighteenth-century culture cannot be readily understood unless they are traced back into the seventeenth century; and it further implies that those same features exercise a determining influence over the period immediately following. At its widest, the long eighteenth century can last from the Civil War of the 1640s to the accession of Victoria in 1837: virtually two centuries, in fact, engulfing not only the Restoration but the Romantic period. A new category, the 'Long Restoration', appears to be emerging to claim definition for a stretch from 1650 to the 1730s. At the same time, Romanticism often appears to claim the territory of the mid-eighteenth century, at least in the dubious format of 'Pre-Romanticism', a term sometimes used to denote those poets emerging from the spell of Alexander Pope who do not quite summon the energy to become William Wordsworth. As with all attempts to demarcate literary history into convenient periods, the term 'long eighteenth century' involves some distortion and suppression. There are in reality no clean breaks and fewer epochal moments than is strictly convenient for the parcelling out of literary history: writers live through change and catastrophe and literary modes outlive their historical matrix. But 'the long eighteenth century' is, by virtue of its very vagueness and adaptability, more neutral and innocent than most such terms. Less thematically loaded than 'Romantic', 'Enlightenment' or 'Augustan', less narrow than 'Restoration', the term suggests that we always need to bear in mind the limits of our literary periods, and what lies across and outside them.

The *Contexts* series already has a volume covering Romantic literature, and therefore the coverage in the present volume goes no further than 1790.[1] This is also a reasonably convenient point in history to stop: the outbreak of the French Revolution in 1789, the dethroning and eventual execution of the French king, the reaction of British writers and politicians to the ideals of the revolutionaries and the decay of those ideals in the Terror, all belong with the story of Romanticism. If the execution of a king stands as one bookend to the period, it is reasonable to look to a comparable event to begin our version of the long century. The corresponding moment I have chosen is 1660, the Restoration of the exiled Charles II to the English throne. Charles I (his father) had been executed in 1649 and for the next eleven years England had been governed as an experimental republic under the leadership of Oliver Cromwell. The return of monarchy was as decisive a cultural moment as it is possible to imagine, and the effects on literature were both obvious and significant: though there were no more civil wars in England, there were several moments of deep political crisis, and the cultural reverberations of the debate on monarchy continued until the French Revolution polarized debate once more.

Within this 130-year span one might identify several sub-periods: the age of Dryden, the age of Pope, the age of Johnson, and so on; or one might divide it by the shifting sands of political organization. The idea of cutting the period into shorter chronological parcels would have the merit of treating an author's works more as a single unit, but a span of 20 or 30 years is not a context, it is a period, and it would be impractical to allot a particular contextual character to an essentially arbitrary chunk of time. It has been decided, therefore, to look at the writing of the period as a whole under eight different aspects: the situation of writers; religion; politics; town, country and nation; the wider world, concepts of selfhood; gender politics; and 'history' itself, meaning the sense of the past the literature embodies and feeds on. Several other areas could legitimately be suggested. Traditional treatments of 'backgrounds' to literature would devote more space to abstract philosophical and scientific ideas (here largely subsumed within the category of 'belief'), or to 'sister' arts such as painting, architecture or music, which scarcely feature here. Other books construe 'context' in a more literary way, treating the history of literature under generic rubrics such as satire, the novel, or panegyric. My choice has been to concentrate on those aspects of the world with which writers were most forcibly and productively engaged, in the belief that in this literary period, perhaps exceptionally, it is that kind of outward engagement that marks and structures the texts we read. Much of what we regard as culturally 'modern' could be said to have originated in the period: the division of labour, the growth of international capitalism, the development of party politics, the industrial revolution, new definitions of empirical science, a new sense of the individual self as politically and economically autonomous and psychologically deep. Other aspects present a history with which we are still dealing: the British Empire grew, and hit crisis in America; the slave trade was put on an institutional footing, and came under determined and successful fire from abolitionists. Writers are principal agents in many of these developments, and principal commentators in others. A new sense of a mass market in literature emerged, with a new class of author to supply the demand; women readers, and women writers, came into prominence.

Some writers with particularly wide interests, such as Johnson, inevitably appear in virtually every chapter; some texts, such as Milton's *Paradise Lost*, engage with several of these focused 'contexts' (it is religious; it is political; it presents an archetypal version of male–female relations). Some of the categories overlap: gender politics is quite closely linked with discussions of the patriarchal origin of government, and with ideas about the formation of selfhood. In the course of the book, however, there is a designed shift in chronological emphasis: the early chapters on religion and politics have centres of gravity much closer to the beginning of the period than the end, because that is where the main debates that set the agenda for the whole period were played out. The final chapter, in which the period's assessment of early history is examined, shifts from the appropriation of classic Greek and Roman culture by Milton and Pope to the proto-Romantic search for an early British native authenticity, leaving us on the verge of new literary interests. Alongside this there is a self-conscious shift from a male perspective (politics and religion constituting, officially at least, a male domain) to a female one: Johnson's literary history, through which the 'situations' of writers are initially viewed, is eventually supplanted, or supplemented, by that of Clara Reeve, which slants towards the female domain of romance.

This volume attempts a fairly thorough coverage in that it includes all the usual suspects of the academic literary canon, but also tries to give consideration to writers whose work is only gradually emerging into the light of critical attention (in the main, women writers). No attempt to apportion a strictly 'fair' amount of space is made: if anything, more attention is devoted to less familiar works, such as Manley's *Adventures of Rivella* (1714), than to obvious classics, such as Richardson's *Pamela* (1740). This is partly because *Pamela* has had the advantage of 250 years of continuous critical commentary, while *Rivella* was until recently scarcely known; but it is also because the collocation of (in terms of canonical acceptance) 'major' and 'minor' works is useful in pointing up the workings of particular historical contexts: why does one work become dominant while the other is marginalized? This method also has the effect of establishing a kind of contextual link between texts that might not otherwise be considered as having a connection, and thereby illuminating a wider context: *Rivella* and *Pamela* are both, for all their differences, meditations on gender politics, the power of sex, and the problematic identity of women who write.

Each chapter contains a document. We have, in order, a bookseller's contract, a letter from a scientist to a clergyman, a segment of a political essay, part of a report on agriculture, some clauses from an international peace treaty, a chapter from a philosophical treatise on human nature, an extract from an early feminist treatise, and part of a controversial argument about the interpretation of history which itself includes discussion of a newly discovered historical document. The documents all have some thematic relation to the context under discussion in the particular chapter. The extract from the treaty in Chapter 5, for example, is a clause from an agreement appended to the Treaty of Utrecht (1713) in which Britain is granted the 'asiento' for legal trade in slaves across the Atlantic. This shows with alarming clarity the methods by which European powers carved up the world and quite calmly disposed of hundreds of thousands of black Africans as if they were cattle, which in turn throws some light on those texts (like Behn's *Oroonoko* and Defoe's *Robinson Crusoe*) which deal with slavery and with the economic exploitation of colonies. The anthropological elements of those literary texts (the study of human differences) can also be traced in this official diplomatic prose. The documents are deliberately varied in character, as pointers to the variety of the external text-world ('contexts') of which literature forms a part. They are also selected to suggest that documentary reality, the textual residue of the real world, can be subject to the same kinds of critical reading as those texts we know as literary.

Note

1 Jennifer Breen and Mary Noble, *Romantic Literature* (London, 2002).

1

Situations

I do hereby promise to pay John Dryden, Esq., or order, on the 25th of March, 1699, the sum of two hundred and fifty guineas, in consideration of ten thousand verses, which the said John Dryden, Esq., is to deliver to me, Jacob Tonson, when finished, whereof seven thousand five hundred verses, more or less, are already in the said Jacob Tonson's possession. And I do hereby farther promise, and engage myself, to make up the said sum of two hundred and fifty guineas three hundred pounds sterling to the said John Dryden, Esq., his executors, administrators, or assigns, at the beginning of the second impression of the said ten thousand verses.

In witness whereof I have hereunto set my hand and seal,

this 20th day of March, 1698/9. **Jacob Tonson**

Sealed and delivered, being first duly stampt, pursuant to the acts of parliament for that purpose, in the presence of **Ben. Portlock**

Will. Congreve

March 24, 1698

Received then of Mr. Jacob Tonson the sum of two hundred sixty-eight pounds fifteen shillings, in pursuance of an agreement for ten thousand verses, to be delivered by me to the said Jacob Tonson, whereof I have already delivered to him about seven thousand five hundred, more or less; he the said Jacob Tonson being obliged to make up the foresaid sum of two hundred sixty-eight pounds fifteen shillings three hundred pounds at the beginning of the second impression of the foresaid ten thousand verses;

I say, received by me,

John Dryden

Witness, **Charles Dryden**

[Samuel Johnson, *Lives of the English Poets*, edited by George Birkbeck Hill, 3 vols (Oxford, 1905), I. 405–6][1]

This pair of documents gives an insight into the production of books in the late seventeenth century. Jacob Tonson (1656–1736) was the shrewdest publisher of the day, whose choices of author helped to construct the literary canon as we know it; John Dryden was the leading writer of that canon (one of the witnesses, Congreve, was another eminent poet). Tonson had been Dryden's main publisher for many years, a relationship that often nearly foundered over issues of money: Dryden stayed with him because the alternatives were, as he saw them, worse. In some ways this agreement is merely a formal recognition of a less formal arrangement that had been subsisting for some time: Tonson already has the majority of the verses he wants. And it appears to be quantity he is after: 250 guineas for 10,000 verses, or a guinea for 40 verses, roughly a shilling (5p) for every two lines, or sixpence (2.5p) a line. Nowhere does Tonson specify that the lines must be of sufficient quality, and neither writer nor publisher bothers to give a title to this work-in-progress. (In fact it became Dryden's *Fables Ancient and Modern*, a series of verse imitations and translations from Chaucer, Boccaccio and Ovid, published the year of his death, 1700.)

To some extent, the contract and receipt represent an exemplary moment in literary history: the point at which the exchange value of writing becomes particularly evident, a matter of production, sixpence a line. Though he often co-operated with other booksellers to share publication costs, Tonson was in effect a one-man publishing firm, sometimes known as a 'copyright-owning bookseller' as opposed to the proprietor of a bookshop; he was a member of the Stationers' Company, a guild that had been incorporated in 1557 as a trade monopoly with responsibility to monitor training and limit press activities. Its role in censorship had all but vanished, but its agency as a guarantor of copyright was confirmed by the first copyright statute of 1709 – a shift from political control to economic regulation not uncharacteristic of the period as a whole. Once bought, Dryden's work became Tonson's property: though there were at this time gestures towards a royalty system, notably in extra money for a second edition, in essence writers of this period sold their work outright, for a flat fee.

In 1696, just before this contract, Gregory King estimated that the average yearly income of a baronet was £880; of esquires, £450; of other gentlemen £280.[2] Dryden was thus earning himself roughly the equivalent of a gentleman's income for one year. The income of artisans, craftsmen and tradesmen was probably more like £40–£50 per year; the poorer branches of the clergy were earning about this also. A poetry book the size of the one proposed by Tonson normally cost about five shillings (25p), a sizeable proportion of the weekly income of anyone below the gentry. A novel might cost the same. Any book that cost ten shillings (50p) was an expensive book. Individual poems were normally published in grand formats, costing anything from sixpence to eighteen pence (2.5–7.5p), though these were often 'pirated' in unofficial cheap editions. Print runs were normally of the order of 1000 copies, giving some indication of the small size of the reading public.

Material conditions such as these were much in the minds of writers of the period. The Tonson–Dryden documents were first published in a biography of Dryden by Samuel Johnson (1709–84). Towards the end of his life, and the end of our period, Johnson agreed to contribute prefaces to a collected edition of English poets to be published by a large consortium of booksellers. The fifty-two prefaces that he provided became known collectively as *Lives of the English Poets*, though their proper title is *Prefaces Biographical and Critical* to the *Works of the English Poets*. They were published between 1779 and 1781 and form a fitting final literary monument for a writer who by the time of his death had become a kind of self-made national institution, and whose own 'literary life' would, seven years after his death, be embodied in the first truly modern biography, James Boswell's *Life of Samuel Johnson, LL.D.* (1791). These 'prefaces' contain Johnson's most careful literary criticism, but modern readers are often surprised by how much biographical material they contain. The quality and reliability of Johnson's research is unequal but it is usually not negligible, for Johnson was always convinced of the importance of the material reality of a writer's life, and few writers knew more about the effects of circumstance on writing than he.

The son of a provincial bookseller, Johnson had left Oxford University early, from financial or political difficulties, and had abandoned a mediocre career as a schoolteacher to try for a literary life in London. He worked as a journalist, reporting (and partly fabricating) parliamentary debates, as a miscellaneous essayist and reviewer, and as a translator. His poem *London* (1738), for which he received ten guineas, and which sold for a shilling (5p), brought him to the notice of the then leading poet, Alexander Pope (1688–1744), and he gradually achieved a certain eminence. In 1746 he was commissioned by a group of booksellers to produce a dictionary of the English language, an enormously laborious task, for which he was promised £1575. His *Plan of an English Dictionary* (1747) was dedicated to Lord Chesterfield, who as a noble patron was supposed to lend support of various kinds, financial and social. Chesterfield did almost nothing to help him. When the *Dictionary* appeared in 1755, after a belated attempt on Chesterfield's part to make up for this, Johnson wrote him a letter of dignified fury, denouncing his feeble patronage. This document is generally taken as the death knell of the idea of aristocratic patronage of the arts, though in fact it persisted for some decades after this. In 1759 Johnson published an 'Eastern tale', *Rasselas*, for which he was paid £100 (with a further £25 for the second edition; it sold for five shillings, 25p). He used the money to defray the expenses of his mother's funeral. In 1765 Johnson published, by subscription, an edition of Shakespeare. He was awarded an honorary doctorate and a state 'pension' for services to literature. When he died he was buried among the poets in Westminster Abbey.

Johnson's progress was scarcely the easy ascent to grace suggested by a bald career outline: he was never rich and his position was often complicated by political discomfort and strong personal conflicts. But no-one knew the material conditions of writing and publishing in eighteenth-century England better than Johnson. He had grown up in a bookshop, he understood the physical processes of book production, from paper to bookbinding, he knew how copyright law worked and how to draw up a contract. He also understood how hard writing was, what a precarious and laborious means of support it formed, and how prone writers were to social and psychological difficulties. The *Lives of the English Poets* constitute an insider's guide to literary life of the previous hundred years.

The series began with Abraham Cowley, but by the beginning of our period his working life was all but over (he died in 1667). The next poet in the series, however, was John Milton (1608–74), who had in 1660 the greatest of his poetic work ahead of him. He had been very active as a political writer on the parliamentary side during the Civil War and had acted as 'Latin Secretary' to the Council of State under the Protectorate; at the Restoration, having written a last-ditch attempt to defend parliamentary government against monarchy, he was arrested but released, apparently after intercession by other writers, such as Andrew Marvell (1621–78). He returned to poetry, burying his political views in the religious epics *Paradise Lost* (1667) and *Paradise Regained* (1671) and the biblical tragedy *Samson Agonistes* (1671). *Paradise Lost* was the single most influential poem of our period, and with hindsight dominates the literary landscape. But Johnson notes that it was no smash hit. Milton sold the copyright to Samuel Simmons for five pounds, their agreement stipulating that a further five would be paid when 1300 copies of the first edition had been sold. A further five pounds would be forthcoming upon similar sales of the second and third editions, none of which were to exceed 1500 copies. The second edition did not appear until 1674, the third not until 1678; Milton's widow sold her claim outright in 1680, after which the copyright was acquired by Jacob Tonson, who by means of a lavishly illustrated folio edition (1688) turned it into an eighteenth-century bestseller.

Johnson traces the publication history of the poem in some detail, because he has a case to make. 'The slow sale and tardy reputation of this poem have been always mentioned as evidences of neglected merit and of the uncertainty of literary fame', he writes (I.143). But Johnson sees this in the reconstructed context of book-trade history and a particular culture of readership:

> The sale, if it be considered, will justify the publick. [. . .] The call for books was not in Milton's age what it is at present. To read was not then a general amusement; neither traders nor often gentlemen thought themselves disgraced by ignorance. The women had not then aspired to literature, nor was every house supplied with a closet of knowledge. . . . of that middle race of students who read for pleasure or accomplishment and who buy the numerous products of modern typography, the number was then comparatively small. (I.143)

Johnson proves this assertion by pointing out how few editions of Shakespeare there had been between 1623 and 1664. He goes on:

> The sale of thirteen hundred copies in two years, in opposition to so much recent enmity and to a style of versification new to all and disgusting to many, was an uncommon example of the prevalence of genius. (I.144)

Furthermore, after the Revolution of 1688, when political change made Milton once more a hero, the reputation of his greatest poem was assured. Thus the greatest 'text' of our period can, perhaps must, be read in a complex 'context', made up of the writer's personality (to which, in Milton's case, Johnson was hostile), the political situation, the economics of authorship, publication and reading, and the changing parameters of literary history.

Milton represented the case of an author with moderate independent means, educated at Cambridge, who might easily have become a clergyman. But Johnson's authors come from a wide variety of backgrounds. Samuel Butler (1613–80) was the son of a farmer who received patronage from various court figures and wrote satire from a royalist position; Johnson tells his story as an archetypal one of disappointed hopes. Writing of the first part of *Hudibras*, Butler's satire against the religious wing of the parliamentary side, Johnson recounts:

> When it was known, it was necessarily admired; the king quoted, the courtiers studied, and the whole party of the royalists applauded it. Every eye watched for the golden shower which was to fall upon the author, who certainly was not without his part in the general expectation. (I.204).

But the expected reward, in Johnson's narrative, is perpetually delayed, and Butler dies in poverty. At the other end of the social scale stood aristocrats like John Wilmot, Earl of Rochester (1647–80), who wrote verse for private, non-economic circulation in manuscript. Rochester's life was a deliberate exercise in performed excess: he was a court figure who got away with bad behaviour of every imaginable kind, until disease killed him. Johnson is especially withering on the subject of a man who had the advantages of position, wealth and intelligence, and who threw them away.

> Thus in the course of drunken gaiety and gross sensuality, with intervals of study perhaps yet more criminal, with an avowed contempt of all decency and order, a total disregard to every moral, and a resolute denial of every religious obligation, he lived worthless and useless, and blazed out his youth and his health in lavish voluptuousness, till, at the age of one and thirty, he had exhausted the fund of life, and reduced himself to a state of weakness and decay. (I.221)

The return of the court in 1660 had entailed the return of court authors, the aristocrats whose writings had little to do with the marketplace and everything to do with an elite, scribal culture in which manuscripts were circulated amongst a high-class coterie as evidence of wit and learning. Johnson always had a special degree of contempt for those who engaged with the world from a position of power that they then abused, and his comments on aristocratic writers always bear in mind the advantages they are born to: the Earl of Dorset's works are 'the effusions of a man of wit', and no more (I.308). The tradition of the nobly born author, writing for his aristocratic peers and decidedly not for publication, persisted to the end of our period and beyond, though there is a noticeable falling-off of the breed during the eighteenth century; eight such figures were included in Johnson's series, the last of them, George Lord Lyttelton (1709–73) bringing the work to a close. For Johnson, aristocratic writers had too much protection from the world and too little need to cultivate their talents, or to engage a readership: Lyttelton's poems 'are the works of a man of literature and judgment, devoting part of his time to versification. They have nothing to be despised, and little to be admired'; one poem only 'contains much truth and much prudence, very elegantly and vigorously expressed, and shows a mind attentive to life, and a power of poetry which cultivation might have raised to excellence' (III.456–7).

Much more to Johnson's taste was the middling sort of writer: born to some position, some education and some money, but needing to engage with the world through a profession in order to build a career. One of his key cases was that of Dryden, from which we have already quoted. Dryden was born into a relatively well-to-do family with Puritan leanings and was educated at Westminster and then, like Milton, Cambridge where he attended Trinity College (1650–54). During the last years of the Commonwealth he worked, also like Milton, for the government. On the death of Oliver Cromwell in 1658 he wrote some impressive *Heroic Stanzas* in his memory, perhaps with less personal investment than Marvell's equivalent *A Poem upon the Death of his late Highness the Lord Protector*. But at the Restoration, unlike Milton, he quickly turned to the court, writing *Astraea Redux* to celebrate the return of Charles from exile. He was elected Fellow of the newly founded Royal Society in 1662, married a noblewoman in 1663, became Poet Laureate in 1668 and Historiographer Royal in 1670. He was, in many ways, the definitive state author; his *Annus Mirabilis*, on the Great Plague and the Great Fire of London (1665–6), was presented as a kind of state epic, with Charles again in heroic light, and his best-known poem, *Absalom and Achitophel* (1681) was written at the king's suggestion. When James II, a Roman Catholic, succeeded to the throne in 1685, Dryden became a Catholic, adhering to this faith when James departed the throne in 1688 to be replaced by the Protestant William of Orange and Queen Mary; he lost his state positions on this occasion. Just as Milton had fallen foul of a contrary regime, so Dryden found himself without state patronage.

Dryden, however, had maintained alongside his court position a successful career as a dramatist. In the seventeenth century, writing for the stage was the only effective means of making money from literature, partly through regular 'benefit nights', on which the takings went to the author, and partly through publication of the plays: Pope's line in *The Dunciad* about 'Genial *Jacob* [Tonson], or a warm third Day' refers to these twin possibilities. Dryden sought public favour and economic return in the most competitive of literary markets; he produced prose comedies, adaptations of Shakespeare for what conceived itself as a more sophisticated audience than Shakespeare's, and several 'heroic tragedies' in verse. He succeeded in both these aspects, not least because his published plays were often prefaced by skilful essays in literary criticism, giving the resulting texts a sheen of intellectual respectability and founding the practice of criticism in a wholly professional and authoritative context. Johnson positively declares that these essays (for which he had great respect) were supplied 'to increase the value of his copies' (I.366). After 1688, however, Dryden strove to enhance his income from non-theatrical writing, translating the Latin satires of Juvenal and Persius into English (1693) and producing an influential verse translation of Vergil's epic *Aeneid* and other works (1697). The latter appeared by subscription, a form of publishing in which pre-publication agreement to pay a certain amount for a book is secured from a number of purchasers, whose names are then listed at the front of the book. This had the advantage of offsetting the large investment costs of typesetting and printing associated with such major projects; and it further enabled the project to appear, to a degree, collaborative: the named purchasers were seen to be sharing in a kind of cultural project, to be supporting the arts in an act of dispersed patronage. Many of Dryden's individual works were dedicated to a noble patron, who would be expected to pay for the privilege. But whereas an aristocratic patron might once have funded, on a variable and uncertain basis, some kinds of literary production, with subscription publishing a much wider social range (including aristocrats but also gentry, professional men and indeed anyone who cared to pay a guinea or so) could participate in high-culture literary production. Neatly enough, the translation was still dedicated to patrons – indeed, there were three of them. Johnson remarks:

> In 1697 he published his version of the works of Virgil; and, that no opportunity of profit be lost, dedicated the *Pastorals* to the lord Clifford, the *Georgicks* to the earl of Chesterfield, and the *Eneid* to the earl of Mulgrave. This oeconomy of flattery, at once lavish and discreet, did not pass without observation. (I.387)

The deal netted Dryden some £1200, a stunning amount in 1697; the publisher was, naturally, Tonson, and the success of the venture led to the more fluid publishing agreement we have already examined.

It is therefore useful that Dryden's economic and political context varied so greatly over the course of his life. Johnson follows these aspects of Dryden's career attentively, and details Dryden's various quarrels with his fellow authors, most of whom were competitors or opponents on political grounds. But there is a strong economic thread to the narrative. Johnson suspects (rightly) that Dryden's salary as poet laureate was irregularly paid, and notes stories of other payments: for example, the Duchess of Ormond, wife of the dedicatee of the *Fables*, is supposed to have paid Dryden £500 for the book. He further calculates that since the *Fables* actually contained 'about twelve thousand verses', Tonson must have paid Dryden more than the £300 originally stipulated – though he also suspects that Tonson was a fairly ruthless employer. Dryden was, in Johnson's view, the supreme poet-critic represented in *The Works of the English Poets*, and it is noteworthy that his career represents so many different aspects of the profession in our period: state support, aristocratic patronage, cultural patronage, income from the theatre, professional literary criticism, and hard-nosed agreements with unyielding publishers.

Johnson's major contrast with Dryden is Alexander Pope, and in the biography of Pope, the biggest and in many ways the best of the set, he mounts a considered and subtle comparison between the two poets in terms of their works and critical attitudes. But the contextual contrast is also telling. Pope was born in 1688 into a Catholic family, and the course of his life was strongly influenced by his adherence to that faith in a strongly Protestant system. Unable to attend university, he educated himself by reading widely and by conversing with literary men such as the dramatist William Wycherley (1641–1715). In 1709 he published a set of *Pastorals* in a miscellany at the behest of Tonson, for which he received ten guineas; but his influential verse *Essay on Criticism* was published by a much lesser-known bookseller, William Lewis, and his hugely successful mock-heroic poem *The Rape of the Lock* was published by Tonson's rival Bernard Lintot, who paid him £7 and £15 for separate versions. Lintot also published Pope's *Windsor-Forest* (1713; 30 guineas). It was with Lintot that Pope struck the bargain of his life, a deal to translate the *Iliad* of Homer. Modelling the project on the Dryden–Tonson *Works of Virgil*, Pope managed to obtain particularly favourable terms from Lintot, who was anxious to appear a high-class publisher and to catch the commercial wave of interest in English translations of iconic classical writers. Pope and his friends were assiduous canvassers for subscriptions, and Johnson reports the result:

> The encouragement given to this translation, though report seems to have overrated it, was such as the world has not often seen. The subscribers were five hundred and seventy-five. The copies, for which subscriptions were given, were six hundred and fifty-four; and only six hundred and sixty were printed. For these copies Pope had nothing to pay; he therefore received, including the two hundred pounds a volume, five thousand three hundred and twenty pounds four shillings, without deduction, as the books were supplied by Lintot.

'By the success of his subscription', Johnson noted, 'Pope was relieved from those pecuniary necessities with which, notwithstanding his popularity, he had hitherto struggled.' Johnson records Pope's hostility to noble patrons like Lord Halifax and his principled refusal to call on such government support as he could muster for financial relief. Pope was thus the closest of all Johnson's literary ancestors to Johnson's own situation as a truly professional author, subsisting wholly by engagement with the marketplace.

The dedications of Pope's poems are normally to figures markedly less aristocratic than Dryden's; when Pope dedicates, it is usually a public gesture of friendship, between equals, rather than a covert appeal for funds. Pope could afford to do this because of astute management of his talent.

Though his family was well-off, Pope needed little parental finance; nor did he ever make money from the theatre, or from state patronage, or (to any extent) from noble patronage. His fortune was self-made, from poetry almost exclusively. His first published work had appeared in 1709, the year of the 'Copyright Act' that, for the first time, formally invested the ownership of copyright in the author of a text, rather than in the person of whoever published it. Though the implications of the Act took two generations to work out, Pope was unusually quick to spot the power it gave to authors, and once established he set about freeing himself from the dependence on publishers, setting up his own printer and booksellers and financing his publications himself. This gave him a quite unprecedented power over the content, appearance, timing and layout of his work and enabled him to comment with lofty authority on the travails of less successful writers toiling in the literary marketplace. His father had been a relatively solvent linen merchant; Pope was by some distance the most efficient literary 'merchant' of the period.

A much less successful literary merchant was Richard Savage (1697–1743), a disaster-prone writer whom Pope attempted without much success to help and with whom Johnson spent much time as a struggling writer in London. Savage claimed to be the illegitimate son of a union between the fourth Earl Rivers (whose name was Richard Savage) and Anne, Countess of Macclesfield; the claim has never been settled, but it has iconic use in rendering the impoverished writer as the illicit offspring of a decaying aristocratic system. Savage entered the theatre as actor and playwright, producing much run-of-the-mill work; he found himself a series of patrons, but quarrelled with all of them. His hopes of government support proved groundless. Savage was condemned to death after killing a man in a pub brawl in 1727, but was reprieved; he produced elaborate versions of his life-story in several poems (*The Bastard*, 1728, and *The Wanderer*, 1729, in particular). After failing to gain the post of Poet Laureate, he was awarded a pension by Queen Caroline and invested himself with the parodic role of 'Volunteer Laureate'. By this point he had also become acquainted with Pope, who used him as an informant in his war on literary enemies. Savage was a member of a large, indistinct group of writers who appeared to make some kind of living out of writing without ever producing anything very notable: Pope characterized these men as the 'Dunces' and their literary home as 'Grub Street', and Savage was able to supply him with sufficient inside knowledge to make Pope's satire *The Dunciad* an extremely well-informed and accurate (though tendentious) satire on professional writers. By the time Johnson met him, around 1737, Savage was in financial trouble, sponging ready money off acquaintances without much acknowledgement or gratitude, and his literary output was declining fast. As he was on the way down, Johnson was on the way up, and Johnson was evidently attracted by Savage's rebellious independence as much as he was intrigued by the self-destructive course this led the poet to take. In 1739 Savage was sent to Wales with money raised by Pope and others, but he was imprisoned for debt in Bristol in 1741 and died in prison there in 1743. Johnson produced a biography of Savage soon afterwards in a kind of testimony to the importance of Savage's example (he was paid 15 guineas, and worked fast). The size and intensity of the text (which was reprinted as part of the *Lives of the English Poets* series 37 years later) are out of all proportion to Savage's actual achievement as a writer. For Johnson he is a mythic type: at once a feckless, irresponsible Bohemian and the victim of social injustice. The story of his birth is accepted completely; his trial for murder is in effect a speech for the defence. On the other hand, Savage is let down by his lack of discipline, his 'entire subversion of all economy' (I.387) and an imagination which promises more than it can deliver. Johnson had shared Savage's hand-to-mouth existence in London, and had considerable sympathy for the struggles faced by the talented professional writer with the world against him; his account of Savage's inevitable decay into helpless and unhelpable alienation is both a warning to others and an example of a fate easily shared.

Johnson was himself renowned for helpfulness to other writers, especially at moments of economic stress; when his friend Oliver Goldsmith was under threat of arrest for debt, for example, Johnson arranged for the publication of his novel, *The Vicar of Wakefield* (1766), to provide funds for his release. Johnson's biographies offer a kind of harsh, knowing sympathy to each subject, and an unrivalled sense of the situations of writing – the 'contexts' that texts are produced by and engage with. As the chronological series of the *Lives* progresses, the subjects show a rather more settled relation to both political and economic circumstance. Many, like Johnson himself, came to London in search of a literary career, with mixed success: James Thomson (1700–48); William Collins (1720–59); David Mallet (1698–1765). A few, like William Shenstone (1714–63) had somewhat shaky independent means, and wrote from a position of semi-retirement in the country. One, Thomas Gray (1716–71) was an academic; others, such as Samuel Garth (1661–1719) and Mark Akenside (1721–70), were doctors. John Dyer (1699–1758) started out as a lawyer, became a painter, and ended up as a clergyman. Others, like Isaac Watts (1674–1748) were career clergymen who wrote in their spare time, or writers who took holy orders to stabilize their professional position, such as Edward Young (1681–1765). Of these, the most notable was Jonathan Swift (1667–1745), who maintained a solid if unrewarding career as Dean of St Patrick's in Dublin while devoting himself to anti-establishment satire of an exotic, anarchic and often filthy kind.

The *Lives* are not, of course, a complete guide to every possible form of writerly situation in the period. Only poets are included, so Johnson has nothing to say of those writers mainly eminent for drama, such as William Wycherley or William Congreve (1670–1729); he has, however, a life of Nicholas Rowe (1674–1718), a lawyer by training who decamped to the theatre and produced an edition of Shakespeare for Tonson in 1709. Matthew Prior (1664–1721), another inclusion, was a court figure employed as a state envoy; he wrote poems (for Tonson) as a sideline. His imprisonment on political grounds and subsequent release produced a two-guinea subscription edition of his poems, more or less as a vote of sympathy, which raised, according to Johnson, some 4000 guineas. Joseph Addison (1672–1719) was a poet and critic who later held state office. His associate Sir Richard Steele (1672–1729; not in the series) was a soldier before he was a journalist, dramatist and theatre manager; he later served as MP and was perennially investigating entrepreneurial get-rich-quick schemes, most of which failed. Writers such as Daniel Defoe (1660–1731), whose verse was a minor sideshow to his colossal output in journalism and fiction, do not get a look in (Defoe was a businessman and government spy as well as a writer). As a major player in the so-called 'Rise of the Novel', Defoe figures alongside Samuel Richardson (1689–1761), by profession a printer; Henry Fielding (1707–54), a lawyer by training and eventually a conscientious magistrate; Tobias Smollett (1721–71), trained as a doctor; and Laurence Sterne (1713–68), another clergyman. While aristocratic poets began to go out of fashion, Horace Walpole (1717–97), son of the political superman Sir Robert Walpole, had sufficient financial independence and status to launch a whole new genre, the 'gothic novel' in 1764.

Most male writers in the first half of our period thus had some profession other than writing which was their main initial support. Most had studied at either Oxford or Cambridge, then the only two universities in England, or at one of the Inns of Court, where legal training was given. Occasionally writers made it out of very 'low' situations: John Bunyan (1628–88) was a brazier by trade, but published for God rather than Mammon; Robert Dodsley (1703–64) started out as a footman (or minor servant), wrote poems about his 'station' (*Servitude*, 1729, and *The Muse in Livery* 1732) and became a dramatist and successful bookseller. Some had minor government positions; some wrote propaganda for hire on behalf of the government; some wrote for newspapers and the many literary periodicals that sprang up during the period. There also existed something of an amorphous body of writers with no visible means of support: classically educated, often with legal training, subsisting in the public sphere as gentlemen of letters, a sort of democratic version of the aristocratic coterie.

One category of writer conspicuously missing from Johnson's series, and from the discussion so far, is the woman writer. There is not a single woman among Johnson's fifty-two poets. This is hardly Johnson's fault, since the choice of poets in this act of canon-formation was largely set down by the booksellers who commissioned the series, but it was an omission repeated by later collections of British poetry and no doubt contributed to the neglect of poetry by women in later literary history. Actually, as we shall see, there was considerable depth and variety to women's writing over the period, though women who made a living from the pen were rare and conspicuous. The situation of female writers was different in several ways from that of male ones. Women could not attend the universities or law colleges and thus could not gain higher education other than by exceptional means. They could not enter the majority of the higher professions at all: there were no women lawyers, doctors or clergy. Women who needed to work for money were largely confined to retail trades; a number were involved in book-selling, though often in rather peripheral capacities. Women could not vote or take public office, which necessarily limited access to political life; few women writers ventured into the male arena of party politics. Married women were to a large extent legally and financially subject to their husbands, which in some cases limited their scope as writers.

Disabling as this catalogue of privation now seems, in practice women found many ways of circumventing limitations. For one thing, writing was in some ways the most innocent means of developing a public identity, since it was not actually prohibited and could be seen as a suitable accomplishment for an educated woman (along with drawing and music). A few families educated their daughters in the same way that they educated their sons, as far as university level, and several women availed themselves of their father's libraries to continue the process. Publication was sometimes a different matter, since it could be regarded as immodest; but many women writers did publish their work without very powerful opposition and, indeed, with significant help from male writers such as Swift, Richardson and Johnson. Aristocratic women had an inbuilt advantage here, since they were often the most highly educated. High social position, with the absence of financial need, evidently helped Margaret Cavendish, Countess of Newcastle (1623–73), Lady Mary Chudleigh (1656–1710), Anne Finch, Countess of Winchilsea (1661–1720), and Lady Mary Wortley Montagu (1689–1762), to gain a level of respect as writers. Amongst non-aristocratic women, the safest model was that of Katherine Philips (1632–64), known to her admiring contemporaries as 'the Matchless Orinda'. She produced one volume of poems just before dying of smallpox; literate and sensitive, the poems were unimpeachably 'female' in that they celebrated female friendship without political aggression. They were also not published for financial gain, though there was clearly an appeal to cosmopolitan fame in them. Anne Killigrew (1660–85), from a similarly respectable background, also died of smallpox before she could establish her career, and her poems were published posthumously by her father with a brilliant prefatory poem by Dryden.

Much more difficult was the model of Aphra Behn (*d.*1689), perhaps the purest example of a professional woman writer for the whole period. Biographical details are scant and contemporary sources unreliable and obviously elaborated, but it is generally accepted that Behn lived for a while in the English colony of Surinam in South America, perhaps travelling there with her father; from this experience she produced a novel, *Oroonoko* (1688). On her return she acted as an English spy in Holland, but always protested that her services to the Crown (she was an enthusiastic royalist) were undervalued and unrewarded. After several unsuccessful petitions for payment, she produced a play in 1670, following this with some seventeen further dramas. To a surprising extent she appears to have been accepted by the predominantly male theatrical establishment, and she was also praised as a poetess, by Dryden among others. Despite this intense literary activity, she was perennially in debt, and in 1683 bargained hard with Jacob Tonson for an edition of her poems; he had offered £25 for the copyright and she begged for £5 more, pleading 'I want extreamly or I would not urge this'.[3] When she died she was buried in Westminster Abbey, in recognition of her poetic ability. But her reputation was much more complex than that of Philips or Killigrew: some of her verse was reckoned to be indecent, some of the female characters in her plays too pushy, and her own independence as a woman writer no doubt coloured the views of her more conservative contemporaries. Once the Stuarts had been ousted from the throne, her Tory sympathies became an embarrassment. Fascinating as her career was, she was not a model that women writers could easily imitate.

The stage certainly offered opportunities, and women could and did compete with men in the arena of drama. In the season 1695–6 six new plays by women were performed. Susanna Centlivre (1669?–1723), whose husband's career as 'yeoman of the mouth' (cook) to George I was notably less distinguished than her own, was perhaps the most popular dramatist of the period 1710–20, earning some twenty guineas a time for the copyright of the plays and several hundred pounds from successful performances. No woman writer could make a living from poetry: women could contribute to journals such as *The Gentleman's Magazine* (published from 1731, with Johnson a main contributor from 1737) and some, like Mary Jones (*d*.1778) were well-enough respected as poets to be invited to become a regular critic for the *Monthly Review*; but writing was not a career as such for most women. Some worked as schoolteachers; one, Mary Chandler (1687–1745) was a successful milliner in Bath, who educated herself through reading and established sufficient reputation as a poet to be visited and praised by Alexander Pope.

There were notable casualties, and some hard-won successes. Elizabeth Thomas (1675–1731), the daughter of a lawyer who educated herself through reading, tried to supplement her meagre fortune with writing, but died in poverty after a period in prison. Some did make significant sums, often through subscription arrangements that muted the economic reality of book-buying into an act of charitable support. Mary Barber (*c*.1690–1757), for example, was encouraged by Jonathan Swift, who helped her gain an impressive list of subscribers for an edition of her poems in 1734. Swift also promoted the interests of Laetitia Pilkington (*c*.1708–50), who wrote for hire and tried a number of jobs, but spent much of her time in London soliciting subscriptions for an edition of her poems which never appeared. Charlotte Lennox (1729?–1804) was much respected by Samuel Johnson and Samuel Richardson, who organized the publication of her successful novel *The Female Quixote* in 1752; but schemes for a subscription edition of her poems repeatedly came to nothing, partly through her importunity, and she worked as a translator and editor through the 1760s without ever gaining a reliable income. Johnson took the destitute blind poet Anna Williams (1706–83) into his house, and organized a volume of her *Miscellanies* which raised her £300. Near the bottom of the social scale came Mary Leapor (1722–46), who worked as a servant in a country house and whose verse circulated in manuscript amongst an appreciative local audience; a subscription to establish her with a 'competence' was begun, but she died of measles before the volume of her poems was published. Mary Whately (1738–1825), from a similar background, was supported by the poets William Shenstone and John Langhorne, and published a volume of poetry with 600 subscribers in 1764. A friend of Johnson's, Elizabeth Carter (1717–1806) was given the same classical education as her brothers, and continued the process with intense self-directed study; she published a well-respected translation of the ancient philosopher Epictetus in 1758. The subscription brought her nearly £1000, enough to render her independent.

Behn's lead as a female novelist was not really followed until the controversial work of Delarivier Manley (1663–1724), a Tory sympathizer with a colourful history, whose *New Atlantis* (1709) gave a lightly veiled and intermittently eroticized account of contemporary London society. A number of similar scandalous, and scandalously successful, fictions followed. The novels of Eliza Heywood (1693?–1756) moved from amorous indulgence (*Love in Excess*, 1719) to domestic morality (*The History of Miss Betsey Thoughtless*, 1751), charting the gradual rise of the 'respectable' – and remunerative – female novel. Henry Fielding's sister Sarah (1710–68) was a well-known novelist and scholar in her own right; Fanny Burney (1752–1840) produced a series of popular novels between 1778 and 1814. Charlotte Smith, plagued by the financial mismanagement of her husband, produced a much-read volume of *Elegiac Sonnets* in 1784; the fifth edition (1789) had over 800 subscribers, but for the substantial income she required, Smith had to turn to the novel, producing five substantial fictions between 1788 and 1793.

We started this chapter with a document from a particular version of literary history. The document itself shows fairly clearly a moment in the professionalization of writing, which might loosely be said to have taken place in our period; but this 'profession' was not a constant or stable entity for all writers. Clearly the role of the aristocratic patron declined markedly, as did that of the aristocratic writer, but neither completely disappeared. Political divisions impinged less on writers in the later half of the period than they did on those in the earlier half (though this would change once more with the French Revolution of 1789). Money came to play an increasingly important part in writers' lives, and it was evidently quite possible for some writers to earn a living without anything but their intelligence to aid them; at the same time, most writers belonged to some other profession and wrote with that security behind them. Johnson, one of the few completely professional writers, gives a particular view of a particular kind of literary history in the *Lives of the English Poets*, outside which lies another history: journalism, the theatre, the novel. Women writers engage in these genres, and in the bare possibility of writing for a living, in particular ways. The work that emerged on the basis of these material conditions we can now revisit in other contexts.

Notes

1 Subsequent references to this edition are placed in the text. A guinea was variable in value but generally about 21 shillings, or £1.05. Multiplying 1700 values by 100 gives a rough idea of their purchasing power in modern terms: the bargain would be worth about £30,000 today.

2 King, *Natural and Political Observations* (1696).

3 *The Gentleman's Magazine*, May 1836, 481. There is a noticeable falling-off of the breed during the eighteenth century.

2

Writing and belief

When I wrote my treatise about our system, I had an eye upon such principles as might work with considering men for the belief of a Deity; and nothing can rejoice me more than to find it useful for that purpose. . . . As to your first query, it seems to me that if the matter of our sun and planets, and all the matter of the universe, were evenly scattered throughout all the heavens, and every particle had an innate gravity towards all the rest, and the whole space through which this matter was scattered was but finite; the matter on the outside of this space would, by its gravity, tend towards all the matter on the inside, and, by consequence, fall down into the middle of the whole space, and there compose one great spherical mass. But if the matter was evenly disposed throughout an infinite space, it could never convene into one mass; but some of it would convene into one mass, and some into another, so as to make an infinite number of great masses, scattered at great distances from one to another throughout all that infinite space. And thus might the sun and fixed stars be formed, supposing the matter were of a lucid nature. But how the matter should divide itself into two sorts, and that part of it which is fit to compose a shining body should fall down into one mass and make a sun, and the rest which is fit to compose an opaque body should coalesce, not into one great body, like the shining matter, but in to many little ones; or if the sun at first were an opaque body like the planets, or the planets lucid bodies like the sun, how he alone should be changed into a shining body, whilst all they continue opaque, or all they be changed into opaque ones, whilst he remains unchanged; I do not think explicable by mere natural causes, but am forced to ascribe it to the counsel and contrivance of a voluntary Agent.

[Isaac Newton to Richard Bentley, 10 December 1692; in Bentley, *Sermons Preached at Boyle's Lecture*, edited by Alexander Dyce (London, 1838), pp. 203–4.]

This document is the opening of a letter from Isaac Newton to Richard Bentley in 1692, and it demonstrates the use of scientific material in theological argument. In 1662 the Royal Society was founded by royal charter to promote experimental science or 'natural knowledge'; in 1667 Thomas Sprat (1635–1713) produced a *History* of the Society, commending its attention to empirical evidence, formal procedures and exactness of detail. Sprat was not a sceptic: he was a clergyman, and ultimately a bishop. Science and faith were not opposed at this point in history. Newton (1642–1727) was the pre-eminent exponent of a new science of physics ('our system'), principally in *Philosophiae naturalis principia mathematica* (1687) and *Opticks* (1704). While in later centuries the delineation of a mechanistic universe would fuel scepticism about God's role in creation, if not outright atheism, for Newton and his followers the perfection of the system was evidence precisely of God's wisdom. Newton himself had a profound interest in religious history, bordering on obsession, and his own religious views were not orthodox: but the *Principia* has a theological sense behind it.

Richard Bentley (1662–1742) would make his name as a brilliant but arrogant textual critic and domineering Master of Trinity College Cambridge (the mock-notes in Pope's *Dunciad* take a rise out of his tendency to over-confident emendation of classical texts). He applied his scholarship, again controversially, to the text of the New Testament in the 1720s; for that matter, he produced a bizarre edition of Milton's great religious poem, *Paradise Lost*, in 1732. But in 1692 he was the clergyman who gave the first 'Boyle lectures', in a series founded in the name of Robert Boyle, another eminent scientist, designed to use the findings of science to support orthodox religious belief. He gave eight lectures, variously called *A Confutation of Atheism from the Origin and Frame of the World* and *Matter and Motion cannot think*, and as part of the process he corresponded with Newton; four of Newton's letters to him were later published, an extract from the first of which is reproduced above.

Restoration fictions

The Restoration of Charles II in 1660 brought to an end, officially at least, the religious warfare that had culminated in the execution of his father, Charles I: the episcopalian hierarchy of the church was reinstated and a new Church of England Prayer Book was issued in 1662. Academics at the universities of Oxford and Cambridge were largely in holy orders. But 'Dissenters' (those Protestants who did not accept the authority of the

Church of England) did not simply evaporate. The more fervent of the evangelical and antinomian sects of the Civil War period disappeared, but Presbyterians, Congregationalists, Unitarians and Baptists represented something of what those groups had stood for. Quakers, under the charismatic and unyielding leadership of George Fox (1624–91), gradually strengthened their position despite public persecution; his *Journal*, a record of the working of the 'Inner Light of Christ' in his preaching and suffering, was published in 1694. They gained social acceptance in the eighteenth century as it became evident that their belief in absolute honesty transferred into trustworthy business dealings and employment practice.

At the other end of the political spectrum, Roman Catholics were even more problematic. The Great Fire of London in 1666 was blamed on a Catholic plot, and from 1678 a frenzy of suspicion against Catholics was spurred on by the perjury of Titus Oates in the so-called Popish Plot, supposedly a design to kill Charles and set his Catholic brother James on the throne. Some factions in parliament sought to exclude him from the succession on this basis (the 'Exclusion Crisis'). When James did succeed in 1685, he issued a Declaration of Indulgence promising freedom of worship to Dissenters (and Catholics). But the French king's persecution of Protestants made Catholicism look suspect, and James was ousted in 1688 in favour of the Protestant William of Orange and Mary. The 'Indulgence' was superseded by the Act of Toleration (1689), which specified freedom of worship to dissenting groups, though not Catholics (or Unitarians, who denied the divinity of Christ). There were occasional cries of 'The Church in Danger' from those who thought the sectaries made too much of the opportunity of freedom of worship; Defoe's *Shortest Way with Dissenters* (1702) demanded, in an ironic imitation of such high-church views, the extermination of Dissent (unfortunately for Defoe, himself a Dissenter, the irony was missed and he was put in the pillory). But power remained in hands of those who qualified as Anglicans under the Corporation Act (1661) and Test Acts (1673 and 1678), though Dissenters evolved the practice of 'occasional conformity', taking the sacrament in an Anglican church once a year to meet the statutory requirements for taking office, but avoiding it for the rest of the year. In 1709 a high-church clergyman, Henry Sacheverell, preached two sermons in which he argued that Dissenters, with the connivance of the government, would destroy the Church of England; he was prosecuted, but public opinion was noisily on his side and the government itself fell as a result.

Punitive anti-Catholic legislation of various kinds continued to be a feature of the political landscape into the eighteenth century, affecting Catholic poets like Dryden and Pope directly. Catholics could be required to live no closer than ten miles to London; they could be subject to double taxation; they were debarred from inheriting or purchasing land, and from educating children as Catholics. After the Jacobite rising of 1715 controls on Catholics were tightened; even as late as 1780 an attempt to repeal anti-Catholic legislation led to the 'Gordon Riots' in which certain parts of London were laid waste by arson and mob violence.

Amid this volatile array of forms of belief and worship, writers were variously committed. Samuel Butler's masterwork was *Hudibras*, a rough, energetic satire gleefully depicting the hypocrisy and cowardice of the 'Saints' (the Presbyterians and Independents of the Civil War period). But John Milton, whom some would count as one of those very Saints, transformed his experience of the war and interregnum in a very different way. Milton had vehemently opposed the episcopal system of Charles I, but he was also opposed to the 'new forcers of conscience' who came to power in the Civil War. He maintained a vast collection of biblical passages under the title *De Doctrina Christina* but could not publish it under Charles II; it contains some fierce defences of freedom of conscience. Milton did not attend Church of England services, relying instead on the supremacy of Christ and personal conviction. *Paradise Lost*, of which Milton had conceived the first ideas in the 1640s, was published in 1667 (with some 'heretical' slants on the nature of the Trinity excised) and later revised into twelve-book form. It was both a bold theological attempt 'to justify the ways of God to men' (I.26), and explain the process of the Fall, and an even bolder attempt to provide a true English poetic epic using biblical material, splicing pagan epic with Christian theology.[1] Milton chose the evolving freedom of blank verse rather than the order of rhyme, but retained the verbal discipline of a Latinate syntax.

The story itself holds few surprises: Chapter 3 of the Book of Genesis tells in a few verses of the seduction of Eve by the serpent, of the eating of the forbidden fruit by Eve and Adam, and of their expulsion from paradise. This is the Fall, the original sin of disobedience to the Father; all Milton's readers knew what was going to happen. But Milton invents and supplies a huge cosmological and psychological narrative, explaining why humanity fell in this way, and continues to fall. The epic is not told in linear fashion, from Creation onwards, but begins with the fallen angels (principally, Satan) lying on the burning lake of Hell after an unsuccessful war with God. There is a risk in this, for it presents punishment rather than crime, allows Satan to display a kind of heroism, and presents a brilliantly imagined scene; but this is part of understanding our own fallen and fallible condition. The poem tempts its readers as much as Satan tempts Eve; but there is enough to prevent identification with Satan if we read properly. Satan (the angel formerly known as Lucifer), who plays no role in the Genesis narrative, quickly emerges as the leader of the group and the first centre of consciousness offered by the poem. What marks Satan out is his ability to conceal internal torment from everyone but the reader: he makes bold claims about the near success of the war against God and his own 'courage never to submit or yield', but Milton makes it plain that this is a front: 'So spake the apostate angel, though in pain, / Vaunting aloud, but racked with deep despair' (I.125–6). By an impressive imaginative logic, Satan turns his imprisonment into freedom, claiming he brings to Hell 'A mind not to be changed by place or time' (I.253):

> The mind is its own place, and in itself
> Can make a heaven of hell, a hell of heaven.
> What matter where, if I be still the same [. . .]
> Better to reign in hell, than serve in heaven. (I.254–6, 263)

In this spirit Satan creates an alternative court and summons his legions to a sort of parliament. A debate takes place in which the option of continuing war with God is played off against the possibilities of some sort of peace. But it is essentially a sham, since the 'monarchal' Satan has already decided to try to corrupt God's new creation, the world of Adam and Eve. He is, naturally, appointed leader of the mission that he has invented, and he sets off on a journey through the darker, chaotic aspects of the cosmos, one of the earliest 'space voyages' in English literature.

This brings him to the allegorical figures of Sin and Death, presented as foul, oversexed monsters. Sin, it transpires, was Satan's own creature, born from his brain in the form of a daughter, with whom he copulated and who then conceived Death, who in turn repeated the incestuous process. This appalling process of self-involved procreation lies in direct contrast to God's own ability to produce a son, not to mention Adam, by mere thought and word (and without female agency); it is also a gross and guilty parody of the trinity. Practising his smooth rhetorical skills on Sin, who figures as a sort of cast-off mistress, Satan proceeds to Earth, watched by God, who foresees his eventual success. The devils left behind had got themselves into a theological tangle, disputing

> Of providence, foreknowledge, will and fate,
> Fixed fate, free will, foreknowledge absolute,
> And found no end, in wandering mazes lost. (II.559–61)

But God knows the answer; he is insistent that his foreknowledge of the event does not make the event happen. Adam is 'Sufficient to have stood, though free to fall' (III.99), as were all the angels; 'if I foreknew, / Foreknowledge had no influence on their fault' (III.118–19). And God gives us some foreknowledge too, by declaring that since Satan and his kind 'by their own suggestion fell, / Self-tempted, self-depraved' (III.129–30), they shall receive no mercy, but that since Adam and Eve are deceived, humankind shall at length be redeemed. Something must be offered, however, to appease his justice, and the son offers himself: the Christian sacrifice is scheduled before anyone has a chance to Fall.

Satan's courage and leadership in the face of this untouchable power have often, since Romantic accounts of the poem, been taken as a sign of secret sympathy on Milton's part. But there is more than one sort of courage, and Satan's is not only already doomed and futile, but strictly self-seeking, a kind of monomaniac revenge for defeat in battle. Moreover, it is not self-mastery but self-exploration: finally, a kind of narcissism. In public Satan goes so far as to deny having been created by God at all, claiming that he and the other rebels were 'self-begot, self-raised / By our own quickening power' (V.860–1). Despite the claim, we learn of his intense misery in the opening of Book IV, when he alights near Eden, for he now embodies Hell:

> horror and doubt distract
> His troubled thoughts, and from the bottom stir
> The hell within him, for within him hell
> He brings, and round about him, nor from hell
> One step no more than from himself can fly
> By change of place . . . (IV.18–23)

What is claimed as freedom is actually a confirmation of damnation; his secret soliloquy (IV.32–113) is in effect a confession of God's justice.

God, in order 'to render man inexcusable', as the 'Argument' to Book V has it, sends the angel Raphael to Adam to warn him and Eve of Satan's design. This gives Milton the opportunity, in Books V–VIII, to describe in duly epic terms earlier events such as the war in heaven and the creation of the world through God's son. This is out of chronological order but has the psychological effect of focusing those narratives on Adam, who tells Raphael in return what he remembers of his own origin. The individual man thus has the full theological picture. The individual woman, however, does not, and it is on her secondariness and narcissism (already established by her own 'autobiographical' narrative in Book IV) that Satan goes to work in Book IX. Adam's curiosity about the cosmos (perhaps mirrored in our appreciation of Milton's depiction of it), is firmly discouraged by Raphael, but Eve's curiosity and ambition make her an easy prey for Satan: after all, he understands temptation and the will to power.

In his guise as the serpent Satan gives his best rhetorical performance yet, encouraging her to gain knowledge and power and pouring scorn on God's timid prohibition. Eve's eating of the fruit establishes her as an internalized character of the Satanic kind: it provokes not knowledge, but internal self-deception. In her new state she must decide whether to tempt Adam, or whether to overmaster him by keeping the secret to herself, and finally elects to offer him the fruit out of sexual jealousy of a possible alternative partner for him. Crucially, Adam is not deceived, but eats the fruit anyway, in order to stay with Eve, whatever the cost. Satan retires triumphant to Hell, having achieved the ruination of Paradise: his minions set about paving the road from Earth to Hell. But he and the rebel angels are even less free than they were before; they are condemned to become the thing Satan has pretended to be – serpents, hissing and crawling in Hell in gruesome self-parody. Adam, meanwhile, is presented with a vision of future (biblical) history, which holds out the distant possibility of redemption, before being ejected from Paradise with the possibility of an internal redemption in the heart, a 'paradise within' to comfort him.

Milton returned to his epic account of human history under its divine aspect in *Paradise Regained* (1671).[2] Milton reanimates his serpent into the Satan-figure once more, sending him on a quest to test the 'greater man' spoken of in the opening lines of *Paradise Lost*: that is, the 'female seed' of Eve, the incarnated Christ on Earth. Milton chooses not the heroic and dramatic events of the crucifixion, already assigned as Christ's atonement for the sin of Adam, but Satan's temptation of Christ in the wilderness. Reconvening the parliament of devils, Satan is made to tell of Christ's baptism and God's approval, setting forth the new and more difficult task of deceiving him with 'well couched fraud'. The 'infernal crew' have no hesitation in assigning the task to 'their great dictator', who accordingly seeks Christ out in disguise. Much of the poem is a kind of deliberate, compressed reversal of the tragic epic: the wilderness is a converse Eden, the temptations a playing-out of the earlier scenario in terms of theological debate. Christ opens his role in the poem with a kind of autobiography, reminding us of Adam's and Eve's recollections of their origins:

> O what a multitude of thoughts at once
> Awakened in me swarm, while I consider
> What from within I feel myself, and hear
> What from without comes often to my ears . . . (I.196–9)

Like Adam, Christ is given a kind of psychological interior, as is his mother Mary, while Satan retains his improvisatory personality, performing one role to Christ while his inward life continues to be revealed to us as readers. Christ has to come from the fallen world of human psychology to redeem it; but his answers all fulfil the Old Testament scriptures. Satan offers Christ food, since he has been fasting: the banquet is explicitly a much greater temptation than the apple offered to Eve (II.337–67); but Christ rejects it with contempt. He is offered power, glory, earthly rule, but remains constant under pressure, declaring that true model of kingship is internal. It is largely a debate-poem, with Satan becoming less and less disguised in his assaults on Christ's virtue as Christ does what Eve failed to do: he understands the theological truth behind the offers that Satan makes, and is proof against them. Milton displays his characteristic ability to argue the wrong side of the question, granting Satan considerable rhetorical power: much of the time what Satan is doing is praising Christ's intelligence, while trying to defeat it. Most of all he is curious as to what or who Christ actually is; but Christ's firmness strips away Satan's pretences and we learn what *he* is: when Christ tells him he is doomed, his 'inly racked' reply is:

> I would be at the worst; worst is my Port,
> My harbour and my ultimate repose,
> The end I would attain, my final good. (III.209–11)

But while Satan has rhetoric on his side, the full power of pagan classical literature and thought, Christ has scripture. It is no contest: he is himself the 'Word' incarnate. In a last-ditch attempt to tempt Christ, Satan places him on top of the temple in Jerusalem and suggests he throw himself off and demonstrate that the angels will protect him, as the scriptures say; but Christ has read further: 'Also it is written / Tempt not the Lord thy God; he said, and stood'. But Satan falls, crashing back to Hell, leaving Christ to the care of the angels. Christ has a human self, a history: but he does, strictly speaking, nothing, winning by mere resistance alone.

Milton produced one more version of theologically invested poetry: *Samson Agonistes*, published with *Paradise Regained* in 1671 as Milton's valedictory poem. Milton fused the classical Greek model of tragedy with the biblical story of Samson's seduction by the Philistine Dalila, his subsequent blinding and enslavement, and his final victory over his enemies in death.[3] The degraded hero is visited by several figures offering advice, hostility, comfort, seduction (in the shape of Dalila, his own 'Eve'). Finally, Samson, having rejected all counsel and all compromise, understands not only his own responsibility for his downfall, but his continuing potential to act at the crucial moment, and destroys God's enemies when they least expect it.

Where Milton's unfamiliar style took time to reach an audience, John Bunyan's prose templates for religious experience were more immediate hits. Bunyan (1628–88) was the son of a brazier and had worked at that trade; he had fought on the parliamentary side in the Civil War and by 1653 had joined a non-conformist church in Bedford, where he preached. In 1660 he was arrested for preaching without an official licence; while in prison he wrote *Grace Abounding to the Chief of Sinners* (1666), a spiritual autobiography of a particularly intense kind. Bunyan gives a confessional account of his sinful childhood in miserable circumstances, his providential escapes from death (near-drowning, encounters with poisonous snakes), his time in the army and his awakening to a sense of sin and redemption. At one point while Bunyan is playing a game, 'a voice did suddenly dart from Heaven into my soul, which said, Wilt thou leave thy sins and go to heaven, or have thy sins and go to hell?'. He has visions of the path to God's kingdom. He also has appalling temptations prompted by the Devil:

> In these days, when I have heard others talk of what was the sin against the Holy Ghost, then would the tempter so provoke me to desire to sin that sin, that I was as if I could not, must not, neither should be quiet until I had committed that; now, no sin would serve but that; if it were to be committed by speaking of such a word, then I have been as if my mouth would have spoken that word, whether I would or no; and in so strong a measure was this temptation upon me, that often I have been ready to clap my hand under my chin, to hold my mouth from opening; and to that end also I have had thoughts at other times, to leap with my head downward, into some muck-hill hole or other, to keep my mouth from speaking.[4]

This desperate sense (delivered in a single, driven sentence) alternates with a sense of being saved, of loving Christ, of being within God's mercy: 'so my soul did hang as in a pair of scales again, sometimes up and sometimes down, now in peace and anon again in terror' (65). Bunyan portrays his protracted psychological struggle with 'the tempter', who tries to get him to betray Christ, and the compulsive physical forms this struggle takes, with breathtaking frankness. And the process is not ended by his call to the ministry, since he gives at the end a checklist of the 'seven abominations in my heart' and confesses: 'I have sometimes seen more in a line of the Bible than I could well tell how to stand under, and yet at another time the whole Bible hath been to me as dry as a stick; or rather, my heart hath been so dead and dry unto it, that I could not conceive the least drachm of refreshment, though I have looked it all over' (102). Bunyan's book presents unmediated religious experience, beyond the reach of conventional church-bound practice, in which direct contact with God (and the Devil) marks every aspect of life.

During a second period of imprisonment Bunyan probably finished the first part of *The Pilgrim's Progress* (1678). Bunyan relates an allegorical vision in which Christian, bearing a burden (Sin) on his back, leaves the City of Destruction on the advice of Evangelist (scripture) and embarks on a pilgrimage to the Celestial City (Heaven). He engages with, and departs from, various plausible characters such as Mr Worldly Wiseman (who embodies the conventional moral sense and self-interest of the 'Latitudinarian' clergy of Bunyan's day), Pliable (who has not resolution enough to succeed) and By-Ends (who adopts whatever is the policy of those in power, regardless of principle). He passes through various significant places, corresponding to mental states, such as the Slough of Despond (a marshy area representing the kind of depression and fear delineated in *Grace Abounding*); the House of the Interpreter (meaning a kind of ability to translate one's experience into religious terms), and the Castle of Giant Despair (a sense of lost faith). The burden of Sin is removed on the site of a cross (Christ's crucifixion), but there are further trials to come. He fights a verbal and physical battle with the rhetorically adept devil Apollyon, which perhaps owes something to Christ's encounter with Satan in *Paradise Regained*. In Vanity, a town, Beelzebub and Apollyon set up a Fair where all manner of empty worldly successes (property, power, honours) can be bought. Christian's companion Faithful is burnt to death here, in a martyrdom alluding to Christ's; he gains access to the Celestial City immediately, but Christian has further to go. He takes Hopeful with him, and various points of the theology of damnation and salvation are thrashed out in their debates; Hopeful also rescues Christian as he loses confidence in the river of Death that they must cross to enter the Celestial City.

The narrative was immediately popular. Saturated with biblical imagery, written in accessible, vernacular English, with marginal glosses to aid in interpretation, it placed a universal scheme of personal spiritual deliverance within a recognizable psychological and social frame: the characters have a kind of fictional life and plausibility of their own, and the landscape has elements of seventeenth-century England about it. A second part, narrating the progress of Christian's family (his wife Christiana and their children) along the path set out by Christian, appeared in 1684; in a kind of optimistic reversal of the road laid by Sin and Death between the world and hell in *Paradise Lost*, Christiana is helped by Great-heart to follow the signs towards salvation and confirm Christian's route-map to salvation. These books too gained high reputation despite their origin in the non-scholarly world of what some would call 'mechanick preachers'. *Pilgrim's Progress* was a popular gift to children, and much read in non-conformist circles, though not only there; Johnson, a stalwart of the Church of England, admired its 'invention, imagination, and the conduct of the story', adding as evidence of its solid status in literature, 'Few books, I believe, have had a more extensive sale.'[5]

Anglicans and others

In a state where blasphemy was a serious criminal offence, free-thinking was very heavily policed and atheism not voiced openly. Rochester was one of the very few poets who made any kind of open assault on orthodox pieties. In his *Satyr Against Reason and Mankind* (*c.*1675)[6] Rochester voices an attack on reason, the supposedly 'divine' element of mind, which he claims misleads people into 'doubt's boundless sea', and promotes the 'light of nature', or instinct, instead. He debates with a 'formal band and beard' (clergyman), who utters the traditional praise of reason as man's access to the celestial:

> Reason, by whose aspiring influence,
> We take a flight beyond material sense,
> Dive into mysteries, then soaring pierce
> The flaming limits of the universe;
> Search heaven and hell, find out what's acted there,
> And give the world true grounds of hope and fear. (66–71)

But Rochester protests that this is Adam's sin of pride, a 'supernatural gift that makes a mite / Think he's the image of the infinite' (76–7). Better to act according to bestial instinct than follow such reason, Rochester argues, adding in a vitriolic attack on the hypocrisy of the clergy for good measure. He does, however, hold out the mere possibility of 'a churchman who on God relies' (191), 'Whose pious life's a proof he does believe / Mysterious truths, which no man can conceive' (214–15).[7]

The 'formal band and beard', if not such a churchman, did indeed come for Rochester in the end, in the shape of the Whig bishop, Gilbert Burnet, who visited Rochester on his death-bed and claimed to have converted him after long, searching conversations.[8] The Orthodox Church of England position was articulated, naturally enough, from pulpits such as Burnet's; but in 1682 Dryden (at that time an Anglican, acting in his capacity as the state's poet) published *Religio Laici* ('the religion of a layman') in an attempt to voice a moderate, straightforward piety in poetry, opposing the proscribed views of Catholics and the separatist interpretations of Dissenters. In 1687, during the brief reign of the Catholic James, Dryden published *The Hind and the Panther*, a complex debate poem using animal figures to debate the claims of Roman Catholicism (represented by a milk-white hind) against those of the 'spotted' panther, or Church of England; the intent of the poem is to propose an alliance between the Catholic and Anglican churches against the Dissenters and the Whigs.

Out of this contrary culture came one of the most remarkable literary texts of the period. In 1704 Jonathan Swift published anonymously *A Tale of a Tub*, an unclassifiable book consisting partly of an allegorical history of the Christian church and partly of a satire on contemporary writing embodied in the figure of a hack author, too vain and venal to keep out of his own text. The main story concerns three brothers, Peter, Martin and Jack, who on the death of their father inherit a coat with plain instructions not to alter it in any way. It soon becomes clear that the three brothers represent Roman Catholicism (Peter), Anglicanism (Martin, from Martin Luther) and Protestant Dissent (Jack, from John Calvin). The coat is the Christian religion, and the will and its instructions represent Scripture. The brothers, however, soon start finding excuses to modify their coat (their faith) in accordance with prevailing fashions (theories and theologies), using increasingly bizarre and nonsensical reading strategies to justify the practice (that is, they misread scripture for non-theological purposes). Soon the three brothers quarrel, Peter claims to be the eldest brother (though Swift carefully makes it clear that no-one knows which brother/religion is the oldest) and locks the will/Bible up. Swift makes much rude fun of the Catholic doctrine of transubstantiation (whereby the consecrated bread and wine of the mass become the body and blood of Christ) and of an alleged tendency for Catholic priests to claim authority of interpretation; on the other hand, Jack, though he stays with Martin for some while, is also suspect in his masochistic desire for punishment (suffering was a mark of purity among Dissenters) and his conversion of scripture into a variety of physical objects such as an umbrella or night-cap (suggesting that Dissenters saw *everything* in terms of the Bible). Martin, as the representative of that church of which Swift was a priest, fares less badly: he tries to unpick the additional ornaments on his coat, where Jack ends up furiously tearing his to pieces (versions of a return to primitive worship from papal corruptions).

Through the work runs a concern with the bizarre corruptions of the spirit by the body. Swift uses the prevalent scientific empiricism espoused by the Royal Society to produce a number of ludicrous theories about the 'mechanical operation of the spirit'. Some of these are religious in character, as when Swift mockingly invents the sect of Aeolists, for whom 'inspiration' is a matter of (bodily) wind. Some are more widely satirical, Swift identifying certain political activities with madness caused by hydrostatic aberrations in the 'spirit'. At the core of Swift's concern is language: how can the merely material residue of writing reliably embody meaning and intention, if something so plain – and authored by God – can be the source of so much controversy and misinterpretation? The illogical extreme of this problem is found in the example of the Hack whose digressions interrupt the *Tale*; a devotee of fashion (like the brothers), the Hack values above all things the proliferation of interpretation, misreading, translation, and misprision. He claims, proudly, to have written 91 pamphlets in the service of 36 different political factions; he loves mysteries, signs, emblems, shadows, and symbols, and anything that contributes to interpretative chaos. Not surprisingly, the Hack is convinced of the political utility of madness.

The comic history of the church thus allows Swift to comment on a whole range of social and theoretical practice: he uses mechanistic science against itself, he attacks abuses in learning and scholarship, he impersonates a hack writer to expose unprincipled textual proliferation in the modern book trade. The text was controversial for its apparent levity with regard to holy matters. (Swift considered that it had upset Queen Anne so much that his progress towards a bishopric was personally obstructed by her.) Swift issued an 'author's apology' in which he pointed out that the objectionable passages were ironic and that the book was designed to attack abuses in religion, not religion itself. But this apology (which was again anonymous) appeared as yet another textual element of what was intended as a mock-book, peppered with fragments and gaps, deliberately unfinished, a sort of offensive, viral imitation of the textual, if not scriptural, certainties people lived by.

Nature and Nature's laws

Elsewhere Swift published a sardonic summary of Anthony Collins's *Discourse of Freethinking* (1713), a highly controversial pamphlet arguing that the state had no right whatever over private belief. Bentley was another who responded. Collins was a friend of the philosopher and political theorist John Locke, who himself wrote much on matters of toleration and religious belief. Towards the end of the seventeenth century, there was to some extent greater freedom to dissent intellectually from authorized and orthodox positions; John Toland, one of Milton's early editors, advocated in *Christianity Not Mysterious* (1697) a 'natural' or inferred religion rather than a spiritual message delivered by revelation and the church. While the Newtonian system could produce evidence for a creator, to some theologians this produced a merely 'natural' religion, an ethical but not a sacramental faith, leaving every man to fend for himself without the intervention of 'revealed religion' and its ministers. George Berkeley, a bishop who challenged Locke's system of knowledge, could establish God as the universal perceiver whose constant perceptions keep the universe in existence, but this again said little about salvation or Christianity as such.

One poet who had some attraction to 'deism', as the tendency towards natural religion was known, was, surprisingly, Alexander Pope.[9] As a youth Pope had read much religious controversy in his father's library, finding himself a Catholic and a Protestant as each argument took hold, but as an adult he remained firmly Catholic. As a member of a sect all but proscribed by law, Pope trod extremely carefully in religious matters, always promoting the scholar Erasmus as a model of ecumenical seriousness and avoiding doctrinally sensitive issues. He called his atheist friend Samuel Garth 'the best good Christian he, / Altho' he knows it not' on ethical grounds, and declared:

> For Modes of Faith let graceless zealots fight;
> His can't be wrong whose life is in the right.[10]

He was also attracted to the work of William Whiston (1667–1752), who succeeded Newton as professor of mathematics at Cambridge, and gave the Boyle lectures for 1707. Whiston was ousted from his Cambridge post in 1710 for Arian views (the denial of the divinity of Christ) and developed increasingly bizarre theories. But in 1713, at the invitation of Addison and Steele he gave lectures on astronomy in London coffee-houses, which Pope attended and which opened a kind of imaginative vista for him: 'This minute . . . I am above the stars, with a thousand systems round about me, looking forward into the vast abyss of eternity, and losing my whole comprehension in the boundless spaces of the extended Creation, in dialogues with W[histon] and the astronomers . . .' he wrote to a friend.[11] After Newton died in 1727, Pope proposed a somewhat blasphemous epitaph, which did not make it onto Newton's monument in Westminster Abbey:

> Nature and Nature's Laws lay hid in Night.
> GOD said, *Let Newton be!* and All was *light*.

But Pope's greater debt to Newton is found in the *Essay on Man*, published in four anonymous epistles 1733–4, and not immediately recognized as Pope's, such was its skill in avoiding religious positions that would reveal the orientation of its author. Pope's diagrammatic scheme considers 'the Nature and State of Man, with respect to the Universe' in Epistle I; Epistle II looks at Man's nature 'with Respect to Himself, as an Individual'. The third epistle considers social issues, and the fourth, the pursuit of happiness. Pope ostentatiously picks up the challenge of Milton's desire to 'justify the ways of God to men' by claiming to 'Vindicate the ways of God to Man (I.16). Pope shares with Milton a concern to damp down an aspirational curiosity about the universe which covers for a self-seeking pride; 'Know then thyself, presume not God to scan / The Proper Study of Mankind is

Man', he advises, echoing Raphael's warnings to Adam about knowing his place. 'Tis but a part we see, and not the whole' (I.60), he reminds us, at the same time giving us more access to that whole than we had before. For, like Milton, Pope must also satisfy human curiosity in some degree, by giving imaginative access to the invisible world. Several times Pope appears to imagine what it would be like to see beyond our own sphere, in order to suppress the desire to do so:

> Thro' worlds unnumber'd tho' the God be known,
> 'Tis ours to trace him only in our own.
> He, who thro' vast immensity can pierce,
> See worlds on worlds compose one universe,
> Observe how system into system runs,
> What other planets circle other suns,
> What vary'd being peoples ev'ry star,
> May tell why Heav'n has made us as we are. (I.21–8)

The 'He' is an imaginary super-sage who does not exist, but it is hard not to identify him with Pope, or Milton, or the reader, during Pope's exploration of a cosmos he maintains we cannot see. In the second epistle, Pope neatly accepts Newton's brilliance as the scientist of the exterior cosmos but points out that he knows nothing of how consciousness, the inner cosmos (or 'Study of Mankind'), works:

> Could he, whose rules the rapid Comet bind,
> Describe or fix one movement of his Mind? (II.35–6)

Pope, who uses a number of physics-based analogies to provide evidence of moral system, then supplies a rudimentary human psychology, with two operative principles working together in social union: 'Self-love, to urge, and Reason, to restrain' (II.54). The real story of universal struggle is between the principle of outgoing, appetitive action, and the social conscience that allows it to function without damage; the loss of either principle means collapse. Epistle III discovers the principles of connection and system through the chain down to atoms, then applies the principle to the forces which make political society viable. Self-love and love of society can be considered as a sort of heroic couplet in the world: each provides an antithetical but essential dynamic context for the other. The final epistle interestingly begins to skew the systematic symmetries of the first three, as Pope's talent for satiric observation begins to overmaster his adaptation of Newtonian physics to the moral world. Pope acknowledges that there are problems of inequality and human error that cannot easily be assimilated to the somewhat glib formulations he, Pope, has previously offered. His answer is to rediscover a scheme for individual relationship with God – not in a Bunyanesque sense, by which the world is an irrelevant sideshow to the matter of one's salvation, but in a way that renders relation to the world a path to the celestial city:

> God loves from Whole to Parts: but human soul
> Must rise from Individual to the Whole. (IV.361–2)

Pope employs the simile of ripples on a lake, expanding from the motion of a dropped pebble: ripple follows ripple as 'self-love' comes to overflow 'Friend, parent, neighbour . . . His country next, and next all human race', until the 'o'erflowings of the mind' take in the whole chain of being 'And Heav'n beholds its image in his breast'.

Pope's emphasis is not on the theology of the Fall at all but on the state of the cosmos as it stands. In place of Milton's epic struggle there is a system; the darkness of Milton's chaos is replaced by a great chain of being in which everything has an appropriate rank; the presence of evil owes nothing to the personality of the Devil and is revealed as a necessary, though misunderstood, part of God's plan. An uncharacterized God is left alone in his perfection. The poem attracted wide European interest, and was accused of deism for its lack of attention to formal religious worship. The Swiss theologian Jean-Pierre de Crousaz produced two essays disputing the theology of the poem; one was translated by Elizabeth Carter, a close friend of Johnson, who translated the other. William Warburton (1698–1779), a clergyman who had already set himself against Pope's friend and mentor, the deist-inclined Bolingbroke, came to the rescue, rendering the poem more consistent and orthodox than it actually was. It was a good career move: Pope entrusted Warburton with revision of his other work, and eventually, and partly through the career advancement brought on by his friendship with Pope, Warburton became Bishop of Gloucester.[12]

Oh! for a closer walk with God[13]

In the mid-eighteenth century the Church of England was still a dominant feature of national life and religious culture. Several of the writers of our period were, as noted, clergymen, and clergymen feature fairly prominently as characters in fiction: the good-hearted Mr Williams in Richardson's *Pamela*, the comic but sound Parson Adams and the soberly redemptive Doctor Harrison in Fielding's *Joseph Andrews* and *Amelia*, the sentimental hero of Goldsmith's *Vicar of Wakefield*. It was not quite straightforward: the clergyman-novelist Sterne, already in hot water for writing the popular but slightly scandalous *Tristram Shandy*, gained himself further notoriety by publishing his own sermons as *The Sermons of Mr Yorick*, to cash in on the popularity of a character in his novel. And religious sensibilities were not, of course, confined to the practice of the Church. In this section we will look at the ways in which a private sense of religion developed later in the period.

Dissenting habits of self-examination and searching for signs of providence found a prominent literary form in Defoe's epochal first novel, *Robinson Crusoe* (1719). In 'Puritan autobiography' as it is sometimes known, the workings of God's grace in individual lives were recorded for the edification of other believers.[14] Bunyan had used storms and tempests to represent terrors of God and 'Castaway' to signify one cast out from God's favour and grace. In *Robinson Crusoe*, famous for its portrayal of such a castaway on a tropical island (see Chapter 4), the higher purpose is to record Crusoe's growing sense of sin and repentance (the name even suggests 'crucifixion' or 'crusade', though the link is not made explicit). Crusoe is warned by his father against going to sea, and the warning stands in the tradition of Adam and the paternal prohibition: Crusoe pursues forbidden fruit in the wider world. It is his 'original sin' (198). He is warned by various minor disasters against the plan: he should be like a 'true repenting prodigal [son]' (32), but he is more like Jonah causing trouble for the ship that he is on (37). Shipwrecked on an island, he is cast out from God's grace; yet also plucked out by providence, alone among the crew, who otherwise all drown. Providence also sees to it that he accidentally manages to sow some barley (a parody of the 'sower' parable); he reads the Bible and is comforted by phrases from it, repents during sickness, keeps the sabbath, weighs up God's mercy to him, and notices a strangely providential ordering to the days on which significant events have happened to him. Up to a point, his autobiographical self is regulated by reference to a specifically Christian schema, though as we shall see there is more going on in the novel than that.

These habits of self-scrutiny and journal-keeping were commonly associated with dissenting forms of worship. Methodism, though it has some features in common with these 'puritan' sects, was initially an offshoot of the Church of England; the brothers John (1703–91) and Charles Wesley (1707–88) began 'methodical' exercise of religious study and duty while at Oxford, stressing the importance of frequent communion and holy living. In 1738 John had the experience of conversion, feeling his heart 'strangely warmed' by the belief that his personal sins had been atoned for by Christ's sacrifice. Thereafter he devoted his life to itinerant ministry, often preaching (as Fox the Quaker had done) in the open air. Methodism, which remained technically within the Anglican fold until Wesley began ordaining his own clergy for overseas missions, was especially important among the industrial poor, where populations surged faster than official parishes could be created, and though Wesley himself was an authoritarian, no threat to social order at all, his democratic approach to salvation incurred considerable suspicion within the Anglican hierarchy. Methodists were also accused of 'enthusiasm', pointedly defined by the orthodox Johnson as 'A vain belief of private revelation; a vain confidence of divine favour or communication'. Their confidence in salvation and the 'inward light' – a kind of personal hotline to God – was offensive to more anxious Christians, and their emotional display was often characterized as a cover for some kind of sexual fervour. When Fielding makes the villainous Blifil 'turn Methodist' at the end of *Tom Jones*, he does so to contrast Blifil's calculating hypocrisy with the solid virtues of mainstream Anglicanism, as represented by Jones and Allworthy.[15]

Johnson, who admired Wesley's abilities, but disapproved of his religious views, led a fervently religious private life, keeping an angst-ridden diary of his sins and failings. He was an orthodox Anglican but not a regular communicant, and was for much of his life beset by fear of death, anxieties about the state of his soul, and the possibility of damnation. He had had strict religious instruction from his mother, who made him learn texts from the *Book of Common Prayer*, and confined him on the Sabbath to reading *The Whole Duty of Man*, a standard devotional text. At Oxford he responded strongly to *A Serious Call to a Devout and Holy Life*, the work of a high-churchman, William Law. After this he continued to study the Bible, to write private prayers of great intensity for himself, and to provide sermons for a clergyman friend. His profound sense of sin surprised his friends and admirers, who comforted him in his last days by reminding him of the strong moral tendency of his literary work.

Johnson was particularly dismayed by the growth of intellectual atheism in his time, especially in the arguments of the philosopher David Hume (1711–76), who attacked the evidence of the Christian miracles, and disputed the 'argument from design' (the essence of what Bentley took from Newton). He happily committed most theology and metaphysics to the flames on the grounds that it lacked 'experimental reasoning' and empirical validity. Hume rejected all forms of religious belief as projections of human need, though he was careful not to state this openly. Nonetheless, his work was placed on the Roman Catholic Index in 1761 and was deeply offensive to pious believers. Johnson was also antipathetic to Edward Gibbon, once a Catholic convert and latterly a cheerful atheist, who upset many clergymen with his sceptical portrayal of the history of the early Christian church in *The Decline and Fall of the Roman Empire*.

Johnson's own tendency, despite his loyal and very learned Anglicanism, towards a private religious melancholia, is reflected in some of the later poetry of our period. Edward Young, a dramatist and poet who had taken holy orders, published *The Complaint: Or, Night Thoughts on Life, Death and Immortality* (1742–5), a huge series of rambling reflections on death and immortality which enjoyed considerable European vogue. Johnson admired its piety and gave it a favourable review in the *Lives*. The biggest monument of the 'graveyard school' of melancholy, reflective verse, Young's *Complaint* was later illustrated, along with Robert Blair's *The Grave* (1743), by William Blake, who drew inspiration from the dark imaginings of these pious poems.

The tendency for such visionary apprehensions to become pathological was noted by Johnson, always aware of such a possibility in his own case. In his life of William Collins he notes how the wild imagination of the poet had descended into religious melancholia, with the New Testament as his 'only book'. On the other hand, he was disposed to defend his friend Christopher Smart (1722–71), during that poet's confinement in a madhouse between 1756 and 1763: 'I did not think he ought to be shut up. His infirmities were not noxious to society. He insisted on people praying with him; and I'd as lief pray with Kit Smart as any one else'.[16] Smart, who had held a fellowship in Oxford and worked as a hack author for London publishers, had produced a series of prize poems celebrating the 'Attributes of the Supreme Being', as well as other, more sociable work. Pope apparently dissuaded him from producing a Latin version of his *Essay on Man*. His confinement in fact gave him some peace from the life of a hack writer, and he used it to produce some extraordinary experimental poetry on religious themes. *Jubilate Agno*, which was left unfinished and unpublished on Smart's release, was an attempt to produce a kind of antiphonal, incantatory poetry based on Hebrew psalmody. It contains the much-quoted lines on Smart's pet cat, 'For I will consider my cat Jeffrey', which become, in the context of the menagerie of animals included in the poem, not so much an eccentric series of observations on cat behaviour as an example of the ways in which creatures worship God simply by being themselves. Language is pushed to the point of an all-inclusive devotional music. *A Hymn to David* (1763) is, by contrast, an elaborately formal, carefully wrought song of praise to the Bible's chief ruler-poet (David was held to be responsible for the Book of Psalms), using numerical structures and alphabetic clues to produce a spiritual pattern. Smart went on to produce a further series of hymnic offerings, including a book of poems for children. His source is a redeemed language: the order of theology is already there in the words, not in contemplation of Newton's ordered cosmos.

Another writer of hymns was William Cowper (1731–1800), a man periodically subject to Bunyanesque fits of suicidal melancholia: 'such a dejection of spirits as none but they who have felt the same can have the least conception of. Day and night I was on the rack, lying down in horrors and rising in despair'. This depression took a religious form, and looked to religion for cure:

> I particularly remember the barren fig tree was to me a theme of inconceivable misery, and I applied it to myself with a strong persuasion upon my mind that when Our Saviour pronounced a curse upon it He had me in His eye and pointed that curse directly at me. I turned over all Archbishop Tillotson's sermons in hopes of finding one upon that subject . . . desirous if possible to arrive at a gentler interpretation of the passage than my evil conscience would suffer me to fasten upon it.[17]

After confinement in an asylum he was lodged in the house of a clergyman, and came under the influence of John Newton, an evangelical curate within the Church of England, with whom he wrote the *Olney Hymns*, a series of prayerful self-examinations and exhortations (1779). In periods of relative tranquillity he wrote, like Smart, social verse and satire, but a mournful vein of isolation, fear and loss always recurred. One of his poems, 'Verses supposed to be written by Alexander Selkirk' was based on the story of a marooned sailor that was one of the sources of Defoe's *Robinson Crusoe*; in Cowper's verse, Selkirk can claim 'I am monarch of all I survey' but his alienation from humanity and from religious practice is almost complete. Towards the end of his life Cowper wrote 'The Castaway', invoking a stormy scene from the circumnavigation of George Anson of 1740–4, in which a sailor was swept overboard and lost. Cowper's poem elaborates in calm, sympathetic measure the despair of the man overboard, before a final appalling shift in which it becomes clear that the real 'castaway' is the man who feels abandoned by God:

> No voice divine the storm allay'd,
> No light propitious shone,
> When, snatch'd from all effectual aid,
> We perish'd, each alone:
> But I beneath a rougher sea,
> And whelm'd in deeper gulfs than he.[18]

Notes

1 Passages are quoted from John Milton, *Paradise Lost*, edited by Alastair Fowler (London, 1971).
2 Passages from this and *Samson Agonistes* are quoted from the texts in John Milton, *Complete Shorter Poems*, edited by John Carey (London, 1971).
3 Judges XVI.
4 Bunyan, *Grace Abounding and the Life and Death of Mr Badman*, edited by G. B. Harrison (London, 1928), p. 34.
5 Boswell, *Life of Johnson*, II.238.
6 Passages are quoted from the text in *The Poems of John Wilmot, Earl of Rochester*, edited by D. M. Vieth (New Haven and London, 1979).
7 That reason was in harmony with revelation was one of the tenets of the 'Cambridge Platonists', the chief manifesto of which was Ralph Cudworth's *The True Intellectual System of the Universe* (1678).
8 Burnet, *Some Passages of the Life and Death of the Right Honourable John Earl of Rochester* (1680).
9 Deism was another named target of Dryden's *Religio Laici.*
10 'A Farewell to London in the Year 1715', line 15, and *Essay on Man*, III.303–4.
11 Pope to John Caryll, 14 August 1713; *The Correspondence of Alexander Pope*, edited by George Sherburn, 5 vols (Oxford, 1956), I.185.
12 A then influential work combating the intellectual premises of deism appeared shortly after Pope's *Essay*: Joseph Butler, *The Analogy of Religion* (1736).
13 Cowper, *Olney Hymns*, I.
14 The first sequel to *Robinson Crusoe* was secular in character, but the third, *Serious Reflections . . . of Robinson Crusoe* 'with his vision of the Angelick World' (1720), interpreted the adventure in more Bunyanesque spirit.
15 See also Richard Graves, *The Spiritual Quixote* (1773), a novel which satirizes Methodist failings.
16 Boswell, *Life of Johnson*, I.397.
17 William Cowper, *Letters and Prose Writings*, edited by James King and Charles Ryskamp, 5 vols (Oxford, 1979–86), I.8 and 26.
18 Cowper, *The Task and other selected poems*, edited by James Sambrook (London, 1994), p. 319 (lines 61–6).

3

Court and parliament

The next place of Scripture we find our author builds his monarchy of Adam on, is 3 Genesis 16: 'And thy desire shall be to thy husband, and he shall rule over thee.' 'Here we have,' says he, 'the original grant of government,' from whence he concludes . . . 'that the supreme power is settled in the fatherhood, and limited to one kind of government, that is to monarchy.' For let his premises be what they will, this is always the conclusion; let 'rule' in any text be but once named, and presently absolute monarchy is by divine right established. . . . But we will . . . consider the force of the text in hand. The words are the curse of God upon the woman, for having been the first and forwardest in the disobedience, and if we will consider the occasion of what God says here to our first parents, that he was denouncing judgement, and declaring his wrath against them both, for their disobedience, we cannot suppose that this was the time, wherein God was granting Adam prerogatives and privileges, investing him with dignity and authority, elevating him to dominion and monarchy. For though as a helper in the temptation, as well as a partner in the transgression, Eve was laid below him, and so he had accidentally a superiority over her . . . yet he too had his share in the fall, as well as the sin, and was laid lower, as may be seen in the following verses, and 'twould be hard to imagine, that God, in the same breath, should make him universal monarch over all mankind, and a day labourer for his life, turn him out of Paradise to till the ground . . . and at the same time advance him to a throne, and all the privileges and ease of absolute power.

[John Locke, *The First Treatise of Government*, *c*.1681, Chapter 5, paragraph 44]

Locke appears to have written first versions of this and the following essay during the prolonged period of political unease of 1679–82. He was rebutting the arguments of Sir Robert Filmer (*d*.1653), whose many defences of the divine right of kings had been published during the contest between Charles I and parliament; his *Patriarcha* was not published until 1680, when similar conflict was brewing. Filmer propounded the view that monarchy was the natural form of government because God had originally handed power to the first patriarch, Adam, and all men (and, of course, women) were bound by that original grant and tenure. Locke's treatises were eventually published in 1690, when they appeared as part of the political theory that justified the Revolution of 1688. Locke supplied an alternative theory of political society that became the standard Whig viewpoint: that power derived from consent, from a 'contract' or 'compact' mutually agreed between people:

> Men being . . . by nature all free, equal and independent, no man can be put out of this estate and subjected to the political power of another without his own consent. The only way whereby anyone divests himself of his natural liberty and puts on the bonds of civil society is by agreeing with other men to join and unite into a community for their comfortable, safe, and peaceable living one amongst another in a secure enjoyment of their properties, and a greater security against any that are not of it. This any number of men may do, because it injures not the freedom of the rest; they are left as they were, in the liberty of the state of nature. When any number of men have so consented to make one community or government, they are thereby presently incorporated, and make one body politic, wherein the majority have a right to act and conclude the rest. [From: John Locke, *The Second Treatise of Government*, *c.*1681, Chapter 8, paragraph 95.]

These two positions, patriarchal monarchy against consensual parliamentary democracy, were the poles on which political discussion of the period turned.

Restoration, crisis, revolution

1660 marks the restoration of a king, Charles II, whose father (Charles I) had been beheaded by the English parliament for high treason against the people of England. The status of the king, and the court that surrounded him, was far from a settled issue in the period, and the aftershocks of the Civil War continued to be felt for a century or more. The religious settlement of 1660 was, like all the other arrangements of the Restoration, also political, a return to pre-1641 ideas of government. The son of the executed king returned, the decrees of Cromwell's parliament were annulled, surviving regicides were rounded up and brutally executed.

Milton retreated into a religious and ostensibly non-political poetry. But his political pamphleteering had been saturated with biblical reference: he once likened Charles I to Pharaoh, and there were plenty of observers who, after the Plague and Fire of 1665–6, saw those phenomena as providential curses sent against Charles II's Pharaoh-like rule. Given the connections between intense Bible study and the events of the Civil War, it would be surprising if Milton's late poems were not open to a political reading. The war in heaven draws much imagery and energy from the Civil War. Satan, to some extent, represents the ambition and self-seeking aspects of the rebel leadership that caused the golden chance of Godly revolution to disintegrate. A moment of agreement in the rebel parliament leads to the narrator's outburst against parliamentary infighting:

> O shame to me! Devil with devil damned
> Firm concord holds, men only disagree
> Of creatures rational, though under hope
> Of heavenly grace: and God proclaiming peace
> Yet live in hatred, enmity and strife
> Among themselves, and levy cruel wars,
> Wasting the earth, each other to destroy . . . (II.496–502)

But Satan is also Charles, plotting, ambitious, hypocritical, proud, deceitful, luxurious, and lustful. In *Paradise Regained*, Christ responds to Satan's offer of a short cut to sovereignty:

> Yet he who reigns within himself, and rules
> Passions, Desires, and Fears, is more a King . . .
> But to guide Nations in the way of truth
> By saving Doctrine, and from error lead
> To know, and knowing worship God aright,
> Is yet more kingly . . . (II.466–7, 473–5)

This is precisely the test of governance that Charles II had so miserably failed, and much of what Satan offers Christ sounds like a description of worldly appetite and power of the kind identified with the Restoration court. The description of the Roman emperor Nero in lascivious luxury is designed by Satan to tempt Christ's very purity, with the suggestion that Christ should at once take over the reins of empire, and 'expel this monster from his throne / Now made a sty, and in his place ascending / A victor people free from servile yoke!' (IV.100–02). It might be a temptation for Milton himself, as the exponent of political freedom who had been instrumental in removing a previous 'monster'; yet Christ is unmoved. Cheap, worldly solutions are no use at all; what matters is constancy and faith. His kingdom will be the end of all kingdoms; the Romans are not worth saving, since they have thrown away the triumphs they have won through their own corruptions.

> What wise and valiant man would seek to free
> These thus degenerate, by themselves enslaved,
> Or could of inward slaves make outward free? (IV.143–5)

It is not hard to see further contempt for the failure of the English people to capitalize on their defeat of tyranny. In *Samson Agonistes*, a tragedy about the English, their chosen status, their blindness, their fall from grace, their possibilities for redemption, Milton also has Samson ('Eyeless in Gaza at the mill with slaves', 41) denounce Dalila's country in a way that appears to embody some of the same critique:

> No more thy country, but an impious crew
> Of men conspiring to uphold their state
> By worse than hostile deeds, violating the ends
> For which our country is a name so dear;
> Not therefore to be obeyed. (891–5)

But perhaps to be destroyed, in his last-ditch, unexpected effort.

Milton circumvented political power by claiming a higher poetic authority. Dryden, who knew Milton well enough to request his permission to turn *Paradise Lost* into a rhymed play, picks up this cue, though he writes openly at the behest of the court that Milton detests. In 1662 Dryden writes:

> When our great monarch into exile went,
> Wit and religion suffered banishment . . .
> At length the Muses stand restored again
> To that great charge which Nature did ordain.
> ('To my Lord Chancellor', 17–18, 23–4)

The verse from then on is all, in one way or another, related to that 'great charge'. Unlike Marvell, who to some extent abandoned poetry for practical politics and prose attacks on Charles, such as *An Account of the Growth of Popery and Arbitrary Government in England* (1676), Dryden used poetry to do his political talking. During the connected traumas of the Popish plot and Exclusion crisis, Dryden used a quasi-religious poetry in forceful service of the state position. The lack of a legitimate heir from Charles's marriage was complicated by the tempting presence of a number of illegitimate ones, thanks to Charles's well-known sexual profligacy, and the most eligible of these was James, Duke of Monmouth, an attractive, and Protestant, figure on whom much of the opposition to James focused. The leader of this opposition, Anthony Cooper, Earl of Shaftesbury, was charged with treason in 1681 and Dryden wrote his best-known poem, *Absalom and Achitophel*, in support of the court's case.

Dryden picked on the story of Absalom's rebellion against his father David (from the second book of Samuel) and turned it into a version of current events, with Monmouth as Absalom, Charles as David, and Shaftesbury as Achitophel, the evil counsellor. This was not unnatural: in the Civil War it was often argued that events were replaying events from the Bible, or that biblical events could be read in a 'typological' fashion to refer to current events. But there were also several advantages in this strategy. The action was transferred away from the white heat of the political moment to a relatively safe zone of fictional representation; the readerly energy normally available for resisting partisan accounts of events is instead forced to participate in decoding the typology of the poem; and (perhaps most telling) biblical authority is brought on side. Dryden has tricky problems to deal with here, not least the fact of Charles's sexual incontinence. This aspect of court life had been mocked in several satires by Rochester, including a particularly offensive one that had got him banished from court for a while; and Pepys, a government official, commented privately on the state of play at court in his *Diary*.[1] But Dryden's writing was officially in the service of Charles. He takes a tolerant, libertine line, appearing to mock modern religious restrictions and favouring David's godlike ability to procreate.[2]

> In pious times, ere priestcraft did begin,
> Before polygamy was made a sin;
> When man on many multiplied his kind,
> Ere one to one was cursedly confined;
> When nature prompted, and no law denied,
> Promiscuous use of concubine and bride;
> Then Israel's monarch, after Heaven's own heart,
> His vigorous warmth did variously impart
> To wives and slaves; and, wide as his command,
> Scattered his Maker's image through the land. (1–10)

In fact, this right to reproduce the godlike image becomes crucial in the poem, for while David's reproductive power is authentic ('With secret joy indulgent David viewed / His youthful image in his son renewed'), Achitophel is (like Milton's Satan) capable only of a bestial parody of this creative archetype, producing

> . . . that unfeather'd, two-legged thing, a son:
> Got, while his soul did huddled notions try,
> And born a shapeless lump, like anarchy. (170–2)

Achitophel is, like Satan, the best of a bad bunch of fallen angels, multi-talented intellectually and politically, but without personal principle or restraint. He is 'Resolved to ruin or to rule the state' (174), a highly Satanic formulation. Crucially, he could gather honours naturally, but prefers rebellion: he 'Disdained the golden fruit to gather free, / And lent the crowd his arm to shake the tree' (202–3), another Satanic implication. Also in the wake of Satan comes Achitophel's charming rhetoric, a 'venom' itself laced with suggestions of Satan's perversion of Eve: 'Believe me, royal youth, thy fruit must be, / Or gathered ripe, or rot upon the tree' (250–1). Urging Absalom to seize the chance for kingship, Achitophel uses a Miltonic image to disparage David's status: he 'like the Prince of Angels, from his height, / Comes tumbling downward with diminished light' (273–4).

David is of course himself the supreme poet, his 'tuneful harp' celebrated in the main narrative; but Achitophel mocks David's 'old harp, on which he thrums his lays' and his poetry as 'some dull Hebrew ballad in your praise', linking his supposedly diminished royal power with diminished poetical creativity. Achitophel is not merely a Satanic rhetorician; he is a Satanic theorist and poet, audaciously using the resources of Milton's powerful poem of sin and redemption against the most powerful poet and king. But Dryden is, of course, a step ahead of him, and offers a Miltonic frame outside Achitophel's own perceptions. Absalom is tempted, and Dryden makes Achitophel perceive it: 'Him staggering so when Hell's dire agent found . . .' (373). The Miltonic inversion of syntax underscores the direct identification of Achitophel with Satan.

As in Milton's poem, representation is political; the right of representation, like the right of reproduction, belongs with some official incarnation of divine authority. But this is disputed: for the Jews in the poem (representing God's chosen people, the English), kings and gods alike are things they can choose to make and remake.

> God's pampered people, whom, debauched with ease,
> No king could govern, nor no God could please;
> (Gods they had tried of every shape and size,
> That god-smiths could produce, or priests devise): (47–50)

This draws on the story of the Golden Calf in the book of Exodus, where the Jews, freed from Egyptian tyranny, devise themselves an idol to worship, against the express command of the God and the leader (Moses) who has freed them. The Jews

Now wondered why so long they had obeyed
An idol-monarch, which their hands had made;
Thought they might ruin him they could create,
Or melt him to that golden calf, a State. (63–6)

Achitophel later echoes this Lockean theory of democratic sovereignty directly, telling Absalom 'the people have a right supreme / To make their King; for Kings are made for them' (409–10), a perversion of the loyal sense that kings have duties to their people. To Achitophel's hand comes the Popish plot, which Dryden sees as largely fictional and imaginary, yet dangerous in its representational power because it allowed Shaftesbury to overstate the danger from James in order to promote the interests of Monmouth. Its chief witness, Titus Oates, is invoked in the verse as Corah: 'Erect thyself thou monumental brass' (633), Dryden writes, rendering Corah a kind of self-made combination of irrepressible perjury ('brass') and a true record of the dead ('monumental'), but at any rate a self-producing improviser, another Satan-figure.

This is a contest in both poetry and politics; it is a question of who has the right to author things: children, poems, fictions, sovereigns. Dryden is the poet laureate, speaking at the behest of the Lord's anointed king, conveniently aligned with a biblical poet, whose rebellious son, everyone knew from the Bible story, was defeated (and killed). Dryden has a large section setting out his own loyal political theory of sovereignty, but in the end the creator/king who almost too freely 'scattered his Maker's image through the land' at the beginning of the poem, is offered a platform to speak. And speak is all he has to do; once he represents himself, the battle is over. The easy-going producer of offspring is now the royal supreme; the last 90 lines are given over to his decree, which reclaims both the political high ground and the poetic initiative:

Kings are the public pillars of the state,
Born to sustain and prop the nation's weight;
If my young Samson will pretend a call
To shake the column, let him share the fall . . . (953–6)

Dryden has David/Charles shift the poetic ground to a different Miltonic source, *Samson Agonistes*, to remind everyone not only that he is king, but that he knows the biblical text on which political stability is founded. Resistance is useless, and after David has spoken, 'Willing nations knew their lawful lord'.

The poem appeared a week before Shaftesbury's trial, and Dryden's optimism was unfounded. The case against Shaftesbury was thrown out by a Whig jury and his supporters immediately coined a medal in celebration.[3]

For Dryden this was a further usurpation, since the right to reproduce coin was also a royal prerogative, akin to 'scattering his maker's image through the land'. He responded with *The Medal. A Satire against Sedition*, a much bitterer, more direct satire, in which the aesthetics of the celebratory coin are turned on their head: 'So like the man, so golden to the sight, / So base within, so counterfeit and light' (8–9). A second part of *Absalom and Achitophel* was largely written by Nahum Tate, but Dryden did contribute two hundred lines on the politics of verse, including an attack on Thomas Shadwell, a Whig sympathizer (and rival dramatist). He had already made a greater assault on 'the True-blue Protestant poet T.S.' in *Mac Flecknoe*, written in 1678 and circulated in manuscript, though not published until 1682. For his central idea Dryden develops the motif of a kingdom of Dulness, ruled by Richard Flecknoe, an Irish priest and poet of low repute (he had already been lampooned by Andrew Marvell), who seeks to pass command of his realm to his most natural heir. The tone of the poem is set by the contrast between the 'high' heroic language of royal command and the 'low' actuality of Shadwell's situation. The main figures are comically self-congratulatory, even as they condemn themselves. Flecknoe is compared to the Roman Emperor Augustus (3), he had 'governed long', was 'worn out with business' and had resolved 'to settle the succession of the State'; but his 'Realm' is only that of 'Nonsense' (6) and his statecraft only to 'wage immortal war with wit', that is, good poetry. Shadwell is chosen, as the one who alone 'stands confirmed in full stupidity'. Flecknoe pursues this solemnly ludicrous praise of his dull 'son' for nearly fifty lines, before breaking down 'In silent raptures of the hopeful boy'. Shadwell is then enthroned as a 'mighty Prince' (88) in the theatre sponsored by Charles II for the training of child actors, a scene (for Dryden) of surpassing puerility. Situated on the ruins of an ancient defensive work (the Barbican), now a red-light district giving 'Scenes of lewd loves, and of polluted joys' (71), the child actors seem to emerge promiscuously from a welter of illicit sex to enact their own mock-heroic commentary on usurped authority: here 'queens are formed, and future heroes bred', here 'infant punks their tender voices try, / And little Maximins the gods defy' (75, 77–8). The attendants at the coronation similarly belie a high calling with a low physicality.

Much of the language of the poem is only just short of pure heroic idiom. The opening of the poem sounds a warning note for the 1680s:

> All human things are subject to decay
> And when fate summons, monarchs must obey. (1–2)

Though the nature of *this* monarchy is soon discovered, the statement reminds us that a serious issue, the coronation of a false monarch and the usurpation of power, lies behind the comic futility of Shadwell and the child actors: it is all too easy to use the language of power. The image of false kings haunted the literature of the period.

Revolution

In 1685 Charles died and his brother the Catholic James succeeded, crushing a doomed rebellion by Monmouth. The Whigs, who opposed his Catholicism on principle and suspected him of trying to increase his own power, hoped that he too would fail to produce a legitimate heir, but in 1688 a son duly appeared and it was necessary for the opposition to act. In the event James absconded to France, the protestant prince William of Orange (married to Mary, James's daughter) landed at Torbay and the bloodless or 'Glorious Revolution' was accomplished.

The ousting of James II in 1688 was known to its supporters as the Glorious Revolution, partly to distinguish it from the decade of bloodshed that had led to the interregnum in 1649. In fact, the bloodlessness was largely confined to England: James's supporters were forcibly put down in Scotland, and the situation in Ireland was still worse; the Battle of the Boyne, at which James was decisively defeated, was hardly without bloodshed. Nonetheless the struggle was not prolonged. The Convention which met in 1689 and turned itself into parliament by simply decreeing that it was so, looked for political common ground. William and Mary were crowned, but parliament was careful not to overplay the revolutionary nature of what it was doing. James was accused of illegal and tyrannical acts, as his father had been; the Bill of Rights asserted that he had in effect abdicated through flight, leaving parliament with a duty to find a new sovereign. As an argument it was not pretty but it was sufficient for a majority of those with power to give consent.

Some refused to take the oaths of allegiance to William, tendered to those who took public office as a means of sanctioning the new regime: these were 'non-jurors'; some maintained a belief that James was the true king who would and should return: these were 'Jacobites'. There were many, including some who thought James was a poor king, who could not reconcile themselves to the idea of a king ruling at the behest of parliament (*de facto*) without the clear title from hereditary right (*de jure*), and the shock of this triumph for parliamentary authority was felt throughout the period. Many Tories held to the notion of passive obedience and non-resistance to the sovereign, however poor his rule; most Whigs adhered to the notional liberty of the individual subject and the rule of law as established by parliament, though there was no lack of authoritarianism about that. The latter was not democracy in the modern sense, since suffrage was exclusively male and largely confined to certain classes of property holder. But this was the beginning of the end of direct rule by the sovereign, except in the most technical sense; England moved from a magical, semi-divine monarchy (an image which persisted in the dimming hopes of Jacobite circles), to a pragmatic, essentially secular rule. The European wars which were a consequence of the fall of the Stuarts required substantial government borrowing, and the consequent 'National Debt' and the foundation of the Bank of England in 1694 put professional fiscal administration more clearly in control of policy than it had ever been, much to the annoyance of Tory-inclined writers. The Tory gentry found itself subject to heavy land taxes, while Whig financiers were perceived to benefit, directly or otherwise. While party politics was hardly watertight, some fairly hard identities were now available.

The last Stuart

Deprived of his court posts after 1688 (they went, to add insult to injury, to Shadwell), Dryden retired to the literary marketplace, peppering his work with Jacobite snipings. William died in 1702, once again without issue, leaving the throne to Queen Anne, James II's Protestant younger daughter, and the last Stuart ruler of Britain. By the Act of Succession, the throne was to pass to the Elector of Hanover, the nearest blood relations of the royal line who were also Protestants (Anne's own children all died young). Anne tried to recapture something of the glamour and confidence of the 'divine' Stuarts: reviving a magical practice abandoned by William and Mary, she 'touched' for the King's Evil, a skin disease (scrofula) thought to be cured by the monarch's touch. On the other hand, she was evidently the last of her line, filling in time before the Hanoverian accession. Britain was at war with France for virtually the whole of her reign, with a series of victories credited to the Whig-inclined general Marlborough. But in 1710 the Whig 'Junto' or ministry collapsed, after the impeachment of Sacheverell, and a Tory majority was returned. This brought to the fore Robert Harley and Henry St John (later Viscount Bolingbroke), who for four years, until the death of Anne, ran a Tory ministry, bringing the war to an end.

Writers of this period did not have to declare political allegiance, but most of them leaned one way or another. Defoe managed to write, like Swift's Hack, on behalf of more than one political party, and acted as a government spy for Harley and other ministers inside several journals.

Literary clubs and gatherings tended to develop a bias: Will's, where Dryden presided, seems to have been relatively non-partisan, but after his death Addison transferred the literary proceedings there to Button's, which was clearly Whig in orientation. The Kit-Cat club was political, and Whig, in origin, and it was mainly Whig writers (Addison and Steele among them) who attended meetings, which were held at the house of the publisher Jacob Tonson. Matthew Prior was expelled for joining the Tories after 1710. Swift managed initially to maintain friendly relations with both Addison and Steele, publishing in their popular literary journals *The Tatler* and *The Spectator*, as did Pope. Addison himself created two popular characters in *The Spectator*, the Tory squire Sir Roger de Coverly, and the Whig merchant Sir Andrew Freeport, who maintain cordial relations, though Sir Roger comes in for some gentle ribbing for his country beliefs, and dies in the end. Addison's phenomenally successful neoclassical drama *Cato* (1713), on the theme of virtuous resistance to tyranny, was claimed by both Whig and Tory (Pope wrote the Prologue). The ending of the war and the question of the Hanoverian accession began to polarize matters further. Swift, who later wrote a *History of the Last Four Years of Queen Anne* on the basis of his eye-witness experience of political manoeuvring in the period, began writing highly charged propaganda for the Tory cause, undermining Marlborough by pointing out how expensive he was and how ludicrously self-aggrandizing his vast palace at Blenheim looked. (He was also, less publicly, attempting to hold together the increasingly fragile alliance between Harley and St John). During this time Pope came to Swift's attention partly through *Windsor-Forest* (1713), his most avowedly Tory poem in celebration of the coming peace.

Pope had already written *The Rape of the Locke* (1712, revised as *The Rape of the Lock* in 1714), a poem which, despite its delicate social nuance appears to have some playful Jacobite resonances: the card-game in Canto III, with its spookily animated cards and warlike manoeuvrings, sometimes suggests the context of the long-running political war with France, and sets out a political context for the forthcoming 'rape' of Belinda's hair (a lock which she repeatedly demands that the Baron 'Restore', a political keyword). Pope and Swift, with the political satirist (and royal doctor) John Arbuthnot, the poet and clergyman Thomas Parnell, John Gay, and Robert Harley himself, formed the Scriblerus club in 1714 as an elite group of Tory wits, to kick around satirical ideas and mock the 'works of the unlearned'. The group was short-lived: on Anne's death, Harley was imprisoned on suspicion of treason, Arbuthnot lost his court post, Swift returned to Ireland. St John cast in his lot with the Jacobites and fled to France.

A Jacobite rising in 1715 against the newly installed George I and in favour of the son of the deposed James II was fairly quickly defeated, but for Pope it had the effect of intensifying attacks on him as a Catholic and (therefore) suspected Jacobite sympathizer. Two of his friends were arrested for complicity in the plot. The accession of the Hanoverians brought Whigs back to power and increased activity against acknowledged Catholics and suspected Jacobites. This process also led, after some infighting among the Whigs, to the political rise of Sir Robert Walpole ('the Robinocracy'). It was he who masterminded the great political show-trial of Pope's early career. In 1723 Francis Atterbury (Bishop of Rochester) was sent into exile as the ringleader of a further Jacobite plot in England, and, as a close friend of the accused, Pope was called to give evidence in the House of Lords, though he was not himself accused of treasonable dealings. Walpole, who had directed the surveillance operation that detected Atterbury, secured his own position partly on the basis of the fear of a Catholic/Jacobite invasion, and he was in effect prime minister (though without that title) until 1742. His skill in managing George I on one hand and parliament on the other made him the undisputed leader of government; to enemies he was the Great Man, Merlin, Screen-Master General, and a host of other nicknames which paid backhanded tribute to his apparently magical powers. He was especially adroit at using the new administrative machinery to dispense patronage and influence and bolster loyal support in the House of Commons, where, as first minister, he decided to stay (rather than electing to depart to the Lords). He was also a shrewd, if blunt, debater, and stuck largely to practical and pacific policies which would reduce taxation and avoid exacerbating inherited political tensions – except those that were useful to him.

Atterbury's trial is one of the things that lies behind some of the political satire in one of the great monuments of the Scriblerian alliance, Swift's *Gulliver's Travels* (1726). Swift was rapidly burning any bridges that might have existed between himself and Sir Robert Walpole; in 1724 he had written the *Drapier's Letters* to stir up protest against what he saw as a corrupt scheme to produce a cheap copper coinage in Ireland. These *Letters* had been denounced as seditious and in *Gulliver's Travels* Swift took even more risks, indirectly representing Walpole's regime as a criminal gang running the country on a system of bribery. The somewhat intricate process by which evidence was gathered against Atterbury, which relied to some extent on decipherment of supposedly coded messages, is ridiculed in *Gulliver's Travels* in the passage where 'informers' practise reading strategies not unlike those of the brothers in *A Tale of a Tub* in order to deduce sedition from any text: 'Our brother Tom has just got the piles' becomes 'Resist: a plot is brought home; the Tour'.[4] All the puzzled comments Gulliver makes about courts and ministers in one way or another lead back to Swift's antagonism towards Walpole's political machine. We learn that politics in Lilliput is largely dependent on facility at rope-dancing; the best rope-dancer, Flimnap, is a clear portrayal of Sir Robert Walpole. When Flimnap falls off his rope 'he would have infallibly broke his Neck, if one of the *King's Cushions*, that accidentally lay on the Ground, had not weakened the Force of his Fall' (26); but the 'King's Cushion' is here the Duchess of Kendal, one of George I's mistresses, known to have helped Walpole retain power. And Swift contrives to give trivializing versions of other key political tensions from the Britain of his time: Lilliput is racked with strife between the high-heels and the low-heels (Tories and Whigs respectively).

Next on the scene was Pope's *The Dunciad*, which first appeared in 1728 and which set its face squarely against the Whig establishment and the Hanoverian kings. Following Dryden's *Mac Flecknoe*, it mockingly celebrates the coronation of Lewis Theobald, one of Pope's literary enemies, as the new King of Dulness; the poem proclaims 'Still Dunce the Second reigns like Dunce the first', a clear allusion to the recent coronation of George II. Many of the writers assaulted in Pope's bibliography of Dunces were not only personal enemies of Pope's but friends or employees of Walpole's government, and Dulness herself bears a more than passing resemblance to Queen Caroline, wife of George II, who was held by the opposition to be in cahoots with Walpole to run the country behind the King's back.

The same sensibility lay behind the other great Scriblerian success of 1728, John Gay's *The Beggar's Opera*, which had a huge theatre run. In effect this transfers the mock-heroic mode to the stage. The plot was loosely based on the activities of a figure from the criminal underworld, Jonathan Wild, who had been hanged in 1725 for receiving stolen goods. Wild's practice was to run criminal gangs, receiving the stolen goods and either selling them on or returning them to their owners for a fee; he kept up a front by occasionally turning one or other criminal over to the authorities (for which there was a reward). This seemed to Gay to offer useful political metaphors, and his play centres on the activities of a highwayman, Macheath, and a 'thieftaker', Mr Peachum (a Wild figure). Notably, the characters all talk in a high language of honour and business, a sort of mock-heroic effect in the vein of Pope's *Dunciad*, which treats modern, petty, dirty matters in epic language. But there is a further point, for to those of Gay's persuasion, modern government was effectively a kind of highway robbery, a process of intimidation, bribery and reward, based on no principle at all other than the preservation of its own power. Peachum, casting over his accounts (for as a good, if criminal businessman, his accounts are all in order) to find 'a decent execution', his eye falls on 'Robin of

Bagshot, alias Gorgon, alias Bluff Bob, alias Carbuncle, alias Bob Booty', code-names for Walpole and markers of his slipperiness.[5] Later Peachum complains about 'the long arrear of the Government' (that is, its failure to pay rewards for information on criminals) and declares

> Can it be expected that we should hang our acquaintances for nothing, when our betters will hardly save theirs without being paid for it? Unless the people in employment pay better, I promise them for the future I shall let other rogues live beside their own. . . . In one respect indeed our employment may be reckoned dishonest, because, like great statesmen, we encourage those who betray their friends. (136–7)

In case anyone had missed the point, the 'Beggar' whose 'Opera' this is, discloses at the end: 'Through the whole piece you may observe such a similitude of manners in high and low life, that it is difficult to determine whether (in the fashionable vices) the fine gentlemen imitate the gentlemen of the road, or the gentlemen of the road the fine gentlemen' (158). Not surprisingly, the government banned Gay's sequel to the play, *Polly*, and in 1737 invented a new category of censorship to deal with political satire on the stage.Thereafter a 'Licenser' had to read every play before it was acted, and could demand cuts and changes. This put an end to the stage career of Henry Fielding, who had written a number of anti-Walpole satires, and he turned to prose fiction – including a further satire, *Jonathan Wild* (1743), a not very discreet continuation of Gay's use of the criminal figure to get at the 'Great Man' of politics.

In the meantime it was left to Pope to assume poetic command of the opposition. His ethical poems of the 1730s (*Essay on Man*, *Epistles to Several Persons*, and *Imitations of Horace*) are all variously inflected with animus against Walpole and his minions. Even the determinedly neutral *Essay on Man* has a noticeable bias towards Tory rather than Whig political theory. In Book III, Pope finds that a constitution of checks and balances between competing interests in civil society represents 'Th'according music of a well-mix'd State', another example of cosmic ordering (III.294), with king, parliament and commons holding each other in check – a fairly unexceptionable proposition. But he describes the origins of society in a way that, while it concedes a certain amount to 'contractual' theory, occupies more squarely the ground of 'patriarchal' theory. Pope plays off the communitarian system of ants against the hierarchical monarchy of the bees in his description of instinctive forms of organization; but the order of human society properly only begins with the magical emergence of Patriarchs 'by Nature crown'd . . . King, priest, and parent of his growing state' (III.215–16). And Bolingbroke, the 'guide, philosopher and friend' whose intellectual input into the *Essay* the poem celebrates, was of course a disgraced ex-Jacobite and opposition theorist.

Pope's moral commentaries are often addressed to opposition heroes, as with the *Epistle to Cobham*, which Pope wrote after Cobham had broken with Walpole on a crucial vote, or to crypto-Jacobites such as Lord Bathurst. He tends to identify the land as the source of virtue and of commerce, in a way characteristic of Tory sensibilities, and tends to assault the Whig stronghold of the City as the source of an economic individualism which is ultimately criminal in its neglect of social duty and political principle. For those commentators who have tried to redescribe political divisions as 'Court' against 'Country', Pope is clearly of the Country persuasion. In the *Imitations of Horace* Pope squares up to Walpole most directly, taking the persona of the classic Roman poet of urbane social commentary and adapting it for the contemporary situation. There was a basic irony in this: Horace (65–8 BC) was a court insider, with direct access to the Emperor Augustus, and with a noble patron who had bought him a farm to live on. Pope, as everyone knew, was absolutely an outsider, with no voice at court, and no patron; his 'farm', the villa at Twickenham, was bought with money raised from the Homer subscription and had to be located there because, as a Catholic, Pope could be debarred from living in London. In the first poem of the series, Pope presents his satiric position through a debate with William Fortescue, a lawyer who was one of the few men who could claim to be a friend of both Pope and Walpole. Pope was well aware that he might stand in need of legal advice, so close to the wind did his satires sail, and part of the fun of the poem is in the lawyer's fussy presentation of 'safe' advice. Pope claims that complaints against his moderate, centrist poems come only from extremists – he is:

> Papist or Protestant, or both between,
> Like good Erasmus in an honest Mean,
> In moderation placing all my Glory,
> While Tories call me Whig, and Whigs a Tory.[6]

Pope gradually works the poem round to an overt defence of the right of the satirist to name and shame the socially guilty, however high up the political ladder, before jokingly offering the lawyer the (obviously false) promise that this might mean only

> . . . grave *Epistles*, bringing Vice to light,
> Such as a King might read, a Bishop write,
> Such as Sir Robert would approve – . . . (152–3)

In the rest of the series, Pope presents himself as an affable, shrewd, quirky figure of common humanity, for it is important for the man of virtue not to seem alienated. Nonetheless Pope regularly snipes at Walpole's excess of power and his rule through bribery, attacking 'corruption' in just the way the Bolingbroke did in the main opposition journal, *The Craftsman*. Walpole's less popular moves, the proposed Excise Bill of 1733 and his pacific response to alleged Spanish depredations on British shipping, were all duly drawn up in comic array. In the most daring of the series, an epistle exploring the uses of poetry in modern society, Pope addresses Augustus (George II, whose middle name was Augustus) directly, citing Horace's 'decent freedom' with his ruler and 'manly Regard to his own Character' in the corresponding source poem. Pope's freedom, however, is stuffed with irony, from the awesomely insincere panegyric with which the poem opens to the sniggering tribute to George's uselessness on the world stage:

> Oh! could I mount on the Mæonian wing,
> Your Arms, your Actions, your Repose to sing! . . .
> How barb'rous rage subsided at your word,
> And Nations wonder'd while they dropp'd the sword!
> How, when you nodded, o'er the land and deep,
> Peace stole her wing, and wrapt the world in sleep . . .[7]

The reason Pope can do none of this is twofold – one, it would (as it indeed does here) come out as ironic, for 'Besides, a fate attends on all I write, / That when I aim at praise, they say I bite' [satirize]; and two, George has (in Pope's estimation) done nothing worth praising. With a dig at the Poet Laureate, whose job it was to praise the king, and the small army of loyal hack writers who seconded him, Pope closes with a warning: 'A vile Encomium doubly ridicules;/There's nothing blackens like the ink of fools' (410–11).

At the end of the series Pope placed two dialogues as an 'Epilogue', continuing the self-conscious discussion of his role as opposition bard. In the first, a mealy-mouthed friend attempts to persuade Pope towards safe satiric targets and away from the topic of Walpole; 'Pope' counters with the sly declaration that he knows well enough that Walpole in private life, 'uncumber'd with the Venal tribe', is charming enough to 'win without a Bribe' (28–32). But the public system his rule represents is full of targets that need satirizing, and Pope will go on doing just that. In the second dialogue Pope continues the assault on sycophantic writers who support the government, pledging his own support to anyone in virtuous opposition: 'Does the court a worthy Man remove? / That instant, I declare, he has my Love' (74–5).

Pope was much courted by the opposition and was expected to align himself with the 'counter-court' of Prince Frederick, the eldest son of George I, who began a family pattern in falling out violently with his father. Bolingbroke's idea of a 'patriot king', acting in the interests of civic virtue, attracted him strongly. But Pope never really cast in his lot with the Patriot opposition, and a late poem on the political scene, the unfinished *1740. A Poem*, is an indiscriminate demolition of all those who put themselves forward for political power of any kind, written partly in hieroglyphics to resist the kind of decoding that had brought Atterbury down. In the revised *Dunciad Compleat* of 1743 Pope left a vision of culture irredeemably heading for oblivion more or less under government supervision, though by that stage Walpole had resigned from office (he is the 'Palinurus' who 'nodded at the helm' as the realm of Chaos returns at the end of the poem).

The extent of Pope's Jacobite sympathies has been much controverted, with readers finding Jacobite coding in everything from the early *Pastorals* to the last version of *The Dunciad*. There are varieties of Jacobitism, too: active, conspiratorial, sentimental, nostalgic, and mystical, and all of these degrees have been associated with Pope. Like Dryden, he clearly enjoyed sniping at a regime which disabled him; he knew his personal life would have been much easier under the Stuart line, and his faith led him to respect the tradition and continuity which had been interrupted in 1688. On the other hand, he was not blind to the shortcomings of previous Stuart rulers and he was in no sense a *religious* Jacobite or unthinking adherent of the doctrine of divine right. As with Milton, his sense of poetic talent was such that it would always have resisted subservience to earthly authority, and opposition, in some ways, made him the poet he was; his self-made status, isolated but for his friends, suited him personally and ethically. He is in that sense the antithesis of the early Dryden: the poems espouse open warfare against the court, proposing instead the sovereignty of poetry, an anti-court with one occupant.

After Walpole

The relation between literature and political life after the fall of Walpole in 1742 and the death of Pope in 1744 does not have this clear oppositional structure, and poets like Gray largely steered clear of anything but lightweight political comment.

Pope was probably fortunate to miss the last hurrah of the Jacobite cause, the invasion of Charles Edward Stuart, grandson of James II known as the 'Young Pretender', who arrived in Scotland in 1745 and marched as far south as Derby, taking various key towns along the way and causing financial panic in London. But as with all previous Jacobite forays, there were inadequate supplies of military hardware, personnel, popularity, and skill; Charles retreated back to Scotland and what remained of his army was heavily defeated at Culloden in 1746, with particularly brutal reprisals in the aftermath.

Henry Pelham's relatively uncontroversial ministry lasted until his death in 1754, when his brother the Duke of Newcastle took over. He found it hard to manage the Commons from the Lords, and opportunities were presented for the loose cannon William Pitt the Elder to gain access to power. Riding his luck, parading his charisma and claiming credit for the outcome of the Seven Years' War (see Chapter 5), Pitt made a calculated accommodation with the proscribed Tories which allowed them a certain way back into positions of power in return for a broader base of support. He eventually resigned from office in protest at George III's refusal to wage war on Spain, and a rapid series of 'first ministers' followed, each unable to establish any strong footing with either king or Commons. During the 1760s, the radical politician (and rake) John Wilkes (1727–97) caused considerable agitation by championing Whig positions on electoral rights and the freedom of the press, a campaign supported in particular by small businessmen and craftsmen and reflected in the writings of his friend, the clergyman satirist Charles Churchill (1732–64).

One of Churchill's favourite targets was Samuel Johnson. Born into the last years of Queen Anne, and one of the last children to be 'touched' by the monarch, Johnson's family and local background in Staffordshire had some strong Jacobite leanings. One of his earliest professional writing jobs was covering (and sometimes inventing) parliamentary debates for the *Gentleman's Magazine* and his slant on political matters was always, in broad outline, Tory: he defines 'Tory' as 'One who adheres to the antient constitution of state, and the apostolical hierarchy of the church of England, opposed to a Whig'. (For 'Whig' Johnson supplies merely 'The name of a faction'.) In terms of 'hard' politics, as opposed to social or economic issues, his Toryism was well recognized. He favoured monarchy and the church as twin pillars of a stable system of government and order, and disliked Whigs for what he perceived as their economic self-interest, their religious toleration and tendency towards dissent, and their sympathy with republicanism. He openly disliked the two first Hanoverian kings, and their minister Walpole; but the accession of George III and the complete failure of the Jacobite cause after 1746 brought him towards a gradual accommodation with the non-Stuart line. George III was much more interested in literature and culture than his father and grandfather had been, and he collected a very notable library, now part of the British Library. Johnson had a notable conversation in the Library with the king himself, at the latter's desire. Johnson was known to have Jacobite sympathies, but it is extremely unlikely that he was ever involved in any active Jacobite plotting. He respected non-jurors, and it has been forcefully suggested that he himself avoided such public professions as would result in the oaths of allegiance being tendered to him; but there is no final evidence that he positively saw himself as a non-juror.

In his early years he contributed to the opposition to Walpole in the political pamphlets *Marmor Norfoliciense* and *A Compleat Vindication of the Licensers of the Stage* (both 1739). Some aspects of his poem *London* add obliquely to this standard material. Johnson's writings have been extensively tested by those keen to enlist him to the Jacobite cause, and traces of pro-Stuart sympathies have been discovered in his biography of Savage, his play *Irene*, his novella *Rasselas*, the *Dictionary*, the notes to his edition of Shakespeare, and his Latin poetry. In his account of his tour in Scotland, he pays tribute to Flora Macdonald, who helped Charles Stuart escape from Scotland after Culloden. The sum total of these gleanings is neither great nor wholly convincing, but there is no doubt that, like Pope, he had an emotional affinity with the Stuart line, and as with Pope, his acknowledged Toryism and presumed Jacobitism were a target for literary satirists.

In 1762 Johnson had accepted an official pension of £300 per year after some concern about the damage it would do to his reputation, given that he had defined 'Pension' in the *Dictionary* as 'pay given to a state hireling for treason to his country'. At one stage it was seriously proposed that he stand for parliament. Instead he wrote four political pamphlets on behalf of the ministry of Lord North, leader of a relatively stable ministry from 1770–82. Two of these were on domestic issues. *The False Alarm* (1770) answered the popular protests brought about by the exclusion of Wilkes from parliament; Johnson had already clashed with Wilkes, whom he thought a libertine, opportunist, and scoundrel. (One of the high points of Boswell's *Life of Johnson* is his account of a dinner in 1776 at which he arranged for Johnson and Wilkes to meet each other: they were surprisingly cordial together, though their political differences were undiminished.) *The Patriot* (1774) attacked the self-seeking hypocrisy of the opposition in general. The other two pamphlets treated foreign policy issues: *Thoughts on the late Transactions of Falkland's Islands* (1771) defended the ministry's refusal to go to war with Spain over the sovereignty of the islands. *Taxation no Tyranny* (1775) was a pamphlet defending the sovereignty of the British parliament over the American colonies in the wake of the Boston Tea-Party.

The American War of Independence (1775–83) was a rallying moment for proponents of the right of self-government through free elections (though this did not extend, as Johnson acidly pointed out, to the slaves on the plantations).

Johnson lived until 1784, long enough to see the emergence of a new version of dualistic politics in the rivalry between Charles Fox and William Pitt the Younger. Though in his American pamphlet Johnson was expressing a fairly popular view in opposing the claims of the colonists, there was also a groundswell of pro-American sentiment, from Wilkes, Burke and William Pitt the Elder. This movement, which we might think of as a radical forbear of modern democracy, faced its own challenges not long after Johnson's death when the French Revolution of 1789 ushered in the age of popular democracy. But that belongs with the study of Romanticism.

Notes

1 See Rochester, 'A Satyr on King Charles II' (1674); *Complete Poems*, edited by Vieth, pp. 60–1.
2 Marvell's *Mr Smirke: or the Divine in Mode* (1676) was a more serious attack on the power of the clergy.
3 Shafesbury himself fled to Holland and died there in 1683.
4 Swift, *Gulliver's Travels*, edited by Paul Turner (Oxford, 1994), p. 184.
5 *The Beggar's Opera and other Eighteenth-Century Plays*, selected by John Hampden, introduction by David Lindsay (London, 1974), p. 114. Subsequent references are to this edition.
6 *The First Satire of the Second Book of Horace Imitated*, lines 65–8; references are to *Pope: Poetical Works*, edited by Herbert Davis (Oxford, 1978).
7 *The First Epistle of the Second Book of Horace Imitated*, 394–401, 394–5, 398–401.

4

Town, country, nation

> Why have the inhabitants of Birmingham increased from 23,000 in 1750, to 30,000 in 1770? Certainly because a proportional increase of employment has taken place. Wherever there is a demand for hands, there they will abound . . . Thus where employment increases (Birmingham), the people increase: and where employment does not increase (Colchester), the people do not increase. . . . Go to the shipping of the kingdom, it will be found the same: our sailors have increased. Why? Because their employment has increased. . . . Nabobs from the Indies, planters from America, merchants from the Exchange settle in the counties, they farm, garden, plant, improve – they want men, their demand is answered, and was it regular would around every great house . . . support a town.
>
> Go to the villages, the same truth will everywhere be apparent: if husbandry improves, it will demand more labour – that demand is the encouragement of the production of the commodity demanded – and it will be supplied. Who supposes that a county of warrens, heaths, and farming slovens, converted to well-tilled fields, does not occasion an increased demand for hands? And was it ever known that such a demand existed without being supplied?
>
> But the hands, it is said, leave certain villages and go to towns. Why? Because there is not employment in one case, and there is in another – their going to the town proves that they go to employment – they go to that very circumstance which is to increase their number. They go, because they are demanded; that demand it is true takes, but it feeds them.
>
> [Arthur Young, *Political Arithmetic* (1774), pp. 61–4]

Arthur Young (1741–1820) was an agricultural theorist who acted as Secretary to the Board of Agriculture, compiling official reports on the state of farming in Britain. Before that he had undertaken several provincial tours, surveying regional agriculture, transport and industry in order to inform policy in London. In this extract he comments on the economic factors affecting the balance between urban and rural population, an issue of increasing importance during the period. This chapter will examine the relationships between town, country and emerging nationhood, and the writing that informed them.

London

London was extensively damaged by the Great Fire of 1666, though this also presented an opportunity: much ramshackle, wood-based architecture disappeared, to be replaced by a planned central city of stone, with new bridges, new churches and a new St Paul's Cathedral. This London, the city of Sir Christopher Wren, was the centre of political power, with parliament and the court sitting at the west end amidst a penumbra of high-class housing, theatres and other entertainment venues. On the other side of London stood the City, an area mapped by ancient walls but more clearly known, especially after the foundation of the Bank of England in 1694, as the commercial centre of the nation. Dryden's identification of the 'City' as a Whig stronghold, peopled by those who thought that 'Kings were useless, and a clog to trade' is an exaggeration, but not wholly inaccurate in political terms. It is an irony of Pope's career that he was actually born in the City, and had a merchant for a father.

London was the home of the Inns of Court, the training establishments for lawyers, which in turn fed activity in courts such as the King's Bench and the Old Bailey, and a large array of prisons for debtors and convicts. From Newgate prison would emerge, at regular intervals, those prisoners condemned to execution, who took a well-lined route to the gallows at Tyburn (near where Marble Arch now stands). London was the centre of the book trade: while there were some provincial printing presses (notably at Oxford and Cambridge universities), the real business of book production was firmly located in London, along the Strand, around Fleet Street, in St Paul's Churchyard. Coffee houses had begun to proliferate in the Restoration period, especially in the City, where they were quite commonly places to transact commercial business in stock-broking or insurance. Booksellers congregated in the Chapter coffee-house, book auctions were commonly held in such places, and authors used them as accommodation addresses.

The engravings of William Hogarth depict London as alternately vibrant ('Beer Street') and vicious ('Gin Lane').[1] London attracted and repelled writers in similar fashion. One strand of Swift's *Tale of a Tub* works by setting the representatives of the three churches in a worldly (London) environment:

> . . . they quickly began to improve in the good Qualities of the Town; They Writ, and Raillyed, and Rhymed, and Sung, and Said, and said Nothing; They Drank, and Fought, and Whor'd, and Slept, and Swore, and took Snuff: They went to new Plays on the first Night, haunted the *Chocolate*-Houses, beat the Watch, lay on Bulks, and got Claps: They bilkt Hackney-Coachmen, ran in Debt with Shop-keepers, and lay with their Wives: They kill'd Bayliffs, kick'd Fidlers down Stairs, eat at *Locket*'s, loitered at *Will*'s . . .[2]

Swift's poem 'A Description of the Morning' catches more gently the beginnings of early-morning activity in the streets of London. His 'A Description of a City Shower' comically envisages the effects of an epic rainstorm on Londoners, culminating in the disgusting effluent from Smithfield meat-market. The effect is deliberately mock-heroic: a 'beau' (or man of fashion) trapped in his coach is compared to the Greek heroes in the Trojan horse. These poems were published in *The Tatler* (1709 and 1710), one of a new breed of journals which embraced the urban ethos and tried to coat it with urbane values such as sociability and politeness. Gay (whose first play, *The Mohocks* of 1712, made fun of the alleged activities of a violent London gang) picked up the less polite possibilities of urban mock-heroic in his *Trivia: or, the Art of Walking the Streets of London* (1716). Guiding the reader through the dangers of mucky gutters and littered pavements, Gay encounters a series of street figures (fishwives, ballad-singers, footmen) who give London its characteristic sense of bustle. In Book II he ludicrously derives the 'boot-black' (shoe-shine boy) from a sexual union in a dark alley between Cloacina, the supposed Roman goddess of the sewers, and a mortal 'scavenger' or hauler of excrement. This presents a fit metaphor for the kind of poem he is writing: a fun but illegitimate hybrid between a dirty classicism and urban filth.

Pope's 'The Alley', an imitation of Spenser, splices the earlier poet's high-romance language with the scenery and detail of Billingsgate fish-market, for comic effect. 'Epistle to Miss Blount, On her leaving the Town after the Coronation' (1714) mocks Zephalinda's boredom at a return to country life after the excitements of the big city:

> She went, to plain-work, and to purling brooks,
> Old-fashion'd halls, dull aunts, and croaking rooks:
> She went from Op'ra, park, assembly, play,
> To morning-walks, and pray'rs three hours a day; (11–14)

A companion piece, 'A Farewell to London, in the Year 1715', commemorates Pope's own departure from the 'Dear, damn'd, distracting town', comically contrasting his life as a sexually active young writer in London ('This year in peace, ye critics, dwell, / Ye harlots, sleep at ease!') with the 'sober studious days' he must spend translating Homer in the country.

As a Catholic Pope was under pressure to leave London; hence his diplomatic retreat to the margins of town and country upriver at Twickenham. This kept him within easy reach of the capital, but it also gave him a kind of significant distance, an aloof position from which he could comment on the corruptions of Walpole's London. In 1728 he published the first version of *The Dunciad. An Heroic Poem*, which takes the essential joke of Dryden's *Mac Flecknoe*, the mock-coronation of a talentless poet in a seedy London setting, and projects it as a much larger cultural complaint. Pope's main 'hero' was Lewis Theobald, a lawyer turned poet, dramatist and Shakespeare scholar, who had pointed out with devastating (if pompous) acuity the deficiencies of Pope's edition of Shakespeare. In the final version, the hero was Colley Cibber, comic actor and jobbing playwright, who had told a particularly insalubrious anecdote about Pope's sex life in 1742. (He was also poet laureate, giving Pope a chance to stress how things had changed since *Mac Flecknoe*, when Dryden could issue his lampoon with the authority of the state behind him.) The rest of the host of writers named in the poem are enemies of Pope's: libellers, workers in Walpole's propaganda machine, critics. There is no trace of affable coterie about literary London: from Twickenham, Pope can identify the whole scene as corrupt, stupid and venal.

Pope had of course many other models, including a satire on the London college of physicians by his friend Samuel Garth (*The Dispensary*, 1699), and Swift's *Tale of a Tub* in its concerns about contemporary writing. But *The Dunciad* also provides and relies on a much more detailed map of London, in its deft parody of Aeneas's journey from Troy to found a new colony at Rome. The action takes place, in theory, on Lord Mayor's Day, 1720, when Sir George Thorold took office; his procession left the City and ended up in the West End, which is in effect what the Dunces do, as the poem explains:

> The Mighty Mother, and her Son who brings
> The Smithfield Muses to the ear of Kings,
> I sing. (I.1–3)

Smithfield (the meat-market where Swift's messy flood begins, in the 'Description of a City Shower') was

> the place where Bartholomew Fair was kept, whose shews, machines, and dramatical entertainments, formerly agreeable only to the taste of the Rabble, were, by the Hero of this Poem, and others of equal genius, brought to the Theatres of Covent-garden, Lincolns-inn-fields, and the Hay-market, to be the reigning pleasures of the Court and Town. This happened in the Reigns of King George I and II.[3]

The low-life pleasures associated with dirty areas of London come to occupy locations of power (the theatres near the seats of parliament and the court), under the approving agency of the Hanoverian kings. As well as the Lord Mayor's entry into power, therefore, there is a direct target in the coronation of George II in 1727.

Either figure would do to usher in a new reign of 'Dulness', Pope's mock-Goddess or Empress. Her spiritual home is located near to Bedlam, the London asylum for the insane, but this was itself close to Grub Street, which ran through the parish of St Giles, Cripplegate, just outside the old City wall but within City jurisdiction; it was used metaphorically as an indicator of low-level literature and hack writing.[4] The 'Cave of Poverty and Poetry' which lies here sends forth a spawning morass of print: 'Curl's chaste press' (the output of Edmund Curll, rogue publisher and convicted pornographer), 'hymning Tyburn's elegiac lines' (the 'last dying speeches' issued in the name of executed criminals), and so on: 'all the Grub-street race' (I.39–44). In Book II, Dulness announces 'high heroic Games' for her devotees. This episode, a parody of the funeral games of Virgil's *Aeneid*, brings poets, critics, patrons and booksellers to the Strand, a street where many booksellers had their shops. Curll races Lintot for possession of a 'phantom' poet (mocking Curll's habit of ascribing poems to an imaginary 'Joseph Gay', to pass them off as the work of John Gay). Curll falls over in some excrement, metaphorically standing for an illicit publication of his own, but prays to Jove, who uses the prayer for toilet paper, assisted by 'fair Cloacina', here every bit as filth-inclined as in Gay's *Trivia*, but more pertinently aligned with Curll's predilection for sexual dirt to publish. Curll's prayer is duly 'Sign'd with that Ichor which from Gods distils' and he himself is 'Renew'd by ordure's sympathetic force'; he wins the race, only to find the 'poet' evaporate into a suit of clothes which an unpaid tailor reclaims. After a competition in which poets must tickle their patrons to extract money (that is, they must flatter them with their quill pens in doomed and demeaning ritual subservience), the writers are asked to dive in the mud of Fleet ditch.

> This labour past, by Bridewell all descend,
> (As morning pray'r, and flagellation end)

To where Fleet-ditch with disemboguing streams
Rolls the large tribute of dead dogs to Thames,
The King of dykes! that whom no sluice of mud
With deeper sable blots the silver flood. (II.269–74)

Bridewell was a prison for prostitutes and vagrants, where public whippings were carried out as part of the regular 'discipline', here indiscriminately linked with piety ('morning pray'r'); it was situated on the west bank of the Fleet ditch, an open sewer (eventually covered over in 1737) running into the Thames from north London. Fleet street was also very near the centre of journalistic activity, which conveniently suggested the filthy nature of that branch of writing. Pope's lines brilliantly merge a heraldic purity ('sable', 'silver') with actual effluent. Eventually Jonathan Smedley, an especially vicious opponent of Pope and Swift, returns from the deep to tell of his adventures with the 'mud-nymphs' (excrement turned into figures of amorous intrigue by his diseased imagination). Others make their escape to Fleet prison, where debtors were confined; hence Pope's joke about it being a safe retreat, or 'Haunt of the Muses'. Book III is a dream vision, a parody of underworld trips by Odysseus and Aeneas, as well as of the final books of *Paradise Lost*, that allows the hero to view the future empire of dullness in Britain. Beneath the all-too-real streets of filthy London, a nightmare vision lies in waiting.[5] London provides Pope with an instant contrast between modern life and the grandeur of classical epic: put the two together, and the result is ludicrous. But London has real power, real responsibility, in culture as in everything else: what happens in London matters for the nation as a whole. Its criminally dozy fraternity of writers and booksellers was, in occupying the seats of power of every kind, impoverishing national culture.

In contrast, Samuel Johnson, having arrived in London from Lichfield in 1737, was soon an adoptive Londoner who never lived permanently anywhere else; despite strong traces of a regional accent, he preferred the liveliness and sociability of London to the solitude and inactivity of the country. 'The town is my element,' he told Boswell. 'When a man is tired of London, he is tired of life; for there is in London all that life can afford'; 'I think the full tide of human existence is at Charing-cross.'[6] London offered variety, conversation, people learned in all areas; it was the place of most opportunity for everything, and most particularly for writing: Johnson accepted the conditions of the professional book trade as Pope never did. Johnson's main published work on the city, *London: A Poem, in Imitation of the Third Satire of Juvenal* (1738), conveys, however, a significantly darker picture.[7] The main speaker in the poem is Thales, a poet who denounces the city as he leaves for retirement in Wales. Thales (loosely based on Richard Savage), presents a litany of city evils that he will be free from in the innocent countryside.

> Prepare for death, if here at Night you roam,
> And sign your Will before you sup from Home.
> Some fiery Fop, with new Commision Vain,
> Who sleeps on Brambles till he kills his Man;
> Some frolick Drunkard, reeling from a Feast,
> Provokes a Broil, and stabs you for a Jest.[8]

In later years, Johnson would not have subscribed to a naïve opposition between city corruption and rural innocence. But the sense of London as a criminal haven was not entirely fictional. Eight times a year the gaols of London were emptied as people stood trial, largely for offences of theft, which dominate the printed 'sessions papers' that emerged at the end of every 'gaol delivery'. The death penalty was in place for most crimes against property and most forms of violence: deterrence was used in place of detection, for the idea of a police force was regarded as a French-style attempt to infringe traditional English liberties and impose governmental will on the population. Londoners could also watch or read trials for murder, sex offences, forgery, and counterfeiting, especially interesting cases of which resulted in separate accounts of the trial, the life of the criminal, and an account of the execution. Jack Sheppard's repeated escapes from Newgate were recounted in breathless prose, with diagrams of his exploits. As well as a flourishing literature of criminal biography, there was an influence on fiction: Defoe's Moll Flanders is a London-based thief, stalking the dark alleyways of the city and ending up in Newgate under sentence of death, and Colonel Jack begins the same way. Defoe appears to have written an account of Jonathan Wild, whose appeal to the satiric imaginations of Gay and Fielding we have already noted. Fielding himself became a magistrate in 1748, sitting at Bow Street, and devoting himself to raising judicial standards and providing an adequate local police force. His *Enquiry into the Causes of the Late Increase of Robbers* (1751) depicted a London swamped with low commercialism, disgusting night-cellars full of criminal sexual activity, smelly alleyways inhabited by gangs of criminals and corrupt thief-catchers: a kind of prose version of one aspect of Pope's *Dunciad*.

But this view was open to challenge. Unlike many, Johnson thought Gay's association of sexual glamour with the highwayman Macheath in *The Beggar's Opera* did not corrupt the nation's youth.[9] In a *Rambler* essay he even argued against the use of capital punishment, except for murder.[10] His biographical account of Savage's trial for murder in 1727 is a kind of belated speech for the defence. Johnson gave evidence in person at the Old Bailey murder trial of Giuseppe Baretti, an Italian scholar and friend of his who in 1769 killed a pimp in a street brawl after being accosted by a prostitute. He was acquitted, on grounds of self-defence, after Johnson gave his evidence 'in a slow, deliberate, and distinct manner, which was uncommonly impressive'.[11]

Outside the capital

However atrocious London seemed to Fielding in 1750, it was by modern standards relatively small, the north area being particularly undeveloped. Anyone walking up Tottenham Court Road in 1749 would have been looking at open fields; the land behind the British Museum was in 1756 a farm. The contrast between town and country was sharper in eighteenth-century London than it is now. It was also, however, an ancient and literary one, deriving from the traditions of Greek pastoral (Theocritus) and especially from the Latin *Eclogues* of Virgil, translated by Dryden in 1697. These were a classic example of 'apprentice work', Virgil having proceeded to write epic poetry; it is no surprise that Pope's first published work was a set of *Pastorals*. The four poems each represent a particular season and are set at different times of day, from morning to midnight; though classical names are retained the landscape is that of the Thames Valley and Berkshire, where Pope grew up. In his 'Discourse on Pastoral Poetry', later printed with the poems, he claims the mantle of the ancients, favouring appropriately classical gesture and language against the modern view, represented by the poet Ambrose Philips, that a degree of realistic 'simplicity' should be adopted. He had also spoofed Philips's yokels in an earlier essay.[12] John Gay's *The Shepherd's Week* (1714) was, for similar reasons, in mock-pastoral vein, with characters like 'Blouselinda' and 'Grubbinol' going about their rustic business.

The other 'rural' genre available to poets was the Georgic, so called after Virgil's four poems on agricultural matters, also translated by Dryden, with an influential essay by Addison as preface. Displaying an interest in practical matters, these poems stood somewhere between pastoral and epic; a well-known example in Pope's day was John Philips's *Cyder* (1708). Gay's contribution to the genre was *Rural Sports*, addressed to Pope in 1713 to celebrate Pope's ease in the countryside around Windsor and bewail Gay's own confinement in the 'noisie town'. Pope comes nearest to the genre in *Windsor-Forest*, also published in 1713. This presents a glowing, painterly account of the landscape of the royal park at Windsor, as a direct representative of a lost paradise: 'The Groves of Eden, vanish'd now so long, / Live in description, and look green in song' (7–8). The area was originally not a forest in the modern sense, but a royal preserve for the hunting of deer; in Pope's day it presented a mixed landscape of woodland, pasture, and arable land. Pope makes this variety a source of aesthetic pleasure:

> Here hills and vales, the woodland and the plain,
> Here earth and water seem to strive again,
> Not Chaos-lie together crush'd and bruis'd,
> But, as the world, harmoniously confus'd:
> Where order in variety we see,
> And where, tho' all things differ, all agree. (11–16)

Initially Pope is using the conventions of topographical poetry, especially as represented by Sir John Denham's *Cooper's Hill* (1642), set on a small eminence near the politically significant field of Runnymede. Pope presents a kind of georgic idyll, providing a labour-free cornucopia of agricultural supply: 'peace and plenty tell, A STUART reigns' (42). But the overt political gesture also points to considerable disquiet at the destructive nature of some of the traditional activities that take place within the forest area. Hunting becomes a possible code for war, previous rulers such as the Norman William (to say nothing of the more recent William III, Pope's real target) have devastated the idea of communal, civic living that Pope finds there. At the centre of the poem, a mythological account of the nymph 'Lodona' (who, to avoid rape, metamorphoses into the real river Loddon, a tributary of the Thames), suggests the vulnerability of the landscape. Gathering strength from historical example, however, the poem sets out from a historical centre of royal power, Windsor Castle, moving to the Thames at London in a patriotic vision of Britain's future dominance in a new world order.

Pope's confidence in that role was soon dashed, since his reigning 'Stuart', Queen Anne, died a year later. But that movement, *from* rural virtues *to* civic power, is repeated in later poems. In the *Epistle to Bathurst* (1733), an essay on the use of riches, Pope aligns villainous use of money largely with figures from the City: he names several real individuals, many of them caught up in financial scandals, and ends the poem with a deft moral fable, the story of Sir Balaam, a London-based Whig businessman whose catastrophic fall is caused by his unearned financial success. Contrasts of economy are also felt in the country, however. 'Old Cotta' is a miser, living off nettles and neglecting his duties as a landowner to provide employment and local festivity for the community; 'Young Cotta' inherits and immediately dissipates the fortune in the service of 'GEORGE and LIBERTY', cutting his woods for the navy, donating his wool for army clothing and finally selling the estate outright to cut a figure in London as a Whig loyalist. He goes bankrupt. Bathurst himself ('yet unspoil'd by wealth') provides a better example of a stable local economy, and Pope also presents the case of John Kyrle, a paragon of rural virtue from Ross-on-Wye, who runs his modest estate and the nearby village on protective, paternalist lines.

In the *Epistle to Burlington*, also on the use of riches, Pope invents Timon's Villa, a country seat built out of all natural scale for no purpose but to display wealth. Pope ridicules the extravagance of such a monument: various Whig palaces, built by London-based politicians buying up the countryside, have been suggested as the model for this passage, and Pope probably takes details from more than one of them. Timon represents money coming to the country and ruining it; Pope is out for revenge, and prophesies the return of proper agriculture to demolish such inhuman architecture:

> Another age shall see the golden Ear
> Imbrown the Slope, and nod on the Parterre,
> Deep Harvests bury all his Pride has plann'd,
> And laughing Ceres re-assume the land. (173–6)

Moreover, Pope provides a recipe for the foundation of civic and economic success on the stable rural virtues of the ideal landowner:

> His Father's Acres who enjoys in peace,
> Or makes his Neighbours glad, if he encrease;
> Whose chearful Tenants bless their yearly toil,
> Yet to their Lord owe more than to the soil;
> Whose ample Lawns are not asham'd to feed
> The milky heifer and deserving steed;
> Whose rising Forests, not for pride or show,
> But future Buildings, future Navies grow:
> Let his plantations stretch from down to down,
> First shade a Country, and then raise a Town. (181–90)

This is the true ordering of civil society: a stable peasantry, productive in agriculture, happy with their lot, under the supervision of a benign landowner whose care constitutes the origin of all valid political power.

Burlington (a Whig aristocrat), was an architect, while Bathurst (a Tory and sometime Jacobite) was known for his enormous landscape garden at Cirencester Park in Gloucestershire. Pope advised both men on their schemes, but was especially interested in landscape gardening, and Bathurst's estate was consciously laid out with Pope's guidelines in mind. Pope's essay 'On Gardens' in the *Guardian* (29 September 1713) became a classic of the new curvilinear style of gardening. His own five acres at Twickenham were completely remodelled as a sort of miniature version of a country estate, with lawns, groves, copses and 'vistas' or viewpoints. There was a vineyard, a grand walk, three small 'mounts' to give views, a small 'wilderness' (a deliberately irregular and informal zone), as well as a kitchen garden for practical use. It was a highly coded area, a sort of personal landscape poem with aids to reflection on every hand.

In the Horatian imitations Pope makes comic reference to the small scale of his estate as part of his pose of virtuous independence. His gardening contacts often had a kind of political edge. Timon's villa is criticized for its brute symmetries, unnatural scale and mechanical imposition on nature. Instead, Pope counsels, we should 'Consult the Genius of the Place in all' (*Epistle to Burlington*, 57), and ensure that the human design is just a kind of improvement on the (co-operative) natural landscape. Pope's example of such a garden is Viscount Cobham's estate at Stowe, in Buckinghamshire, one of his regular places of resort. This was in the new naturalistic taste in gardening, as against the previous continental model of formal patterns and regular, symmetrical design. It was also, however, a known centre of Opposition activity, dotted about with iconic references to the infighting and 'corruption' of Walpole's regime and the band of principled patriots who opposed it: the garden as political statement.

The tradition of landscape gardening lived on in Horace Walpole, another Twickenham resident, and William Shenstone, who spent most of his fortune turning his country retreat into a model landscape farm (much to the scorn of Johnson, who recounts Shenstone's failure to observe practical economics in his *Life*). Walpole and Shenstone both wrote essays on gardening, which had become an eminent profession: William Kent, Laurence 'Capability' Brown, and Humphrey Repton were all called in by landowners to redesign their estates in long-term projects involving large-scale use of water and trees. The political element of such designs gave way to aesthetic concerns. 'Picturesque' landscape tourism was popularized by William Gilpin, though there are already signs of what is now a familiar worship of landscape in Pope's 'rambles' in the country.[13]

There were other ways of apprehending the natural world, not least in the work of scientists such as John Ray, Robert Plot and Robert Hooke in the seventeenth century. Stephen Hales, a clergyman and neighbour of Pope's, and also a Fellow of the Royal Society, wrote a groundbreaking book on plant respiration (*Vegetable Staticks*) in 1727. Botanic gardens were opened at the universities of Oxford and Cambridge; experimental hybridization of plants began. Gilbert White, a rural clergyman, wrote a series of exquisitely observed letters on the ecology of a small village in Hampshire, which turned into an unexpected bestseller: *The Natural History and Antiquties of Selborne* (1788).

A kind of hybrid between appreciation of scenery, Newtonian science and Georgic practicality is on offer in James Thomson's *The Seasons* (1726–30, with allegorical designs by William Kent). This seeks to lead the urban imagination through a non-urban scene.

> Now from the town,
> Buried in smoke and sleep and noisome damps,
> Oft let me wander o'er the dewy fields
> Where freshness breathes, and dash the trembling drops
> From the bent bush, as through the verdant maze
> Of sweet-briar hedges I pursue my walk . . . (*Spring*, 101–6)

But it is not strictly a landscape poem. It meditates on the yearly pattern as it affects flora and fauna, including humans. Its Miltonic blank verse can include descriptions of non-human nature that are close to the emerging disciplines of ornithology, botany, and entomology, while it also observes the cycle of agriculture, and offers a hymn of praise to God, the 'author' of it all. It is didactic: in Spring, Thomson can write 'Man superior walks / Amid the glad Creation' (170–1), but in Winter he sees 'one wide dazzling waste, / That buries wide the works of man' (239–40). Naturally, it promotes a contrast between the innocence of rural life and the luxurious corruptions of the town:

> The happiest he! who far from public rage,
> Deep in the vale, with a choice few retired,
> Drinks the pure pleasures of the rural life. (*Autumn*,1236–8)

This is not quite to recapture Eden, however, for the poem also takes a cue from Pope's *Windsor-Forest* in querying the country pleasures of fishing (*Spring*) and hunting (*Autumn*).[14] The most conflicted aspect of Thomson's rural view, however, is labour.

Rural labour

Thomson's poem includes a certain view of the rural economy. Hay is made and sheep are sheared in *Summer*, and in *Autumn* there is honey from the bees, and harvest. Thomson acknowledges the necessary 'sweat, and pain' of labour in general (*Autumn*, 44), but his picture of reaping, though it is ordered economically (the 'Master' is wandering up and down counting the sheaves) also suggests the force of a plentiful Nature:

> Before the ripened field the reapers stand
> In fair array, each by the lass he loves,
> To bear the rougher part and mitigate
> By nameless gentle offices her toil.
> At once they stoop, and swell the lusty sheaves;
> While through their cheerful band the rural talk,
> The rural scandal, and the rural jest
> Fly harmless, to deceive the tedious time
> And steal unfelt the sultry hours away. (*Autumn*, 153–61)

Behind such depictions lay some new developments. Still predominantly an agricultural country, Britain began to experiment with new techniques from 1700 onwards. Jethro Tull, a landowner in Berkshire, introduced a method of 'drilling' rows in the soil that improved the processing of nutrients by crops. His *Horse-hoeing Husbandry* of 1731 was taken up by Charles, 2nd Viscount Townshend, who adopted a new method of crop rotation over large areas of land. Another Norfolk landowner, Thomas Coke of Holkham, developed new methods of manuring land. These developments were promoted by large-scale farmers, for the old system of small-scale tenant farming militated against risky innovation. Arthur Young enthusiastically noted the transition after 1760 from the old practices to the new; to feed an increasing population it was necessary to enclose waste-lands, drain marshes, amalgamate smallholdings into large farms, grow 'green manure' crops, and plan for winter feeds. The landscape was changing.

Literary comments on rural life tend not to have much to say about rural labour, just as landscape painting (which, in the work of Thomas Gainsborough, began to emerge as an artistic genre in the period) generally excluded work from the scene. In 1718, while Pope was staying at the Oxfordshire estate of his friend Viscount Harcourt, two young labourers, Sarah Drew and John Hewet, who were engaged to be married, were killed by lightning during a thunderstorm, thus providing Pope with a rare 'occasion' to make verse (an epitaph) out of agricultural labour.[15] A different case was provided by Stephen Duck (1705–56), a self-educated farm labourer, who read Milton avidly, and wrote poetry himself. This was a kind of wonder, as the breathless title page of his 1730 *Poems* shows: Duck was 'Lately a poor *Thresher* in a Barn in the County of *Wilts*, at the Wages of Four Shillings and Sixpence', but his poems

> were publickly read by The Right Honourable the Earl of *Macclesfield*, in the Drawing-Room at *Windsor*-Castle . . . to her Majesty. Who was thereupon most graciously pleased to take the Author into her Royal Protection, by allowing him a Salary of Thirty Pounds *per Annum*, and a small House at *Richmond* in *Surrey*, to live in, for the better Support of Himself and Family.

This presents some sharp economic and cultural contrasts, between sovereign and labourer, salary and wages, Pope's Windsor and the world of actual agriculture. *The Thresher's Labour*, the most interesting of Duck's poems, delineated the 'endless toils' of agricultural work beyond the conventions of georgic or pastoral, though it obeyed other rules: it is written in Popean heroic couplets and uses a conventional store of mythological reference (Hercules, Sisyphus) to establish a poetic idea of 'labour'. Duck the thresher is clearly at the bottom of the tree, beneath the tenant farmer who organizes the work, and the landowner to whom the tenant pays rent. Work is cheerful enough to begin with, with some variety in the cycle of tasks (threshing, mowing, harvesting) and friendly rivalry between the workers. It is also hard, hot, and sweaty: at its simplest, the poem is a complaint:

> Each Morn we early rise, go late to bed,
> And lab'ring hard, a painful life we lead

Duck even dreams about his work. The Master rewards his workers with a huge feast, but the next morning the whole process starts again. This is not how it seemed in Thomson's *Autumn*. Duck escaped to the dubious status of literary freak: Pope and Swift were among those who subscribed to the 1736 edition of his poems, and Duck was ordained as a clergyman, but in the end he committed suicide.

It was more 'natural' for literature to represent labour through known models, and the production of georgic poems continued: Robert Dodsley, himself a former servant, published *Agriculture* in 1753 and John Dyer, a Welsh artist, poet and clergyman, graduated from the topographical *Grongar Hill* (1726), describing the scenery around River Towy, to *The Fleece* (1757), a poem about the production of cloth from sheep's wool.

Some of the literary engagement with rural work rendered it elusive. Thomas Gray's *Elegy Written in a Country Church-Yard* was loosely based on the churchyard at Stoke Poges, where Gray went for summer retreats. It opens with the blanking out of the landscape and the people who work in it.

The ploughman homeward plods his weary way,
And leaves the world to darkness and to me. (3–4)

The sole living representative of rural labour thus walks out of the poem, his fatigue registered but his absence an essential condition of the verse. This is visionary experience: 'Now fades the glimmering landscape on the sight' (5), with the poet-figure alone amid the 'rude Forefathers of the hamlet'. Gray's communion with the villagers is thus only with those who are buried: his lively vision of their early rising, their life in cottages, their wives and children and their 'jocund' and 'sturdy' labour, is founded on the poignant fact that these things cannot happen for the people around him any more.

Moreover, the poem is not addressed to them, but to people of Gray's class: educated, rich, literate. It is an admonition to those who might condescend to or patronise the low achievements of rural life: 'Let not Ambition mock their useful toil, / Their homely joys, and destiny obscure', Gray warns, for 'The paths of glory lead but to the grave'. Gray's argument also opens the possibility that these unnamed men – there is an implicit sense of gender in the poem – might, in different circumstances, have been statesmen, or poets, or generals.

Perhaps in this neglected spot is laid
Some heart once pregnant with celestial fire,
Hands that the rod of empire might have sway'd,
Or wak'd to extasy the living lyre. (45–8)

Then again, Gray argues, it might be better not to have had the opportunity, since the curtailment of any possible ambition also negates the possibility of crime or abuse of power. Better to remain 'Far from the madding crowd's ignoble strife', and to 'keep the noiseless tenor of their way' (71, 74).

There are radical elements in this, though the morality of it is familiar. But the poem splits apart at the end. Gray notes that even illiterate peasants have attempted, forlornly, to provide epitaphs for the dead: 'Their name, their years, spelt by th' unletter'd muse, / The place of fame and elegy supply' (81–2). 'Uncouth' and 'rustic' as these are, they are quite different from the elegy that Gray's poem supplies, in a tortuous shift of syntax, for himself. Gray imagines what will happen if 'by lonely contemplation led', some 'kindred Spirit shall inquire thy fate' (that is, Gray's fate) and guesses that some 'hoary-headed Swain' will supply the visitor with an oral narrative of the strange figure (Gray) who wandered round the parish, reading flat out by a brook, 'Mutt'ring his wayward fancies', like one 'craz'd with care, or cross'd in hopeless love'. He is missed; then one morning his funeral takes place. Gray has the illiterate villager invite the visitor – 'for thou canst read' – to read the epitaph on the gravestone, which is then given in the final three stanzas of the poem. The one thing the poet-figure appears unable to imagine is ever talking to any of the local inhabitants or workers; his presence in this location is totally alien – accepted, but never crossing a certain social boundary established by Gray's literacy and the peasants' work. The other voices in the poem are those of beetles, owls, and the brook, all non-verbal. His most intense communion is with the landscape; connection with the inhabitants remains with those safely dead.

Oliver Goldsmith's *The Deserted Village* (1770) presents an odd counterpart to this elegiac vein. Goldsmith had been studying rural depopulation and agricultural change for some years. Anticipating criticism of the poem's social critique, Goldsmith dedicated it to Sir Joshua Reynolds, President of the Royal Academy and an unimpeachable figure of the London establishment, and staunchly defended his research: 'I sincerely believe what I have written; that I have taken all possible pains, in my country excursions, for these four or five years past, to be certain of what I allege; and that all my views and enquiries have led me to believe those miseries real, which I here attempt to display'. The poem opens with a 34-line invocation of 'Sweet Auburn, loveliest village of the plain'. The village appears utterly stable, a picture postcard with all desirable features in exactly the right place:

> How often have I paused on every charm,
> The sheltered cot, the cultivated farm,
> The never-failing brook, the busy mill,
> The decent church that topped the neighbouring hill,
> The hawthorn bush, with seats beneath the shade,
> For talking age and whispering lovers made. (9–14)

The poet is not 'of' the village, he is an observer, waiting for the return of the actual inhabitants from their labour (which is not described). Though the villagers 'toil' and 'labour', we learn, cheeringly, that 'Health and plenty cheered the labouring swain' (2). The poet sees the villagers only after work, engaged in picturesque rural sports on the village green.

But these 'charms' abruptly disappear, for 'amidst thy bowers the tyrant's hand is seen'; 'One only master grasps the whole domain', enclosing the village and evicting the tenants. This leaves nature, which without human use is seen by Goldsmith as dead and threatening: the sound of the bittern and lapwing, and growth of vegetation in the stream (markers of ecological soundness, to modern ears) are presented as signs of decay. Goldsmith argues that a 'bold peasantry' represent national, and natural, virtue:

A time there was, ere England's griefs began,
When every rood of ground maintained its man;
For him light labour spread her wholesome store,
Just gave what life required, but gave no more:
His best companions, innocence and health;
And his best riches, ignorance of wealth. (57–62)

The changes to this stable union of land and man are blamed partly on 'trade's unfeeling train' (the commercialization of industry and agriculture) and partly on 'unwieldy wealth and cumbrous pomp' (the enclosure of land for enormous private parks and houses). The poet presents alternate scenes of prior happiness and current ruination; the self-sustaining, healthy community of villagers is throughout fiercely contrasted with the corrupt and sickly pleasures of the city. Goldsmith's own role as a figure in the poem is to fill a desolate space with remembered bliss and hope.

In the centre of the poem Goldsmith remembers three houses: the parsonage, the schoolhouse, and the inn, as centres for particular kinds of activity. The 'village preacher' is, like Goldsmith's own Dr Primrose in *The Vicar of Wakefield*, a model of sympathy, if subject to some gentle irony for his over-ready charity. The secular authority in the poem is the schoolmaster, a man of practical skills and knowledge and a source of wonder to the villagers. The village inn constitutes a space where the villagers themselves exert some (gently mocked) authority: here 'village statesmen talked with looks profound, / And news much older than their ale went round'.

These authority figures are all male. Female figures in the poem have a somewhat different function: there is a lone survivor, a 'widowed, solitary thing', living off raw nature, and constituting the 'sad historian of the pensive plain' not in any literary sense but as the definitive incarnation of loss. The land itself is figured as a woman, beginning as a 'fair female unadorned and plain' who has to adopt increasingly extreme versions of costume and adornment in order to attract admiration (287–302). A further female, a village maiden seduced by the charms of wealth and power but abandoned to a miserable death in the city, then re-embodies this sense of the country as vulnerable to rapacity (325–36).

Beyond the destroyed village and the corrupt city lies only emigration to an America that combines a destructively wild nature with poisonous city values. This then becomes the ground of a political allegory: 'Even now, methinks, as pondering here I stand, / I see the rural virtues leave the land'. As the people go, so do 'contented toil and hospitable care', 'kind connubial tenderness', piety, 'steady loyalty' and 'faithful love'. So, indeed, does Poetry ('thou loveliest maid'), unable to flourish in this altered world, a last endangered female. As if to emphasize the loss, the last four lines of the poem were written by Goldsmith's friend Samuel Johnson, emphasizing the poem's firm moral commitment to 'self-dependant power' against the transitory splendours of 'trade's proud empire'.[16]

The poem is addressed to 'ye friends to truth, ye statesmen', not in any sense to the rural labourers themselves, whom the poem conceives of as without literature (despite the school). It is the crowning and unspoken irony of the poem that its celebration of rural life only emerges in the context of that life's absolute obliteration: without the disaster, there is no poem. However, nostalgia and sentiment could have radical effects: Goldsmith clearly upholds the rights of the villagers to their village against the tyranny of landlords and agricultural businessmen, and he is much more focused on the labourers than Gray is. At times the detail amounts to a list of picturesque desiderata for a landscape painting in which the villagers have no more individuality than the village green, their voices a wordless music amidst farm noise. But the idealization of the village constitutes a huge stick with which to beat emergent capitalism, city ethics, and political indifference. And Goldsmith had perceived something of an actual trend. The increase in the 'efficiency' of agriculture, which we noted earlier, meant bigger farms and fewer farmers. Enclosure acts, passed by parliament to allow landowners to cultivate previously fallow common land in and around villages, did force workers off the land and into cities in search of work, in the manner Young approved as economically rational. Between 1761 and 1844 there were nearly 4000 enclosure acts, and eventually rural depopulation was of sufficient concern to raise serious debates in parliament. Goldsmith's poem was unusually prescient.

Nation

Defoe's *Tour through the Whole Island of Great Britain* (1724–6) gave an enthusiastic description of the present state of trade throughout the nation. As he toured the nation in search of agricultural improvement, Arthur Young also took delight in the great increase in manufacturing industry of the latter half of the century, which was most easily observed in the regions rather than London. James Hargreaves' 'Spinning Jenny', which hugely increased the productivity of workers in the spinning of thread, was created at Blackburn in the 1760s, and was soon improved by Richard Arkwright's spinning frame, first modelled in Preston. Johnson visited Arkwright's factory near Ashbourne, surprising the manufacturer with his ready understanding of the new process. The 'Industrial Revolution' created new manufacturing towns such as Birmingham and Manchester; Josiah Wedgwood's factories at 'Etruria', round Stoke-on-Trent, supplied fine pottery to the metropolis. The terrible roads encountered by Bunyan's Christian (and by Young) were improved by turnpike trusts, which created a series of gated toll roads across Britain in mid-century. Young was pleased to observe in the 1770s the development of a network of canals to carry freight. London's dominance as a port began to be challenged by Bristol and Liverpool in the west, conveniently situated as they were for the cross-Atlantic trade (some of it in slaves). It became fashionable to 'take the waters' at spa towns such as Epsom, Tunbridge Wells, Bath, Bristol, Scarborough and Harrogate, which also offered their own social entertainments. (Rochester's poem 'Tunbridge Wells' gives an early sardonic glimpse of the kind of social and sexual interplay that might be found or imagined in such places.) Sea-bathing was also thought to be beneficial to health and was popularized by George III; the seaside holiday arrived.

The wider entity of 'Britain' had scarcely existed at the start of our period: England was the power in the isles. Ireland had its own parliament but was economically subject to English interests and its largely Catholic population was under the thumb of the 'protestant ascendancy'. Addison was among those who served in the political administration of Ireland, while writers such as Goldsmith and Sterne were born there, migrating to literary life in England. Swift, also born in Ireland, fought a long and bitter pamphlet war in an attempt to promote the Irish economy. His most extraordinary contribution, however, was *A Modest Proposal* (1729), in which a Whig 'projector' or businessman comes up with a novel solution to solve the overcrowding among the Irish population: eat the children. The proposer has it all worked out, with facts and figures, and is sure that the peasantry will co-operate with the scheme in their own interest, with the women competing with each other to see who can bring the fattest child to market. He is not joking, though Swift, in a black and bitter way, is; after all, the pamphlet argues in a rare slip of the mask, the landlords have 'eaten' the tenants already.

Also problematic was Scotland. By the Act of Union of 1707, Scotland was formally ruled from London; it had had its own parliament, but this disappeared. Defoe was active in promoting the case for union, both by sending reports of political activity in Edinburgh to Robert Harley, and in his journalism. Scottish writers such as Allan Ramsay had some popular success in the 1720s with distinctive regional ballads, and the Edinburgh-based Henry Mackenzie scored a hit with his sentimental novel, *The Man of*

Feeling, in 1771. The philosopher David Hume was Scottish, as was one of his more notable antagonists, the clergyman poet James Beattie. At the very end of the period, the ploughboy poet Robert Burns (1759–96) performed a somewhat more successful version of Duck's rise to eminence with his *Poems, chiefly in the Scottish Dialect* (1786). Scottish authors who made their way to London, however, such as Thomson and Smollett, tended to be regarded with some suspicion; some of them made an attempt to delete 'Scotticisms' from their speech.

Scotland had been the site of continued Jacobite assaults on the crown: the rising of 1715 was defeated at Sheriffmuir, and the more dangerous one of 1745 wiped out at Culloden. However, a series of military roads and forts and extensive surveying of Scotland, together with the collapse of the Jacobite cause, gradually transformed the unknown region north of Edinburgh into a tourist possibility. Thomson allowed his 'muse' to see 'Caledonia in romantic view' in *Autumn* (880–909); around 1750 William Collins had written 'An Ode on the Popular Superstitions of the Highlands of Scotland, Considered as the Subject of Poetry', in celebration of an imagined landscape of pure magic, which he sent to a Scottish writer, John Home. Gray, who disliked the Lake District, was charmed by the mountains of Scotland. A different sensibility, given critical respectability by Edmund Burke's *Philosophical Enquiry into the Origin of our Ideas of the Sublime and Beautiful* (1757), viewed mountains, rocks and moors as scenes of imaginative splendour and ancient grandeur, an essential psychological need. [17]

Towards the end of the period, 'Britain' had become a known entity, and it was possible to speak of 'British literature'.[18] One text which makes a particular effort in this direction is Smollett's *Humphry Clinker* (1771). This takes a party of ill-assorted travellers from Wales, led by the irascible Matthew Bramble, on a tour of 'Britain'. Told in letters, it allows for the viewpoints of the characters to be given directly, and includes a greater range of voices and reactions than is conventional, matching the local variety of the tour (though some of the 'voices' are louder, and more powerful, than others). It is a 'British' novel in that it takes in not only London and Bath (which Bramble finds disgustingly promiscuous) but a tour of Scotland, figuring as a zone of enchanting self-discovery. A sequence of marriages and a rediscovered long-lost son emphasize the new connections that have been made, before the party returns to Wales.

By contrast, Johnson's *Journey to the Western Islands of Scotland* (1775), records an actual journey Johnson made in the company of Boswell from Edinburgh to the Hebrides. (It includes a tribute to Smollett's cousin, with whom they stayed.) The tour was organized by Boswell, partly out of national pride, and partly to see what would happen when Johnson the devout Englishman encountered a region so alien to him. It was indeed the most remote journey Johnson ever made. The *Journey* tries to see Scotland in historical perspective. Johnson has no time for landscape prospects and comments instead on issues of commerce, education, emigration, the cultural consequences of the Jacobite failure, and the problematic nature of an oral Gaelic culture. In all this Johnson can seem an unsympathetic member of an alien ruling class, but his authorial technique is on many occasions deliberately self-undermining; he is quite ready to narrate comic instances against himself, and the pioneering journey to the edge of British territory, in the Hebrides, is genuinely revelatory. As he ascends a steep hill, the path zig-zags, and Johnson watches his 'baggage' go one way, while he goes the other: the movement is an apt illustration of a geographical reorientation, and a fit emblem of the troubled but ascending path to nationhood.[19]

Notes

1 These appeared in 1751, at the height of concern over the consumption of spirits. Hogarth's famous series 'Four Times of Day' (1738) and 'Industry and Idleness' (1747) present similar contrasts.

2 Swift, *Tale of a Tub*, section ii; edited by D. Nichol Smith, pp. 74–5.

3 Pope's note to I.2.

4 Fielding produced a *Grub-street Opera* in 1731 and associates of Pope set up the *Grub-street Journal* in the 1730s to continue the satiric work of *The Dunciad*.

5 The revised version of 1743 adds a final book in which the reign of a Miltonic chaos is duly established.

6 Boswell, *Life of Johnson*, IV.358; III.178; II.337.

7 An earlier version of Juvenal's attack on Rome, by John Oldham, had appeared in 1682.

8 Johnson, *London*. 224–9; *The Complete English Poems*, edited by J. D. Fleeman (1982), p. 67.

9 Boswell, *Life of Johnson*, II.367. George Lillo's crime drama, *The London Merchant* (1731) offered more conventional sentiments on criminal biography.

10 *Rambler*, 20 April 1751.

11 Boswell, *Life of Johnson*, II.98.

12 *Guardian*, 27 April 1713. For these essays see *The Prose Works of Alexander Pope, Vol. I. The Earlier Works, 1711–1720*, edited by Norman Ault (Oxford, 1936).

13 A good example is his letter to Martha Blount, 22 June 1724, on the landscape views ('more romantick than Imagination can form them') around Sherborne, though this is still based on a country estate, that of his friend Robert Digby.

14 More enthusiastic about hunting was William Somervile, in *The Chace* (1735).

15 Pope wrote three epitaphs on the couple, two 'straight' and one comic. The incident is also mentioned in Thomson's *Summer*.

16 Johnson, however, also admired *The Village* (1783), by an actual rural clergyman, George Crabbe, who objected to Goldsmith's sentimental whitewashing of

the unremitting toil of rural life: he set himself to 'paint the Cot [cottage], / As Truth will paint it, and as Bards will not'.

17 Charles Cotton's *Wonders of the Peake* (1681) stands out as an exceptional early landscape poem, describing the curious geology of the Peak district, though it returns to the 'Country House' genre by celebrating Chatsworth House.

18 See Linda Colley, *Britons: Forging the Nation, 1707–1837* (New Haven, 1992), and Howard Weinbrot, *Britannia's Issue: the Rise of British Literature from Dryden to Ossian* (Cambridge, 1993).

19 Johnson kept a diary of a subsequent tour to North Wales, in 1774.

5

World views

> First then to procure . . . a mutual and reciprocal Advantage to the Sovereigns and Subjects of both Crowns, Her British Majesty does Offer and Undertake for the Persons, whom She shall Name and Appoint, That they shall Oblige and Charge themselves with the bringing into the *West-Indies* of *America*, belonging to His Catholick Majesty in the Space of . . . Thirty Years . . . One hundred and forty four thousand Negroes, *Piezas de India*, of both Sexes, and of all Ages, at the Rate of four thousand and eight hundred Negroes, *Piezas de India*, in each of the said Thirty years.[. . .] That for each Negro, of the regular Standard of Seven Quarters, not being old or defective . . . the Assientists shall pay thirty three Pieces of Eight (*Escudos*) and One third of a Piece of Eight . . . the said Assientists may import and vend the said Negroes in all the Ports of the *North* Sea, and that of *Buenos Ayres* at their Choice . . . as to the other Ports of *New Spain* . . . it shall be lawful to sell them at the best Prices they shall be able to get.
>
> [*The Compleat History of the Treaty of Utrecht*, 2 vols (London, 1715), I.ii.156–9]

The Treaty of Utrecht, signed by Britain, France, Spain and the Netherlands on 31 March 1713 after two years of negotiations, brought to an end the War of Spanish Succession. Officially the war was to determine the balance of power within Europe, but a major element in it was competition for trade to the New World: Europe was, in effect, mapping the rest of the world as colonial territory. Britain gained some new territorial rights, and in this separate treaty, signed with Spain 13 July 1713, an exclusive contract for the provision of slaves. In this chapter we shall examine British relations with the world of Europe and beyond, and look at how imaginative writing responded to these often troubled new zones and the people who lived there.

Many of the writers of our period, including figures such as Dryden and Pope, never left the British Isles, though by education they were pan-

European. Some of Johnson's aristocratic writers (Rochester, Sackville, Sheffield) had served in foreign wars; Prior saw diplomatic service in France during the Utrecht negotiations. The 'Grand Tour' was normally undertaken to complete the education of young men (seldom women) of private means, often travelling with a tutor (James Thomson performed this role), with the ostensible aim of cultivating polite manners and artistic taste. Such tours almost always included France, usually Italy (for the art and ruins), and sometimes extended to Switzerland, Austria and Germany. The less salubrious possibilities of the grand tour were caustically displayed in Pope's *Dunciad* (IV.293–330).

Writers were generally not in sufficient funds to indulge in the full menu of travel, sightseeing, art collecting and loose living. Milton had travelled in Italy, and Addison toured the continent on a government grant in 1699–1703, producing *Remarks on Several Parts of Italy, &c* (1705). Walpole travelled through France and Italy in 1739–41, taking with him the impecunious Gray. Boswell studied at Leiden and travelled through Germany, Switzerland, Italy, Corsica (where he supported General Paoli's struggle for Corsican independence) and France. Similar customized versions of the Tour were made by the historian Edward Gibbon, the actor David Garrick and the politician Edmund Burke. Johnson took a brief tour to Paris in 1775, but a projected trip to Italy came to nothing.

Oliver Goldsmith performed a low-income version of the Tour in 1755–6. A poem begun abroad was eventually published (with 18 lines by Johnson) as *The Traveller: Or, A Prospect of Society* (1764). The poet-figure mounts an Alpine eminence, using the 'prospect' to assess the benefits and demerits of the national characteristics of the Italians, Swiss, French, Dutch and British. Using the couplet form to point up balance and antithesis, Goldsmith finds that the virtues on which each nation prides itself are counterweighted by a related vice or problem. The Italians have the best climate, but as a consequence are addicted to sensual luxury. The Swiss landscape is barren and dangerous, and the peasantry are right to be proud of subsisting on their own labour in self-built huts. On the other hand, this is no idyll: if they lack luxury, they also lack the higher forms of morality and pleasure. In France, such things abound and are a genuine source of pride – just as they also promote ostentation, vanity and jealousy. The Dutch landscape breeds industry and commerce, but also fraud and corruption. 'Creation's mildest charms' centre in the British landscape and climate, where 'Liberty' flourishes; but 'That independence Britons prize too high, / Keeps man from man and breaks the social tie' (339–40). A nation of 'self-dependent lordlings' ends up mired in faction and infighting. It was left to Johnson to find a conclusion above geography: 'Still to ourselves, in every place consigned, / Our own felicity we make or find' (431–2), Johnson writes, rating personal 'reason, faith and conscience' (438) above all local considerations in the determination of happiness.

Other writers went to the continent for health reasons. Fielding went to Portugal for this purpose in 1754, but died in Lisbon, leaving a posthumously published journal of the voyage. Smollett left a dyspeptic record of his *Travels through France and Italy*, completed between 1763 and 1765 in a slightly more successful attempt to restore his health. Smollett was very much John Bull abroad: the inns, manners, and arts of France and Italy all come in for British disgust, and the company of expatriate Britons is much preferred. The landscape around Nice, however, impresses him, as do the classic cities of Pisa, Florence and Rome. Smollett's rank xenophobia led Sterne to caricature him as 'the learned Dr Smelfungus' in his own highly idiosyncratic *Sentimental Journey through France and Italy* (1768). Based on Sterne's own continental trips in the years 1762–5, Sterne borrows the character of the whimsically gallant parson Yorick from his novel, *Tristram Shandy*, to act as the traveller. Yorick is a 'man of feeling', his encounters all exercises in 'sensibility', a flamboyant readiness to sympathize with those in distress, such as the picturesquely deranged Maria, and to weep for caged starlings or abused donkeys. The purity of these feelings is always teetering on the brink of self-parody, however: Yorick evidently enjoys sympathy for its own sake, letting his imagination produce fictional scenes of distress to wallow in at leisure. The book is also driven by a thoroughgoing comic sexuality. Yorick flirts with women from all classes, deriving erotic sensation from having his pulse taken by a shopgirl and helping an aristocratic lady go to the toilet. The book ends with an ambiguous but plainly sexual gesture, with Yorick accidentally catching hold 'of the Fille de Chambre's —'.

Beyond Europe

As Sterne's text occasionally indicates, even such sunny forays into foreign territory were complicated by the fact that for large portions of the century Britain was at war with one or other European power, and often several at once. These wars, in turn, were not merely struggles for power in Europe, but contests for control of trade and empire throughout the world. Britain was a relatively late entrant to the competition for empire, having by the 1660s laid claim only to the American colonies, Jamaica and a few other places. In the seventeenth century Britain began to muscle in more aggressively on international trade, first by harrying Spanish shipping with privateers, then through official investment in both merchant and Royal navies (especially after the Dutch sank English ships in the mouth of the Thames in the 1660s). A charter granting monopoly trading rights was granted to the Royal Africa Company in the first year of Charles's reign. The East India Company, which took over Bombay [Mumbai] in 1668, and the Hudson's Bay Company, enjoyed similar state backing to colonize through economic means. The Royal Society had as one of its aims from 1671 the mapping of the seas, and Charles II appointed an Astronomer Royal to provide better celestial maps for navigation. This produced Greenwich Observatory, later to be defined as zero longitude. Prizes for reliable methods of calculating longitude were offered and the problem was solved by John Harrison's marine chronometers, constructed in the 1750s.

Competition for access to American waters, and Indian and South Pacific oceans, was the motor for much European war in the period. Initially, the Dutch had been the main antagonists, but after the Dutch prince William of Orange came to the throne, France became the clear enemy. The War of Spanish Succession, which began in 1701, set England and Holland against France and Spain, with battles fought particularly in the Low Countries but also in Germany, Italy and Spain. Britain was at war with Spain for much of the 1720s, and the War of Jenkins' Ear was declared in 1739 after the Spanish had been accused of piracy against British shipping. This was submerged in the War of Austrian Succession, which lasted until 1748. The Seven Years' War (1756–63) was virtually a world war, with Britain supporting Frederick II of Prussia against France, Austria, Russia and Sweden, and campaigns fought in Canada, India and the Mediterranean. Britain eventually consolidated its hold on India and Canada, and the Peace of Paris that ended the war in 1763 granted Britain in addition the territories of Senegal, Florida, and several West Indian islands – perhaps the most important moment in the foundation of the British Empire. The American War of Independence (1775–83), however, involved competition with the French once again, and severed the connection between the colonies and Britain.

The War of Spanish Succession had divided poets. Addison, as a devout Whig, had praised the achievements of the English general Marlborough in his poem *The Campaign* (1705) and in his journalism; Swift acted as one of the Tory government's main propagandists in arguing for an end to the war. Pope celebrated the peace in *Windsor-Forest* (1713) in terms of millennial fantasy: Britain's fleets would cover the world's oceans to bring back coral, gold, amber and ruby, and once 'Thames shall flow for all mankind', then the process of imperial expansion is over. The 'new world' will return to look at the old: 'And naked youths and painted chiefs admire / Our speech, our colour, and our strange attire!' (405–6).

Britain will become the entrepôt for the world: 'Till Conquest cease, and Slav'ry be no more', Pope hopes, in a sidelong glance at the *asiento*.

> 'Till the freed Indians in their native groves
> Reap their own fruits, and woo their sable loves,
> Peru once more a race of Kings behold,
> And other Mexico's be roofed with gold. (409–12)

Pope's romance of Empire had already begun; he was partly drawing on established literary models of the New World as an imaginative resource. Aphra Behn's *Oroonoko: or, The Royal Slave* (1688) is set partly in Surinam, a British colony on the coast of South America; several characters mentioned were historical figures.[1] Oroonoko (not a historical figure) is a noble, courageous, handsome prince of 'Coramantien', a region of what is now Ghana, then a port of call for English and Dutch slave traders. His blackness is suitably adjusted for Western tastes:

> His face was not of that brown, rusty black which most of that nation are, but a perfect ebony, or polished jet. . . . His nose was rising and Roman, instead of African and flat. His mouth, the finest shaped that could be seen; far from those great turned lips, which are so natural to the rest of the Negroes. (81)

In many ways, he is a black European, partially educated by a Frenchman in exile, and learning 'civilized' ways from English traders.

Oroonoko's grandfather desires his betrothed, Imoinda, for himself, and the story sounds initially like a conventional erotic novel, kitted out with an exotic African setting; but hero and heroine alike are tricked into slavery, which brings them to Surinam. Oroonoko impresses the white colonists with his obvious nobility: 'the royal youth appeared in spite of the slave'. He does no work; the slaves of the colony treat him as a king and the whites adopt him as a companion. Oroonoko and Imoinda converse daily with the narrator, who continues their education in Western literature. So far as Oroonoko himself is concerned, the novel is anti-slavery; he is a prince, and retains royal dignity even when enslaved by the machinations of villainous whites. He denounces white hypocrisy and the purely nominal Christianity to which they adhere, and is fully supported by the narrator, who views the deputy governor of the colony (a real figure) as 'a fellow, whose character is not fit to be mentioned with the worst of the slaves' (128). On the other hand, Oroonoko participates fully in the original cross-Atlantic slave system, and the colonial position as a whole is not challenged. Whites in Surinam were heavily outnumbered by slaves and Oroonoko's eloquently incited slave rebellion can hardly be allowed to prosper, especially given his natural leadership talents. The uprising is easily crushed by fraudulent promises, and Oroonoko regrets his attempt 'to make those free, who were by nature slaves, poor wretched rogues, fit to be used as Christians' tools' (130). He is whipped and humiliated. Escaping once more, Oroonoko kills the pregnant Imoinda to preserve her from captivity, a gesture that seems initially Roman and heroic (she accepts the fate willingly). But he is tracked down by the smell of her rotting corpse, and his own illness and weakness prevent him from offering more than slight resistance to capture: his bold vision of vengeance is imaginable, but totally unachievable. He is dismembered at the stake, having first torn off pieces of his own flesh to show his contempt for pain. The noble prince is reduced to the bestial body: 'if before we thought him so beautiful a sight, he was now so altered, that his face was like a death's head blacked over, nothing but teeth, and eye-holes' (139). There is nowhere for the narrative that has created him to take him to, and the narrator offers an apologetic account of her own powerlessness (as a 'female pen') to do other than celebrate a vanished nobility.[2]

There is a further element of exoticism in the text beyond the encounter with the fascinating black African, since Surinam itself is a relatively unknown quantity. In the opening pages Behn describes the indigenous inhabitants as noble savages, enjoying a natural morality and paradisal sexual innocence:

> And though they are all thus naked, if one lives for ever among them, there is not to be seen an indecent action, or glance; and being continually used to see one another so unadorned, so like our first parents before the Fall, it seems as if they had no wishes. (76)

Western religion 'would here but destroy that tranquillity they possess by ignorance' (77). Nonetheless, relations between whites and 'Indians' are a matter of compromise; 'they being, on all occasions, very useful to us, we find it absolutely necessary to caress them as friends, and not to treat them as slaves; nor dare we do other, their numbers so far surpassing ours on that continent' (78). It is an unashamed colonial apology, though it comes with a tourist's taste for the exotic: Behn gives enchanted descriptions of the local flora and fauna (the armadillo, for example) and the customs and abilities of the natives. Beyond the coastal fringe lies the darker interior, with potentially hostile animals and peoples, into which the narrator penetrates with Oroonoko as companion. Behn links its inexhaustible wonder with a wealth of natural resources; she regrets that Charles II has too easily ceded the 'vast and charming world', of which the colony was the known edge, to the Dutch (in 1668).

The new literature of exploration included lurid narratives of piratical excess in the Caribbean, sometimes with an ostensible moral condemnation, but usually with a more obvious element of excitement and romance. William Dampier gives a glamorous account of his heroic resistance to the perfidious Spanish (not to mention hostile indigenous peoples) on his privateering voyages round the South Seas in the late 1680s; but Woodes Rogers, in his *Cruising Voyage round the World* (1712), decries Dampier as a pirate. He also gives an account of Alexander Selkirk, a mariner deliberately marooned on an island by Dampier and picked up after four years' solitude by Rogers. This was one source for the most famous shipwreck novel of them all, Defoe's *Robinson Crusoe* (1719).

Defoe drew on the burgeoning literature of exotic travel, including *Oroonoko*: the island on which Crusoe is cast away turns out to be 'near the Mouth of the Great River of OROONOQUE', from which Behn's hero is possibly named. He copies from travel narratives navigational details as an authenticating device (degrees of latitude, dates and climatic conditions are all logged). Again, there is more than one kind of exoticism on offer, for on an early voyage Crusoe is himself enslaved. Escaping with the aid of a moslem boy, Xury, Crusoe is eventually picked up by a Portuguese ship, to the captain of which he sells Xury, in an exemplary colonial moment:

> I was very loath to sell the poor boy's liberty, who had assisted me so faithfully in procuring my own. However, when I let him know my reason, he owned it to be just, and offered me this medium, that he would give the boy an obligation to set him free in ten years, if he turned Christian; upon this, and Xury saying he was willing to go to him, I let the captain have him. (54).

This turns out to be a mistake, as Xury was highly skilled and he and Crusoe had formed a useful team; but it was an economic mistake rather than a personal one.

The main narrative concerns Crusoe's 28 years on an island as the only survivor of a subsequent shipwreck. Crusoe will never 'go native'; he does not so much adapt himself to the island as reconfigure the island in his own image. Crusoe's first reaction to his deliverance is fear, and he spends his first night up a tree to avoid wild animals. He has dropped off the map of European knowledge ('some hundreds of leagues, out of the ordinary course of the trade of mankind', 80) into a wholly alien zone, and must recreate a European system from scratch. From the wreck he reclaims a basic toolkit of Western technology: food, clothing, rope, knives, tools, guns. The haul includes, in a famous moment of irony, money, which Crusoe denounces as useless, before taking it anyway, perhaps as a talismanic reminder of the system from which he is cast out.

Soon he has created a defensive 'fortress' for protection from unknown threats. The focus shifts to domestication, and Crusoe contrives table, chairs, a 'kitchen'. The island becomes a resource; one of his first actions onshore is to fire a gun at a bird on a tree – 'I believe it was the first gun that had been fired there since the creation of the world' (72), and it acts as a sign of Crusoe's dominance over the territory. He finds natural crops: cocoa, tobacco, wild sugar cane, citrus fruits, grapes, melons. He plants corn; he domesticates goats. The landscape has something of Eden about it, but Crusoe's relation to it is always alien: he overcomes fear by the gradual exertion of power.

> I descended a little of the side of that delicious vale, surveying it with a secret kind of pleasure . . . to think that this was all my own, that I was king and lord of all this country indefeasibly, and had a right of possession; and if I could convey it, I might have it in inheritance as completely as any lord of a manor in England. (114)

With his stock of tame animals he becomes, comically, a prince:

> There was my majesty and prince and lord of the whole island; I had the lives of all my subjects at my absolute command; I could hang, draw, give liberty, and take it away, and no rebels among all my subjects. (157)

The peace of this cosy hierarchy is however shattered when Crusoe comes across 'the print of a man's naked foot on the shore' (162). Having longed for company, Crusoe's instinct when the sign of it arrives is a catastrophic reversion to fear, shutting himself up in his 'castle, for so I think I called it ever after this'. He redoubles the fortifications, placing muskets in the manner of cannons on a castle wall. The island, it transpires, is occasionally used by inhabitants of other islands in the region as a location for cannibal feasts, thus justifying Crusoe's sense of the alien as essentially hostile and inhuman. His first response is genocidal, but he comes to question his own authority over what is evidently to them an approved custom, doubts that he can read the will of God in the matter, and recalls as 'meer butchery' the terrible history of the Spanish in South America.[3] Crusoe reaches a compromise by rescuing one individual from a group of cannibals, by firing on them. This mystifies the terrified cannibals and supplies Crusoe with a willing servant. Crusoe's description of Friday (whom he renames after the day of the rescue, identifying him with the European calendar and erasing his tribal name) reminds us to some extent of Behn's defensive account of Oroonoko:

> He had a very good countenance, not a fierce and surly aspect; but seemed to have something very manly in his face, and yet he had all the sweetness and softness of an European in his countenance too, especially when he smiled. His hair was long and black, not curled like wool . . . The colour of his skin was not quite black, but very tawny; and yet not of an ugly yellow nauseous tawny, as the Brasilians, and Virginians, and other natives of America are; but of a bright kind of a dun olive colour . . . (p. 208)

Crusoe has found himself a new version of Xury who will call him 'Master', serve him faithfully, and regard him as a saviour. Crusoe puts defences between himself and Friday, boarding up his innermost sanctum so that Friday cannot get at him at night; but gradually the social relations of authority are established, and Crusoe clothes Friday, teaches him English, trains him in the use of firearms, gives him to understand that cannibalism is not acceptable and converts him to Christianity. They rescue a Spaniard from the cannibals (the offence of proposing to eat a white man helps Crusoe overcome his scruples about killing the 'savages'). This rescue also brings Friday's father, another proposed victim, onto the island, and Crusoe contemplates his domain:

> My island was now peopled, and I thought my self very rich in subjects; and it was a merry reflection which I frequently made, how like a king I looked. First of all, the whole country was my own meer property; so that I had an undoubted right of dominion. 2dly, my people were perfectly subjects: I was absolute lord and lawgiver; they all owed their lives to me . . . (p. 241)

Crusoe appears to need subjects in order to feel properly human himself. And though the language here is comic, the authority which Crusoe founds on circumstance takes on a final, absolute role at the end of the novel. Crusoe rescues the captain of a ship whose crew has mutinied. He ambushes and subdues the crew by drawing up a miniature army and pretending to be governor of the island, thus re-establishing a version of British naval authority. But he is, in fact, governor of the island: he leaves it populated by the mutineers and takes passage to England with the captain he has rescued. We learn that the island is divided up between the inhabitants, that Crusoe sends supplies of necessaries to assist in the colonization, that battles with Caribbean islanders continue. It is to all intents a purposes a functioning colony, of which Crusoe is the owner under the crown.[4]

Crusoe's money, meanwhile, has gone on magically accumulating, and his plantations in Brasil have succeeded without his agency. All Defoe's subsequent fictions have the same romance of money about them, and the same sense of the world as a place to be exploited, gathered in, traversed, mapped and possessed. In *The Adventures of Captain Singleton* (1720) Defoe gives us a mariner who walks across Africa gathering gold along the way and who subsequently enjoys a successful career as a pirate before retiring to enjoy the loot. Moll Flanders endures a life of economic struggle, and is transported to Virginia to work as a convict on a plantation; she eventually returns as a rich planter herself.[5] *The History of the Remarkable Life of Colonel Jacque* (1722) tells of a pickpocket, born similarly into the poorest of London environments, who is kidnapped to work in Virginia; he climbs the career ladder to the post of 'overseer' and becomes a planter himself, using enlightened and 'humane' methods of management to improve the conditions of the slaves – and thus increase their efficiency as workers.

In both *Oroonoko* and *Crusoe* the ex-patriate narrators find themselves the subject of amazed scrutiny by indigenous inhabitants. This reversal (the traveller as exotic) is picked up by Swift in *Travels into Several Remote Nations of the World*, commonly known as *Gulliver's Travels* (1726).[6] This is a parody of travel narrative, and one of its targets is the naïve empiricism by which such narratives authenticate themselves: Behn gives Indian feathers to the theatre, Crusoe takes with him his goatskin cap as a memento, and Gulliver gives some gigantic wasp stings to Gresham College. Like Crusoe, Gulliver is adept technically and shows a good deal of ability with practical projects. Gulliver's four zones of travel are very carefully located in relation to the known world (one near Sumatra, another south of Japan, and so on), with maps and latitudes given, in a deadpan rehearsal of Crusoesque detail. Gulliver cites William Dampier as a fellow travel-writer. But Gulliver does not meet 'uncivilized' races; he comes up against social systems that are already developed, and can thus compare them with his own.

In Book 1, Gulliver is shipwrecked in Lilliput and passes out on land; when he wakes he finds himself pegged down to the grass by a crowd of miniature people, in the first of the disfiguring accidents that befalls him. They are freakish to him, but confident within their own system: it is Gulliver who is the real freak, the dangerous visitor. His pockets are searched, and an inventory of the contents supplied: the objects are unknown to them, even though we can easily work out that they are the familiar accoutrements of a gentleman: handkerchief, snuff-box, comb, pistol. Swift provides, however, an opportunity to look at the familiar as if it were unfamiliar. They find

> A globe, half Silver, and half of some transparent Metal: for on the transparent Side we saw certain strange Figures circularly drawn, and thought we could touch them, until we found our Fingers stopped with that lucid Substance. He put this Engine to our Ears, which made an incessant Noise like that of a Water-Mill. And we conjecture it is either some unknown Animal, or the God that he worships: But we are more inclined to the latter Opinion, because he assured us . . . that he seldom did any Thing without consulting it. He called it his Oracle, and said it pointed out the Time for every Action of his Life. (pp. 21–2)

This circumlocutory description renders the watch strange, and funny. But it also acts as a kind of satirical question against Gulliver, and by implication the average European male he represents: is there some sense in which he does worship technology?

Conversely, Gulliver's assiduous reporting of Lilliputian politics sees the system with the advantage of an unfamiliar, oversized perspective. But Gulliver always fails to note the resemblances between Lilliput and Britain. Civil wars, wars with the rival empire Blefuscu, and endless controversy have been waged over the issue of which end to break an egg at (a travesty of the religious elements in the wars between Britain and France). Gulliver's own fate comes into the balance: having prevented an invasion from Blefuscu by turning himself into a superweapon and hauling their fleet over to Lilliput, Gulliver then resists the Emperor's megalomaniac plans to destroy his opponents, and is accused of treason. Gulliver is surprised at this, but his naïve observations on court politics imply that in British politics such things happen all the time.

What seems remote is thus satirically familiar, just as the familiar is placed in an alien context that will question its normality. In the second voyage, Gulliver is abandoned in Brobdingnag, a land of giants, reversing the perspectival device of the first voyage. Here the fantasy allows us to see human beings hugely magnified, as if through a microscope, and the close-ups of skin are at once fantastically imaginative and dizzyingly repellent. Gulliver is even more vulnerable in this context, even more of a freak. He suffers variously from the attentions of a monkey, a dwarf, wasps and a frog, not to mention the sexual games of the court ladies. The king himself is magnanimous where the emperor of Lilliput was petty, and after being convinced that Gulliver is not actually a clockwork toy (again, a sort of question is being asked) he is curious about Gulliver's own society, giving him the opportunity to discourse at length – and embarrassingly. The king asks highly pertinent questions about political processes, receiving enthusiastic answers from Gulliver that make his home nation look foolish and corrupt.

> He was perfectly astonished with the historical Account I gave him of our Affairs during the last Century; protesting it was only an Heap of Conspiracies, Rebellions, Murders, Massacres, Revolutions, Banishments; the very worst Effects that Avarice, Faction, Hypocrisy, Perfidiousness, Cruelty, Rage, Madness, Hatred, Envy, Lust, Malice, and Ambition could produce. (p. 120)

At the end of the process Gulliver's size has come to represent the diminished expectations of his humanity and the king announces (kindly): 'I cannot but conclude the Bulk of your Natives, to be the most pernicious Race of little odious Vermin that Nature ever suffered to crawl upon the Surface of the Earth' (121). Gulliver is not convinced, and gives as an instance of the king's narrowmindedness his response to Gulliver's proposal to hand him the secret of gunpowder (the secret of Crusoe's mystic and practical power over the cannibals): describing the effects of gunpowder to the king, to whom it is completely unknown, Gulliver unwittingly gives a horrific description of modern warfare. The king is 'struck with Horror' at the picture, and at Gulliver's blithe offer.

In Laputa, Gulliver is a free traveller, commenting on the bizarre activities of the Laputan philosophers. These abstract thinkers inhabit a floating island, the dimensions and technological principles of which Gulliver gives in full detail. Beneath this lies Balnibarbi, always subject to the threat of demolition from the magnetic island that hovers above it (though there is perilous balance here, in that the island itself might suffer in an attack). The hostility to technology continues in an account of Gulliver's travels in Balnibarbi. Here he meets Lord Munodi, a Popean paragon of rural and political virtues, who entertains Gulliver with a view of his stable, productive agricultural system, now under threat from stupid political interference from the Academy of Lagado, a parody of the Royal Society. In the Academy Gulliver finds a whole series of ludicrous experiments (the breeding of sheep without wool, the extraction of sunbeams from cucumbers), which he attempts to view with his usual optimism. But the latter portion of the voyage begins to demolish Gulliver's positive outlook. On a visit to the Isle of Spirits, Gulliver gains access to the spirits of the departed, and discovers that familiar history has been largely falsified, that the blood of noble families is hopelessly adulterated, that celebrated actions in history were largely corrupted by private interest and that there has been a huge falling-off in the quality of civic life since ancient times. Gulliver is further disabused of his confidence in the possibilities of moral life by his encounter with the Struldbruggs, a race of immortals. On hearing of these exceptional beings, Gulliver amuses himself with a fantasy of immortal life, a schematic programme of learning and virtuous acquisition; but the reality is that after the normal period of life, the Struldbruggs descend into an insupportable and obscene senility.

On the final voyage, Gulliver is captain of a ship whose crew mutiny against him: an ominous sign of human faithlessness. Gulliver is rescued by a race of intelligent horses, the Houyhnhnms, whom Gulliver readily identifies as possessing ideal virtues: strength, health, reason. They have no technology at all, no writing (so that all discourse is personal and oral), no political system beyond a kind of public forum, and no word in their language for lying. They thus represent a refuge from the human failings discovered throughout the rest of Gulliver's voyages. Against them stand the Yahoos, a filthy, degenerate race that the Houyhnhnms use as labourers: 'I never beheld in all my Travels so disagreeable an Animal, or one against which I naturally conceived so strong an Antipathy' (215) declares Gulliver. However, when Gulliver is brought close to a Yahoo for inspection,

> My Horror and Astonishment are not to be described, when I observed, in this abominable Animal, a perfect human Figure; the Face of it indeed was flat and broad, the Nose depressed, the Lips large, and the Mouth wide: But these Differences are common to all savage Nations . . . (222)

For the rest of this book, Gulliver is torn between his appalled identification with the Yahoos, whose lustful, acquisitive behaviour bears an increasingly obvious resemblance to the political and social behaviour of humans, and his aspiration to the status of Houyhnhnm. He now denounces his homeland in exactly the way the King of Brobdingnag had done in Book 2.

The Houyhnhnms have only one political question: whether, as a superior race, they should destroy the Yahoos or not. Gulliver's arrival complicates the problem in that it is feared that he will mate with them and produce a race of super-Yahoos: he is banished, poignantly. After his departure he is shot at by a savage, leaving a scar ('I shall carry the mark to my Grave', 276), thus seeming to confirm his now fixed identification of Yahoos with the whole of humanity. But this simplistic equivalence is immediately modulated when Gulliver is taken up by a Portuguese captain (another borrowing from Defoe) who looks after him, clothes and feeds him, and acts a Christian, humane part. Gulliver can only see him as a repellent, filthy Yahoo, which he is evidently not. At home, Gulliver prefers the company of his groom, who smells of horses, to that of his wife and children; he walks like a horse, and talks to his own horses, under the impression that they are Houyhnhnms. Travel has not so much broadened his mind as permanently distorted it.

Towards the end of the book, Gulliver discusses the issue of colonization, admitting that he was 'bound in Duty as a Subject of *England*, to have given a Memorial to a Secretary of State, at my first coming over; because, whatever Lands are discovered by a Subject, belong to the Crown' (285). Crusoe would agree. But Gulliver has 'conceived a few Scruples' on the subject of the 'modern colony' and its acquisition:

> For Instance, A Crew of Pyrates are driven by a Storm they know not whither; at length a Boy discovers Land from the Top-mast; they go on Shore to rob and plunder; they see an harmless People, are entertained with Kindness, they give the Country a new Name, they take formal Possession of it for the King, they set up a rotten Plank or a Stone for a Memorial, they murder two or three Dozen of the Natives, bring away a Couple more by Force for a Sample, return home, and get their Pardon. Here commences a new Dominion acquired with a Title by *Divine Right.*

Though Gulliver specifically acquits the British of such acts, the denial is flagrantly and bitterly ironic.

Gulliver's Travels thus uses the device of imaginary voyages to produce exotic, transformed versions of the familiar, in which it was up to readers to recognize resemblances. This was a particularly popular textual strategy in the eighteenth century, and Swift had already noted its potential during a visit of four Iroquois kings to London in 1710; his hint was written up in Addison's *Spectator* of 27 April 1711. There are many examples of such satirical refocusing in this period, such as Lord Lyttleton's *Letters from a Persian in England* (1735). Eliza Heywood's *The Adventures of Eovaai, Princess of Ijaveo* (1736) shares Swift's political sympathies and casts Walpole as a sexual predator as well as magical politician. Goldsmith's *Citizen of the World* (1762) uses the device of a Chinese visitor to defamiliarize London customs.

Beyond Europe lay a realm of the imagination. The orient was of particular interest since it was one area Europeans did not colonize, and was therefore something of a fantasy zone, to be colonized by the mind. There were some developments in actual knowledge during the period; the Ottoman empire was in decline, reducing hostility and tension along the borders with Europe, and Arabic was being studied more exactly at universities. In 1704 there appeared a French version of the *Arabian Nights*, which was soon adapted for an English audience and proved ready source of exotic imagery for use in satirical tales, erotic romances and moral stories. Lady Mary Wortley Montagu accompanied her diplomat husband on a peace mission to Constantinople (now Istanbul) during 1716–18, and wrote a series of letters about the conditions she found there (published after her death, in 1763). She also attempted versions of Turkish verse, and brought back some oriental medical practises, such as vaccination for smallpox. As a woman she was able to gain access to the Sultan's harem (where she finds herself an object of curiosity, as Behn had done in Surinam), and she pokes much fun at the tall tales told by previous travellers. She observed avidly, disguised in a heavy veil and at one point dressing as a man to gain entry to a mosque.

Literature helped itself to orientalist fantasy. William Collins produced a set of *Persian Eclogues* (1742), and one of Gray's strangest poems is the delicately spooky and ironic 'Elegy on a favourite cat, drowned in a tub of goldfishes', written about an event in the London house of Horace Walpole, who was one of the first to import exotic carp. John Hawkesworth's *Almoran and Hamet* (1761) offers a substantial fable about political power, while Frances Sheridan's *The History of Nourjahad* (1767) relates the sensuous but ultimately delusory adventures of its imaginative hero. William Beckford (1759–1844), a rich traveller and collector who created his own Gothic palace, Fonthill Abbey, produced in *Vathek: An Arabian Tale* (1786) an extravaganza of sensual cruelty for his eponymous hero. The son of a sorceress, Vathek has no restraint whatever, and commits himself in a Faustian pact to the service of the Devil. Sacrificing fifty children, he sets out for an ancient ruined city, in search of the ancient treasures of pre-Adamite sultans. With him goes Nouronihar, a woman equally devoted to unrestrained and amoral sensual gratification. After a rapid series of lavish supernatural adventures, Vathek discovers the worthlessness of the power he has sought and exploited, and is damned, his heart bursting into flames inside his still-living body: a seductively grand vision of living hell.

An Englishman abroad

Johnson's work shows something of the way these world issues penetrate a writer's life and imagination. A more fiercely English figure could scarcely be imagined, but there was always something attractive for Johnson in the cultures he had not seen: his account of Scotland is peppered with references to Borneo, Sumatra, Patagonia, and Africa and on that tour he is reported to have performed an imitation of the newly discovered kangaroo. He was fascinated by India; many of his friends had strong professional connections there, and he considered emigrating. One of these associates was Sir William

Jones (1746–94) judge in the supreme court of Bengal from 1783, who published some pioneering scholarly research on Persian and Sanskrit, as well as some of the earliest English translations from those languages.

Johnson's first published book was a translation of Father Jerome Lobo's *Voyage to Abyssinia*, an account of a Jesuit mission to what is now Ethiopia (1735). His early play, the tragedy *Irene*, is set in a Greece overrun by Turkish conquerors. Much of the action concerns the struggle between Greek liberty and Turkish despotism, but the perverse sexual attraction between the Turkish emperor and Irene, a Greek lady, is also highlighted. Johnson befriended the fake 'Formosan', George Psalmanazar, who had availed himself of the craze for the exotic in 1704 by passing himself off as a native of Formosa (now Taiwan), complete with invented language and customs. Johnson's *Vanity of Human Wishes* (1749), a sober version of Juvenal's tenth satire, invites us to look around: 'Let Observation, with extensive view, / Survey mankind from *China* to *Peru*' (1–2). What the worldview shows is a uniform sequence of human failure; aspiration and ambition seem alike doomed to the status of self-defeating delusion. Examples from English history are coupled with figures from European power-struggles; in imagination Johnson tours Austria, Bavaria, Croatia and Persia to illustrate a kind of community of fate: that aspirant rulers and eminent people of all kinds tend to overreach themselves and fail.

In 1759 Johnson returned to these themes in his *The Prince of Abissinia*, commonly known as *Rasselas* after its central character.[7] Johnson uses the distant realm to envisage a 'happy valley' where all possible wants of the body and mind are readily catered for, but which no-one is allowed to leave. Rasselas is unhappy amid this Edenic richness without clearly knowing why, and imagines life beyond the valley. A tutor-figure, Imlac, who has retired to the valley after a life of travel, recounts to Rasselas his adventures in Persia, Syria and Europe, which mostly (such is the 'vanity of human wishes') end in disappointment. Nonetheless Imlac also understands Rasselas's desire for the unknown: 'some desire is necessary to keep life in motion; and he, whose real wants are supplied, must admit those of fancy' (56). Everyone, in fact, finds the happy valley tedious; in its insistence on pleasure, it is totalitarian and oppressive. Rasselas and Imlac escape from the valley in the company of Rasselas's sister Nekayah and her attendant, Pekuah, and set off to Cairo, where they study human life in different situations. All their hopes of finding a system of happiness are defeated: they visit shepherds in search of pastoral simplicity and find only squalor and envy; a hermit, regarded as a sage, is desperate for company and returns with them to the city; a philosopher who teaches restraint of the emotions is inconsolable on the death of his daughter. When they visit the great pyramid, Imlac acknowledges that they have 'gratified' their minds with 'an exact survey of the greatest work of man, except the wall of China' but declares: 'It seems to have been erected only in compliance with that hunger of imagination which preys incessantly upon life, and must always be appeased by some employment'.

Against these stern laments for the fallacy of the imagination, however, Johnson supplies a sudden new imaginative scope to his novella, for Pekuah is abducted and held to ransom. This adventure, a miniature romance in itself, also affords the princess a valuable lesson: grieving for her lost companion, she decides to resign herself to a convent, but Imlac perceives that this too is a false seclusion, a 'choice of life' which is tantamount to death. Eventually Pekuah is returned, and the episode is in turn displaced by a still more exotic fantasy. The group meet a deluded scientist, a man whose acute knowledge of astronomy has led him to the conclusion that he is actually in control of the forces of nature. From this mad supposition he is slowly rescued by the presence of the socially adept women. In the conclusion 'in which nothing is concluded', each makes an ideal 'choice of life' secure in the knowledge that it cannot be fulfilled, and they return to Abyssinia. The group possess as much power as is possible to possess, they are in the most imaginative realm Johnson can envisage, and still they cannot find a role that satisfies desire. Indeed, it is important that they do not, for fixed identities and resolutions all fail, in the course of the novel: social interaction is privileged above isolation, openness to the new scores more points than a 'choice of life' which will inevitably become a new prison.

There are more practical elements to Johnson's sense of the non-British. One of the ill-assorted inmates of his house was Francis Barber, a black servant, born a slave in Jamaica around 1742 and brought to England in 1750 by his owner, whose son then transmitted him to Johnson's care. The boy was educated and formally freed, but did not get on well with other members of Johnson's household and enlisted in the navy. Johnson requested, through Smollett, that he be discharged from this service, and Barber returned to work for Johnson in 1760, studying further (he could read Latin and some Greek). He married a white woman in 1773 and was present at Johnson's death; he was Johnson's residuary legatee. The relationship was often difficult. But on the issue of slavery, Johnson was firm: 'No man is by nature the property of another', he declared, and he interested himself on behalf of Joseph Knight, a slave whose case came to court in 1777. Opposing the American colonists' appeals for independent power in his pamphlet *Taxation no Tyranny* (1775) he made the telling remark: 'How is it that we hear the loudest yelps for liberty among the drivers of negroes?' He also once famously proposed a toast to 'the next insurrection of the negroes in the West Indies'. Johnson's opinions chimed with a growing unease about the conditions of slave workers and the slave trade that was eventually to become an actual movement for abolition.[8]

Empires of the mind

The admiralty had continued to sponsor naval circumnavigations, such as Anson's voyages of 1740–4 and Byron's of 1764–6, to produce maps and claim territory. These voyages produced their own popular literature and food for the imagination: Byron, having explored the coast of Patagonia (now Argentina), was popularly supposed to have discovered a race of giants, a claim ridiculed by Johnson in his *Journey*. James Cook's voyages were promoted by the Admiralty partly for imperial purposes: the discovery of territories that could be claimed for the British crown and subsequently used as British bases, and the improvement of charts that could be used in naval warfare. But there were scientific and cultural spin-offs. The first voyage was designed to observe the 'transit of Venus' across the sun from the island of Tahiti, but also to see what could be discovered about the largely unknown south Pacific. Cook charted the coast of New Zealand in 1768, claiming the islands for Britain (after some uneasy trading with the Maori). The entire continent of Australia was claimed for Britain in 1770. Cook was accompanied by an eminent naturalist, Sir Joseph Banks, who made a record of flora and fauna and brought news of the kangaroo to Western ears. Cook himself brought home a number of ethnographic items such as paddles and weapons. On a further voyage (1772–5) Cook explored Antarctica and Pacific islands. He then led an expedition to discover the North-West Passage, trying to do it from Pacific to Atlantic, efforts in the other direction having failed. Every avenue was blocked by ice. Looking for somewhere to refit the ships, he landed at Hawaii, where (having initially been welcomed as a god) he was killed during a dispute over a stolen boat.

Tahiti was reported as a version of Eden, without economic necessity or sexual restraint. A resident, Omai, was brought to England in July 1774. Under the patronage of Banks, the barefoot and tattooed Omai was trundled round the highest social circles of London: he was presented at court, attended the races, was invited to dinners and balls. Reynolds painted a huge and classically glamorous portrait of him in priestly vestments. He impressed everyone, including Johnson, with his 'natural' civility and good manners and boosted a strain of primitivism in English thinking that idealized pre-economic island life against the corruptions of civilization. Omai himself played along with and extended this mythology in hopes that his supporters would provide him with the means to reclaim his inheritance on a different island. But such romances tended to sour: Omai returned to Tahiti, laden with useless Western goods like fireworks and a suit of armour, in 1776, died a few years later, disorientated and rootless.[9] Another South Sea islander, Lee Boo, was brought to London in the interests of educational experimentation, and died of smallpox inside six months.

Towards the end of the period, non-European voices began to be heard more plainly. Black servants became fashionable; Hogarth integrated black workers into his vision of the social fabric, often as amused spectators of the corrupt and fraudulent behaviour of the sophisticated white British. Ignatius Sancho was born on a slave ship in 1729 and became a servant, later setting up as a grocer in Mayfair in 1773; here he became known as a man of taste and a talented musician. He was painted by Gainsborough in 1768, and his correspondence with Sterne and others was posthumously published in 1782. In 1789 there appeared by subscription *The Interesting Narrative of the Life of Olaudah Equiano, or Gustavus Vassa, The African. Written by Himself*. This was one of the earliest first-hand accounts of what it was to live as a slave in the British colonies. Equiano was born about 1745 in part of what is now Nigeria, and kidnapped with his sister by slave dealers at the age of ten. At his first sight of white men he is convinced they are cannibals who will eat him, and though this is in some ways a comic reversal of the expected hierarchy of savage and civilized it forms a grim premonition of later abuse. There are further echoes of fictional models: his estranged description of a watch reminds us of the Lilliputians' bemused accounts of Gulliver's belongings. Equiano casts himself as Crusoe's Friday made literate, but as the story develops, Equiano becomes more like Crusoe. Under the relatively benign ownership of a Quaker 'man of feeling' (101), he commences merchant on his own account, and despite the frauds of white men, eventually amasses enough capital to buy his own freedom. Like Francis Barber, he enlists as a sailor; he educates himself and becomes, almost, an establishment figure; he marries a white woman.

The book is also an account of the anthropological observations of an extremely well-travelled man. As a slave he travels on his master's ships up and down the coast of North America and across the Atlantic, at one point being shipwrecked in the Bahamas; as a free sailor and merchant he goes to Portugal, Spain and Italy, attending opera in Naples and observing the eruption of Vesuvius with equal interest. Equiano's African homeland has in its simple plenty the tincture of the noble savage about it, but he also records details of the eating habits, clothes, religious worship and domestic organization of the peoples he observes – Western, American, West Indian, Oriental, Arctic. He expands or eludes the boundaries of conventional travel writing: he is fond of Turkey, one of his reasons being that 'I believe they are fond of black people' (168), circumventing western European perspectives altogether. Without ever having full civil rights, despite his legal freedom, he manages a slave estate himself (his life is not without compromise, and he sees Africa as a huge potential market) and becomes an envoy of the British government in their attempt to establish a colony of freed slaves and other migrants in Sierra Leone. At one point he engages a 'Musquito prince' from North America in dialogue about Christianity. As a black man who had once naïvely attempted to wash his face white, and later consciously whitened his complexion while laying a trap for a white merchant who had cheated him, Equiano offers an unusual perspective on cultural and racial difference.

The *Interesting Narrative* contains, like *Crusoe*, a prominent vein of religious superstition, including a shipwreck prefigured by a dream. As well as a travel book, it is a spiritual autobiography, showing the workings of God in his life and fate. At length Equiano experiences a profound 'conversion' experience, including a vivid vision of Christ on the cross and 'uncommon commotions within' (191), linking him with Methodist experiences of salvation. Whatever the personal significance of this, there is no doubt that it makes him unimpeachable politically: it allows him to criticize the appalling cruelty of nominally Christian slave traders and owners, and it grants him a ready identity among the Quaker and Methodist groups opposing the slave trade. Equiano's *Narrative* was a powerful document in that emerging argument, which had been gaining some momentum since a court decision in 1772 (the case of Joseph Knight) ruled that slavery was not legal on English ground. The *Narrative* was an example of what a slave, given economic freedom, civil rights and education, could achieve: as sailor, entrepreneur, and finally as writer.

Notes

1 Quotations are from *Oroonoko, The Rover and other Writings*, edited by Janet Todd (London, 1992).
2 Thomas Southerne's dramatic version of the story (1695) was markedly more sentimental.
3 Dryden's plays *The Indian Queen* (1664), *The Indian Emperor* (1665) had allowed for the presentation of similar issues.
4 Defoe followed up with a sequel, *The Farther Adventures of Robinson Crusoe* (1719) in which the development of the colony is described.
5 Defoe is using the new 'Transportation Act' (1718), by which convicts could be sent to American plantations for a set time.
6 Quotations are from *Gulliver's Travels*, edited by Paul Turner (Oxford, 1986).

7 Quotations are from *The History of Rasselas, Prince of Abissinia*, edited by D. J. Enright (Harmondsworth, 1976).

8 Some of Cowper's later poems, such as 'The Negroe's Complaint', 'Pity for Poor Africans' and 'Sweet Meat has Sour Sauce; or, The Slave-Trade in the Dumps' were written in support of abolition.

9 Omai's death was reported by Captain Bligh, later the victim of the Mutiny on the Bounty: this too spawned narratives of travel, hardship – and paradisal freedom on the Pitcairn islands.

6

Versions of the self

For my part, when I enter most intimately into what I call *myself*, I always stumble on some particular perception or other, of heat or cold, light or shade, love or hatred, pain or pleasure. I never can catch *myself* at any time without a perception, and never can observe any thing but the perception. When my perceptions are remov'd for any time, as by sound-sleep; so long am I insensible of *myself*, and may truly be said not to exist. And were all my perceptions remov'd by death, and cou'd I neither think, nor feel, nor see, nor love, nor hate after the dissolution of my body, I shou'd be entirely annihilated, nor do I conceive what is farther requisite to make me a perfect non-entity. If any one upon serious and unprejudic'd reflection, thinks he has a different notion of *himself*, I must confess I can reason no longer with him. . . . He may perhaps, perceive something simple and continu'd, which he calls *himself*; tho' I am certain there is no such principle in me.

. . . I may venture to affirm of the rest of mankind, that they are nothing but a bundle or collection of different perceptions, which succeed each other with an inconceivable rapidity, and are in a perpetual flux and movement. Our eyes cannot turn in their sockets without varying our perceptions. Our thought is still more variable than our sight, and all our other senses and faculties contribute to this change; nor is there any single power of the soul, which remains unalterably the same, perhaps for one moment. The mind is a kind of theatre, where several perceptions successively make their appearance; pass, re-pass, glide away, and mingle in an infinite variety of postures and situations. There is properly no *simplicity* in it at one time, nor *identity* in different; whatever natural prepension we may have to imagine that simplicity and identity. The comparison of the theatre must not mislead us. They are the successive perceptions only, that constitute the mind; nor have we the most distant notion of the place, where these scenes are represented, or of the materials, of which it is compos'd.

[David Hume, *Treatise of Human Nature* (1739–40)]

Mind and body

In the seventeenth century a new empirical anatomy displayed the workings of the body as essentially mechanical, hydrostatic, chemical, a matter of tubes and liquids. The old system of medical 'humours', with its division of human characters according to the mix of the humours, gave way to a recognizable form of 'neurology' in the work on the anatomy of the brain carried out by Thomas Willis (1622–75). There were problems with this view of man, since it might be said to leave no room for the soul; the political philosopher Thomas Hobbes scandalously accepted the implications of this in his reasonings on government in the 1650s. Man was a machine like any other; there was no immaterial soul, just a bundle of sense perceptions, and these could be governed as an animal could be trained. The eighteenth century saw what might be termed the invention of the modern self, politically and economically autonomous, and psychologically deep. As theological certainties about identity (the matter of the soul) lost ground the question of selfhood became more of a philosophical conundrum (the mind).

John Locke (1632–1704) argued in his *Essay Concerning Human Understanding* (1690) that the really important question was not the mechanical body, but the mind, the process of acquiring knowledge and selfhood through experience. Unlike earlier philosophers, who postulated an innate sense of virtue, or soul, or knowledge of God, Locke likened the mind of the newborn infant to a sheet of blank paper, an empty 'cabinet', a *tabula rasa* [blank writing-tablet]; through experience the individual accumulated sufficient probabilities and truths to be able to function in the world. There were no innate moral ideas, but these ideas were formed practically enough by the experience of consequences in the world and by the association of one idea with another. The question of identity was thus opened up: the essential aspect of selfhood turns out to be self-consciousness, the awareness of the self in the act of perceiving. Using a number of provocative thought-experiments (if two people share the same consciousness, are they not the same person? is a person asleep the same as a person awake?) Locke arrived at the conclusion that what matters is continuity of consciousness: in effect, memory. Continuity of body is irrelevant: we are what we remember. Locke added a chapter on 'Identity and Diversity' in the second edition of the *Essay* (1694), pushing these ideas even further.

Locke was also providing formulations about identity for legal purposes: accountability in the courts and in commerce, property ownership and transfer, citizenship, the franchise. There was a close fit with Whig political theory, the notion of society as a contract between free individuals. Locke's ideas were popular with Whig-inclined writers such as Addison and Steele, who encouraged through their periodicals the idea that if character was not fixed, it could be disciplined, improved, ameliorated. Locke was the major theorist of education for the eighteenth century.[1] Locke's pupil, Shaftesbury, taught in turn that philosophy was essentially concerned with self-knowledge, with the governance of emotion, and with the production through discipline of perfect self-mastery and autonomy.[2] Sciences of man emphasized self-control and self-development. The eighteenth century saw a huge growth in the discourses of medicine and anatomy, in exercise regimens, dieting, hygiene, discussions of mental health, and psychiatry. Christian disgust at the body gave way to secular concerns about regulation of the body's 'economy'. George Cheyne, a doctor who gorged himself to the point of death around 1720 (he weighed 32 stone) wrote a kind of medical autobiography of his 'cure' through regimented habits of moderation and exercise in *The English Malady* (1733). Another doctor, John Armstrong, harnessed verse to the health services in *The Art of Preserving Health* (1744). These regulatory instructions are in one sense anti-self, as if by the correct 'discipline' selfhood could be rendered neutral, non-problematic, uniform (this was also the great age of the institution: school, hospital, reformatory). But insofar as they were based on empirical study, they encouraged self-examination and self-knowledge as a high moral good.

Locke's ideas did not, however, simply dominate eighteenth-century thinking; they were much less popular with orthodox divines and Tory satirists, who took Locke to be opening the floodgates to moral relativism and theological scepticism. Pope and the other Tory satirists amused themselves with their own thought experiment in *The Memoirs of Martinus Scriblerus* by asking what happens, legally and sexually, when Siamese twins marry. For Swift, indeed, the body was still dominant and he used a technique of reduction to the physical body, throughout his satire:

> Last Week I saw a Woman *flay'd*, and you will hardly believe, how much it altered her Person for the worse. Yesterday I ordered the Carcass of a *Beau* to be stript in my Presence; when we were all amazed to find so many unsuspected Faults under one Suit of Cloaths: Then I laid open his *Brain*, his *Heart*, and his *Spleen*; But, I plainly perceived at every Operation, that the farther we proceeded, we found the Defects encrease upon us in Number and Bulk . . . (pp. 173–4)

Swift satirized biological mechanists with cod-science, but at the same time managed to suggest that the body formed the only 'rational' explanation for much social and political activity in the contemporary world.

As the mind took over the moral functions of the soul, and usurped the body's status as guarantor of the continuity of selfhood, so the body could be seen to be taking revenge in the physiology of madness. The 'age of reason', as the period is sometimes known was possessed and fascinated by the fear of madness and mental disorder, prompting a huge outpouring of theories about the somatic causes of melancholia and hysteria. Locke thought madness was psychological, a fault in the association of ideas; but much of the discourse about madness ascribed it to organic or somatic causes. Cheyne's *English Malady* had speculated about the operations of the nerves in the brain; Nicholas Robinson's *A New System of the Spleen* (1729) argued that malfunctions in the nerve fibres were the cause.[3] In 1758 William Battie attacked the old-fashioned punitive methods of dealing with madness in London's premier asylum, Bethlehem Hospital (the 'Bedlam' of Pope's *Dunciad*), arguing instead for progressive 'management' of mental illness. Towards the end of the period neurophysiology was being challenged by psychology and psychiatry, with practitioners such as William Perfect offering *Methods of Cure, in Some Particular Cases of Insanity* (1778). These issues became nationally important with the derangement of George III in 1788.

Philosophers, meanwhile, continued to see the problem as epistemological and cognitive. Hume, like Locke, saw the principal questions of philosophy in terms of the mind's materials and abilities. Identifying the question of personal identity as of special and recent concern in English philosophy, Hume declares himself more sceptical than Locke about the consistency of selfhood. He equates self with mind, without reference to body, and sees this not as the identity of a single, permanent object, but as a federation or relation of impressions. Hume argues that the mind tends to supply continuity to series that are actually interrupted or to supply unknown and mystical relations between things that are actually distinct. Just as a river is in constant flux and yet is thought of as 'one' object, so the body changes all the time, and yet we call the self identical. Arguing, against Locke, that memory alone is insufficient to account for our sense of identity because it is subject to massive interruptions and error (he implies that imagination is much the greater power), Hume finally announces that 'all the nice and subtle questions concerning personal identity can never possibly be decided, and are to be regarded rather as grammatical than as philosophical difficulties'. There is no unitary, consistent self, because consciousness is atomistic.

Some kind of solution to the mind/body debate in the formation of identity was offered by David Hartley (1705–57). Having considered a career in the church, Hartley found he could not in conscience subscribe to all 39 Articles of the Church of England, so practised medicine instead at Bath. His *Observations on Man, His Frame, His Duty, and His Expectations* (1749) adopted a Lockean sense of consciousness, but tried to ground the processes of self-formation in physiology, the nervous system and workings of the brain. He argued that 'association of ideas' must work through mechanisms of vibration within the matter of the brain, leaving tiny 'vibratiuncles', physical traces of complex ideas. It was a form of neuro-psychology, which eluded the mind/body distinction altogether and showed the possibility of a consistent, unitary selfhood.

Poetic selves

We tend to expect literature to explore the private, psychological self, but for much of the period the presentation of self in poetry takes a rather different form. Milton's identification with the hero of his *Samson Agonistes* is unspoken but probably quite strong. There is, however, no ambiguity about his presentation of 'The Author John Milton' in *Paradise Lost*.[4] In the opening of Book I Milton invites the 'heavenly Muse' to 'sing' the epic of man's fall for him, before manoeuvring himself into a more assertive position.

> I thence
> Invoke thy aid to my adventurous song,
> That with no middle flight intends to soar
> Above the Aonian mount, while it pursues
> Things unattempted yet in prose or rhyme. (I.12–16)

Milton asks the 'Spirit' that once 'Dove-like sat'st brooding on the vast abyss / And mad'st it pregnant' (I.21–2), to do the same for him in poetic terms: 'what in me is dark / Illumine, what is low raise and support' (I.22–3). If this sounds like a prayer to the holy spirit, to 'inspire' Milton in the manner it was deemed to have inspired the writers of the Bible, there are significant changes in the model by Book III. In his invocation to the 'light' in the first 55 lines of that book, Milton 'revisits' the light after the darkness of the two first books, identifying his own motion with the motion of the poem. But since Milton is blind, the works of nature 'a universal blank . . . expunged and razed', he must find comfort in the model of other blind poet/prophets, including Tiresias and Homer. Moreover, the poignant lament for lost sight has a sting in the tail:

So much the rather thou celestial Light
Shine inward, and the mind through all her powers
Irradiate, there plant eyes, all mist from thence
Purge and disperse, that I may see and tell
Of things invisible to mortal sight. (III.51–5)

There is something better than empirical evidence: there is inspiration. In Book VII, Milton hymns 'Urania', Muse of astronomy, for help in celestial imagining, but returns himself to the dangers of earthly life under the Restoration:

More safe I sing with mortal voice, unchanged
To hoarse or mute, though fallen on evil days . . .
In darkness, and with dangers compassed round,
And solitude . . .

With Urania's help, he seeks 'fit audience, though few' (VII.24–31).

In Book IX, Milton celebrates his

celestial patroness, who deigns
Her nightly visit unimplored,
And dictates to me slumbering, or inspires
Easy my unpremeditated verse . . . (IX.21–4)

This is almost secular, a conventional 'Muse': the invocations encode a gradual assumption of poetic identity and power. But even so Milton did not address personal concerns directly, as he had done in earlier sonnets on his blindness and his dead wife: these moments feature as part of the ongoing argument in the poem about creativity and worship.

Rochester, by contrast, has only too many selves in the poetry: each one is a miniature drama in a different character, with no stable core of identity on offer. In Dryden we do not find much 'personal' material, for the personality is that of the state poet. 'Thus have I made my own opinions clear', he writes in *Religio Laici* (451), but the 'I' here is that of the state's ideal layman: unobtrusive, quietist, conformist. 'To the Memory of Mr Oldham' has more in it of what a modern reader would find personal, though the poem is really about a failure of personal contact: 'Farewell, too little and too lately known, / Whom I began to think and call my own . . .'. *Mac Flecknoe* has some private animus, naturally, but there is no ostensible 'Dryden' attached to it – the poem seeks rather to identify Shadwell's poetic corpus with his notorious bodily corpulence.

Shadwell's own works have physical status because they have no mental identity: on the road to the theatre, 'Loads of Shadwell almost choked the way' (103). Shadwell himself was notoriously fat, and Dryden helps himself to some comedy on this score, linking Shadwell's bulk with the tedious materiality of his writing. Flecknoe, for whom Shadwell's 'goodly fabric' (25) is a source of pride, exalts in the contrast between his huge noisy stomach and his tiny ('kilderkin') intelligence:

> Nor let thy mountain-belly make pretense
> Of likeness: thine's a tympany of sense.
> A tun of man in thy large bulk is writ,
> But sure thou 'rt but a kilderkin of wit. (193–6)

Shadwell's life and work is reduced to a body, to corporeal materiality, in the purest form of personal attack (Dryden plays no explicit part in the poem at all, and its circulation was, in theory at least, anonymous).

Swift (whose works were almost all published anonymously), worked by inhabiting the skin of the person or type he was attacking, whether in poetry (in popular ballads) or parodic prose pamplets. His major 'autobiographical' poem was, characteristically, about his absence: *Verses on the Death of Dr Swift* comically envisaged the reactions of friends, enemies and booksellers to the news of his demise – though enclosed within the fiction is a kind of ironic record of his achievements, literary and political.

The case of Pope is more complex. Pope did not believe in the new kind of psychology any more than Swift did: his *Epistle to Cobham* (1734), 'on the Characters of Men' sticks to ready satiric formulations of character-types, arguing that beneath that lies a morass of unknowable motive and counter-motive. For Pope the only constant is the 'ruling passion', a kind of dominant psychological thread that explains and unifies apparently disparate actions. He carried this theory of psychological essences into the *Essay on Man*, where he urged: 'Know then thyself, presume not God to scan; / The proper study of Mankind is Man.'[5] Pope's own position was complex. He wrote no Donne-like love lyrics, no poems of spiritual self-examination in the manner of the Metaphysicals. Saddled with a 'crazy carcase', caused by a long-standing illness that rendered him very short and subject to an increasingly pronounced curvature of the spine, he was always subject to merciless attacks on his physique. His response (apart from attacking in turn) was to control very carefully the dissemination of his work: he edited his own poems, issuing them with a fine engraved portrait disguising his curvature, in 1717, and in the course of his career exerted an unusual degree of influence on his public image. *The Dunciad* was a poem of all-out war; it was also a self-defence, the implied autobiography of the libelled poet. Pope was proud of his letters, but (as with autobiography), publication of such private material was ruled out as a form of vanity. In 1735 he managed to trick Edmund Curll into publishing an unauthorized edition of his correspondence, so that he could legitimately publish an authorized text, showing himself in the light of a faithful friend, erudite conversationalist and spontaneous wit. These textual strategies for careful self-revelation continued throughout the 1730s in the series of Horatian imitations, where Pope's similarities to, and differences from, Horace, are registered in the contrast between original and translation.

In 1735 Pope issued his greatest poetic 'autobiography', the *Epistle to Dr Arbuthnot*. This was, as the preface made clear, in response to a number of attacks on his poetry, his life, and his family. Most notable among these was the poem, written 'in witty fornication' between Pope's former friend Lady Mary Wortley Montagu and Lord Hervey, a Whig intimate of Walpole and Queen Caroline. One of the more effective poetic rebuttals of Pope's poetic agenda, this took pot-shots at Pope's stature, sexual unattractiveness, family background and ludicrous claim to satiric power.[6] Pope actually responded privately to these attacks in a prose *Letter to a Noble Lord. On occasion of some Libels written and propagated at Court, in the Year 1732–3*.[7] But this remained unpublished. Instead he pulled together various scraps, episodes and fragments of verse and melded them into a public apologia, the *Epistle to Dr Arbuthnot* (1735). Importantly, this was an urgent celebration of friendship, a last letter to the doctor who had helped him through 'this long disease, my life' (Arbuthnot, as was expected, died shortly after its publication). One of the main contentions of the Hervey/Montagu *Verses* was that Pope was friendless and outcast, and the poem is designed to show that this is not the case. Indeed, it opens with Pope instructing his gardener John to keep the hordes out:

> Shut, shut the door! good John! fatigu'd I said,
> Tye up the knocker, say I'm sick, I'm dead . . . (1–2)

So far from being shunned by humanity, Pope's poem suggests, his retreat at Twickenham is perennially invaded by crowds of would-be friends seeking to imitate his success: 'By land, by water, they renew the charge, / They stop the Chariot, and they board the Barge' (9–10). Solitude would be welcome, for what these 'friends' want is some of Pope's advantages: talent and money. 'Three things another's modest wishes bound, / My Friendship, and a Prologue, and ten Pound' (47–8).

Hervey/Montagu might poke fun at his body; but flattery is worse:

> There are, who to my person pay their court,
> I cough like Horace, and tho' lean, am short,
> Ammon's great son one shoulder had too high,
> Such Ovid's nose, and 'Sir! you have an Eye—' (115–18)

Pope knows better than any satirist or flatterer what a disaster his body is: he is writing the poem to his doctor, after all, the man who has helped him through 'this long disease, my life'. The poem turns the problem into a defence of self-knowledge.

After shutting out all this worldly noise, Pope meditates on his own poetic autobiography for the benefit of invited eavesdroppers (that is, us, the polite audience). Pope's initiation into poetry was always natural: 'I lisp'd in Numbers, for the Numbers came' (128), and helped into print by a band of respectable poetic godfathers (models of *real* friendship). Nonetheless, self is oppositional in this world. There are three great set-pieces in the poem, each defining what Pope is *not*. He is not 'Atticus', a figure standing for Addison, at lines (193–214), presiding over his little coterie of flattering critics and writers, pretending friendship but jealous and back-stabbing at the core. He is not 'Bufo', a more powerful literary patron, 'fed with soft dedication all day long' in the odious patronage system (231). Above all he is not Sporus, the bisexual, toothless, made-up fop whose poetry and identity Pope savages without mercy:

> Whether in florid impotence he speaks,
> And, as the prompter breathes, the puppet squeaks;
> Or at the ear of Eve, familiar Toad,
> Half froth, half venom, spits himself abroad,
> In puns, or politicks, or tales, or lies,
> Or spite, or smut, or rhymes, or blasphemies. (317–22)

This figure, indiscriminately passing on messages from Walpole (the 'Prompter') to Queen Caroline (Eve) and spouting forth an egotistical display of poisonous lather, is Hervey himself, the 'vile antithesis' against whom Pope proceeds to characterize himself:

> Not Fortune's worshipper, nor Fashion's Fool,
> Not Lucre's madman, nor Ambition's tool,
> Not proud, nor servile; Be one Poet's praise,
> That, if he pleas'd, he pleas'd by manly ways . . . (334–7)

Pope's definitive self-display is thus calculated with extreme care: it is not merely that he shows himself in a good light, but that the whole point of selfhood is an internal consistency that engages with the world in consistent ways. Virtue must be stable, visible, known, whatever the corruptions and contingencies of political and commercial life.

Poetry was thus coming to have an autobiographical status, albeit in a very controlled and calculated way. Prose autobiographies were not normally published during the writer's lifetime, for that would signal vanity.

An exception that proved the rule of modest non-publication was Pope's *bête noire* Colley Cibber (1671–1757), the actor and poet laureate who published *An Apology for the Life of Mr Colley Cibber, Comedian* in 1740.[8] As an actor Cibber was famous for foppish comedy roles, and satirists explained that this was because his whole life was in fact a kind of empty display. The text of his *Apology for the Life* rather bears this out. Asking an imaginary critic 'What will you do with me? Expose me?', he answers, 'Why, dear, sir, does not every man that writes expose himself? Can you make me more ridiculous than nature has made me?' (28). Calling himself 'incorrigible' by any criticism, he declares 'I can no more put off my follies than my skin' (14–15). Allotting to himself 'giddy negligence' he calls himself an 'inconsistent creature' (8).

> But why make my follies publick? Why not? I have pass'd my time very pleasantly with them, and I don't recollect that they have ever been hurtful to any other man living . . . the publick very well know my life has not been a private one (p. 5).

Performance is all there is: Cibber virtually ignores his domestic life, his unnamed wife and children being mentioned merely once, in a deliberately throwaway fashion:

> It may be observable too, that my muse and my spouse were equally prolifick; that the one was seldom the mother of a child, but in the same year the other made me the father of a play. I think we had a dozen of each sort between us; of both which kinds some died in their infancy, and near an equal number of each were alive when I quitted the theatre. (p. 138)

All his judgements are on the effectiveness of actors and performances. It is not merely that this is a theatrical memoir ('a life in the theatre', it might be called): for Cibber the self simply is theatrical, and the book displays aspects of his character just as the stage does. There is no difference, in Cibber's scale of values, between activity on stage and activity in parliament or in the courts: they are all theatres for exposition.

Nonetheless this measure of self-display stood beyond acceptable limits and Pope gratefully took him as hero of brazen overconfidence in the final version of *The Dunciad*.[9]

Where are you?

New possibilities of selfhood over time were explored in the one genre with which Pope had nothing to do: the novel. Defoe's *Robinson Crusoe* gives us 'economic man' of the kind later approved by Adam Smith in *The Wealth of Nations* (1776): free, autonomous, self-interested.[10] That is what makes economies work, in the arguments of eighteenth-century *laissez-faire* capitalism. Crusoe however has to get to this state by gradually discarding the theological baggage of sin and guilt and the temporal imprisonment of the island. As we have seen, that process also renders him an alienated, possessive individual. All Defoe's heroes and heroines have a detached, free-moving selfhood: Crusoe himself is originally 'Kreutznaer', not English at all but from a German settler family. His sojourn on the island reconstitutes him in the role of mastery: the absence of social speech is supplied by his parrot, Poll, who wakes him one morning with the alarming existential question: 'Robin, Robin, Robin Crusoe, poor Robin Crusoe, where are you Robin Crusoe? Where are you? Where have you been?' (152). Since Crusoe has taught the parrot to speak, the question emanates from Crusoe's own narcissism and is answered only by a hierarchy of power: 'where Crusoe is', effectively, is on top of everyone else. He efficiently brings the place of his new self (the island) into economic line with the place where his old self (proprietor of estates in Brazil) has been prospering in his absence. His family, by contrast, has completely disappeared, freeing him from obligation and ties; and though he does marry ('and that not to my disadvantage'), his wife is never named and dies before the sentence which informs us of the marriage is even complete. Having rebelled against his father, Crusoe is never again a family man.

Crusoe is a cross between the Puritan autobiographer and the free capitalist agent (though some historians find the roots of 'possessive individualism' in aspects of self-help and advancement espoused by some branches of Protestantism). The rest of Defoe's heroes branch out ever further into sin-free accumulation of goods. Criminals they may be, and guilty in a technical sense, but the shackle of Bunyanesque guilt is cast off. They tend to use pseudonyms to avoid legalistic identification within a recognized system of authority. They re-invent themselves repeatedly, scoring economic success thereby, and to some degree their hyperkinetic peregrinations constitute a sign of their freedom. 'Family' tends to be a sign of horror: it is eradicated in *Robinson Crusoe*, returns incestuously in *Moll Flanders*, and is (perhaps) murdered in *Roxana*. One of Swift's many tasks in his anti-novel, *Gulliver's Travels*, was to demolish this new type of economic subjectivity, to reveal it as self-seeking, power-hungry, deracinated and deranged.

The emergent novel continued the debate. One of the doctor George Cheyne's correspondents was the printer Samuel Richardson, who burst onto the literary scene with his highly controversial *Pamela: or, Virtue*

Rewarded (1740–1). This is the story of a servant girl whose master (Mr. B) pursues her, separating her from her friends and associates and imprisoning her on his remote estate in Lincolnshire, where she is further pressured by a housekeeper. Mr B. offers to make her his official mistress, then tries to rape her, then arranges a fake marriage. All these trials of her virtue having been resisted, Pamela, realizing that in fact she loves her master, agrees to marry him. The book then deals with the further trial caused by the social unacceptability of this marriage across the class divide. The story is told in the documentary form of letters and journals (mainly Pamela's, but there are several other correspondents), so that the emotional impact of each new sexual and psychological outrage is rendered directly, with no apparent mediation. The novel now gave deep feeling, deep selves.

In *Clarissa: or, The History of a Young Lady* (1747–9), Richardson raised the stakes. The story is essentially simple: virtuous, independently minded Clarissa is destined by her family for a marriage with the hideous landowner Solmes but is pursued by the rakish, Rochesterian aristocrat Lovelace. To avoid the tyranny of her family she escapes with him and he attempts to seduce her, to break down her willed resistance, by placing her in a variety of deceptive situations such as a brothel disguised as a lodging house. Using disguise, impostors, and forgery he attempts to remodel her mental landscape. She withstands everything, even the offer of marriage, and he drugs and rapes her; she dies, and he is killed in a duel by her cousin. But Richardson provides a massive text (again in the form of letters, this time more evenly distributed between the selves on show) to tease out every psychological nuance and inference of this battle of wills. Clarissa is all truth, her letters embodying a biblical sincerity; Lovelace is all performance, quotation, disguise, and forgery, a kind of latterday Satan. He intercepts and interrupts her correspondence with her close friend, Anna Howe, who provides a more worldly viewpoint; access to writing becomes a crucial element of self-expression and power. Clarissa endeavours to maintain her hold on identity in the midst of an environment increasingly distorted and inflected by Lovelace's desires and contrivances. After the rape, Clarissa spends a period necessarily mad, her textual coherence shattered.

Again, this model of experience was not incontestable: Fielding immediately responded to *Pamela* with *An Apology for the Life of Mrs Shamela Andrews* (1741), a wickedly plausible spoof novella containing letters that revealed the 'real' self hidden in Pamela's letters (a conniving, calculating gold-digger).[11] Overt shows of feeling, such as Pamela's, were still transgressive. Fielding's *The History of the Adventures of Joseph Andrews* (1742), supposedly the story of Pamela's brother, replaced such self-indulgence with the certainties of classic satiric identity, the 'type' rather than the individual. In his Preface Fielding sets out his manifesto for the 'comic epic poem in prose', deploying witty 'character' against the indulgences of self-seeking individuality. Joseph reverses Pamela's progress by resisting the advances of his aristocratic mistress, and getting himself thrown out. But his self-discovery is scarcely psychological at all: it turns out (by means of a fairy-tale birthmark) he is the son of the country gentleman Wilson, whose life story is told as an interlude in the main narrative. Identity is thus a matter of sorting out misplaced individuals: Joseph's noble character is perfectly established in his return to his noble origin.

In *The History of Tom Jones, A Foundling* (1749), Fielding provided his answer to *Clarissa* (which, in fact, he admired much more than *Pamela*). Jones is discovered, as an abandoned infant, in the bed of the gentle and childless Allworthy, a country gentleman, who brings the boy up. His putative parents are the schoolmaster and a maidservant. Allworthy's sister marries and has a son, the villainous Blifil, who is brought up with Tom. Where Tom is naturally good-humoured, energetic and generous, Blifil is calculating, mean and hypocritical. Tom loves Sophia, daughter of a rough country squire, who destines her for Blifil, whom she detests. Tom is thrown out after his conduct is falsely maligned to Allworthy, and Sophia escapes the captivity of her father. Despairing of his chances of marrying Sophia, Tom sleeps with various women along the way, including one who turns out to be the woman thought to be his mother. Gradually all the characters are drawn towards London, where Tom's life is threatened by the machinations of Blifil and a crew of vicious aristocrats. But eventually it transpires that Tom is really the son of Allworthy's sister, and the hypocrisy of Blifil is laid bare. Tom marries Sophia, and Blifil is thrown out in his turn.

Johnson, who thought *Tom Jones* a 'vicious' book for its tolerance towards Tom's sexual adventures, commented that Richardson was much the better master of human nature, and that 'there was as great a difference between them as between a man who knew how a watch was made, and a man who could tell the hour by looking on the dial-plate'.[12] But depth of this kind was not what Fielding was after. The hold on formal identity is registered in the style: where Richardson pretends to retreat to the position of a mere editor of correspondence that we can, deliciously, spy on, Fielding presents us with a completely overt mediator, a narrator who announces his presence and intentions and who provides a comic grid of formal perception and intervention between 'life' and 'reader'. The book is elaborately plotted, a fact to which the narrator makes overt reference. The reader is directly addressed, cajoled, bossed around (comically). There is no 'illusion' as such. It is in no sense 'realistic' to assemble a cast of characters called 'Allworthy', 'Thwackum' (the schoolmaster) and 'Square' (the philosopher); the reason Tom is called Jones has less to do with his putative parentage in the novel and more with the need to mark him out as 'anonymous'. Until we find out who he actually is, at the end of the novel (Allworthy's nephew), he has no social role, other than to be the 'foundling' whom the charitable Allworthy takes in. His rule-breaking and sexual philandering is not merely unfocused excess of animal spirits, but a kind of displaced search for a role and a partner at all levels. When he finds out where he belongs, he simply marries the beautiful, intelligent Sophia, and fades immediately into the social wallpaper of English rural life.

Poetry of the mind

Poetry after Pope tended to side with the Richardsonian idea of selfhood. Against the public self-fashioning of Pope came the poetry of the mind. Mark Akenside's *Pleasures of Imagination* (1744) constituted a poetry of mental processes, enacting and promoting those same processes as it traced the structure and activity of the human imagination. William Collins moved away from the public model of heroic couplets to more loosely-constructed *Odes on Several Descriptive and Allegoric Subjects* (1746), exploring emotions such as pity, fear and superstition.

Pope's careful self-implications do not work for other poets. Gray's *Ode on a Distant Prospect of Eton College* positions the speaker on an eminence opposite his old school, but this does not grant him observational power so much as a crippling sense of absence: it is a 'distant' prospect because the scene represents childhood innocence, to which the observing figure cannot return. Gray's *Elegy Written in a Country Churchyard* similarly locates the poet-figure in a non-functioning landscape, that of death; the elegy is in the end not so much for all the dead that lie round but for the blanked-out figure of the poet himself, envisaged as a half-crazed solitary. In the same way, Goldsmith's *The Traveller* conveys a 'prospect of society', as we have seen, using the Popean heroic couplet to do so. But it also places the poet-observer very carefully, modifying the kind of personal power inherent in his high Alpine prospect ('Creation's heir, the world, the world is mine', 50) into an absence from his brother, safe in the domestic setting of his English rectory. The poem is remarkable for its plaintive presentation of the poet-figure, 'Remote, unfriended, melancholy, slow', wandering Europe despite the lure of home:

Where'er I roam, whatever realms to see,
My heart untravelled fondly turns to thee;
Still to my brother turns with ceaseless pain,
And drags at each remove a lengthening chain. (7–10)

Henry's family home is presented as an unchanging place of domestic comfort and efficiency against Oliver's proto-Romantic solitariness, 'My prime of life in wandering spent and care, / Impelled, with steps unceasing, to pursue / Some fleeting good . . .' (24–5). The problem of finding a home which is adequate for the poet-figure (in the sense that Henry's home is adequate for him) remains unsolved, leaving open the potential romance of eternal exile, so popular with the later Romantics. The poet's later defeated wish to return 'home' to the (deserted) village reinforces this model of poetic isolation, another marker of incipient Romanticism.

Who are you?

Another development in literature that seemed to proffer the possibility of regulating the presentation of selfhood externally, was literary biography. Isaac Walton's studies of Robert Hooker (1665) and George Herbert (1670) were to a degree hagiographic and some early biographies had too much of an axe to grind: when Boswell offered Gilbert Burnet's account of Rochester as an example of 'a good Life', Johnson retorted: 'We have a good *Death*; there is not much *Life*'.[13] By that time, however, literature might be said to be ordered biographically: Johnson's *Lives of the English Poets* stood in a long line of biographical compilations such as Giles Jacob's *Poetical Register* (1719–21), and *Lives of the Poets of Great Britain and Ireland*, notionally edited by Cibber's son Theophilus (five volumes, 1753). The collected 'Works' of poets, establishing their literary corpus, invariably appeared with an engraved portrait and a biography. This was in sharp contrast to the seventeenth century: Shakespeare's plays had appeared without any sort of biography and it was not until Rowe's edition of 1709 that an attempt was made to compile one. By the end of the century, the Shakespeare industry had zealously researched (and manufactured) a very large body of anecdotal and documentary evidence about the model poetic 'genius'.

The biography that dwarfed them all was Boswell's *Life of Johnson* (1791), the biggest biography of a private individual there had ever been. Johnson had been the subject of several biographies by the time Boswell (with help from the Shakespeare scholar Edmond Malone) finally managed to get his immensely complex notes in order. Boswell had been researching the biography more or less since his first meeting with Johnson in 1763, asking questions, keeping notes, sorting out Johnson's often complex bibliography. After Johnson's death he pressed Johnson's friends for information, letters and documents, producing a hybrid text consisting of full texts of many letters, interspersed with narrative, psychological commentary, and above all Johnson's powerful conversation. He produced a record of Johnson's essential *oddity*, his inimitable individuality from bodily appearance and habit through impromptu conversational character to literary style. It was a painful hagiography: Johnson's immense wisdom came at huge psychological cost, which Boswell, himself subject to fits of depression and alcoholism, understood only too well. In 1729, for example, he recounts that Johnson was scarcely ever free from such fears: he inherited a 'vile melancholy' from his father, and was early in life 'overwhelmed with an horrible hypochondria, with perpetual irritation, fretfulness and impatience; and with a dejection, gloom and despair, which made existence misery. From this dismal malady he never afterwards was perfectly relieved.'

Johnson had kept a diary of such experiences, an often painful record of his religious guilt, personal misery – and medical symptoms, the diary of self-regulation often involving recording one's weight, medication, and bowel movements over time. One of Boswell's main sources was his own journal, which he kept assiduously, recording his conversations with Johnson and others, his sexual adventures and his plans for self-reinvention. Boswell saw Johnson as a model of psychological strength, a man who conquered his private demons and preserved a model of selfhood against mental disorder. Boswell had a gallery of such men to live up to, pitting his own sense of role-play and improvisatory disorder (he was notoriously fond of the glamorous, rakish figure of Macheath, from Gay's *The Beggar's Opera*) against the perceived firmness of great characters, especially writers.

Diary-keeping had Puritan roots, of the kind we have seen in Bunyan and Defoe; but in our period it also had a wholly secular dimension. Samuel Pepys (1633–1703), 'clerk of the King's ships' under the Restoration, kept the famous diary between 1 January 1660 and 31 May 1669, when his sight began to fail. It was private: the cipher in which it was written was not decoded until 1825. John Evelyn (1620–1706), a friend of Pepys's, kept a diary for most of his adult life (it was not published until 1818). Both men were royalists in politics and had little interest in the 'spiritual autobiography' model of diary-keeping, though Evelyn's is more religious in character than Pepys's: they write about public and private concerns, their reading habits, visits to the theatre, their travels, their contemporaries, and in Pepys's case, his sexual and marital difficulties. Biographers were sometimes helped by diaries of their subjects, or by autobiographies, though neither of these were normally published during the writer's lifetime. David Hume, so sceptical about the coherence of personality, wrote a five-page self-portrait, *My Own Life*, just before his death in 1776; a fragment survives of an autobiography by Johnson; and Gibbon wrote several versions of his memoirs (essentially the growth of his mind rather than his notoriously gross body) for posthumous publication. The sources of writing in the personality, were, so to speak, written out in the life story.

But this too was problematic. The novel which most closely corresponds to these forms is Laurence Sterne's *The Life and Opinions of Tristram Shandy, Gent*, published in instalments (as Sterne's fame grew) between 1759 and 1767 (Sterne died in 1768). Drawing heavily both on the psychological theories of Locke and the available discourses of physiology and anatomy, Sterne produced a teasing, puzzling study of identity and its representations. Tristram Shandy's misfortunes begin not at the Lockean moment of inception into the world of experience, at birth, but during the inept sexual act that produced his body. Interrupted during intercourse by his wife's question about winding up the clock, Tristram's father ejaculates prematurely,

> which scattered and dispersed the animal spirits, whose business it was to have escorted and gone hand-in-hand with the *HOMUNCULUS*, and conducted him safe to the place destined for his reception.[14]

Tristram's life is ruined at conception. Comic as this is, scientifically, it is a significant moment in identity formation and the first in a long line of disasters: Tristram's nose is flattened by crude use of forceps during delivery; he is circumcised (at least) when the sash drops as he is urinating out of a window; and even his name is an accidental truncation of the intended mystical 'Trismegistus'. These primordial sexual cripplings cast a long shadow: the book is full of wounds, illnesses, deaths, failed couplings and other bodily aberrations. Mental development fares no better: his father's grand scheme of education for his son grows more slowly than Tristram himself, so by the time it is ready he has outgrown it. Lockean association of ideas proves intensely fallible as characters mishear, misread and misunderstand each other in comic and random free-assocation. Tristram looks to bodily gesture and posture and the discredited science of physiognomy (the reading of faces for character and meaning) with no better results. Ultimately, as with Swift's *Tale of a Tub*, language breaks down, and Tristram offers the reader blank pages to write on, marbled pages, black pages and diagrams to signify beyond words. Tristram makes text out of the fact that his autobiographical project is doomed: he simply cannot write fast enough to record what he has already lived through, as he lives longer so he must write more, and the project inevitably moves backwards rather than forwards. The text of autobiography unravels, and that is the only identity on offer: 'And who are you, said he – Don't puzzle me, said I.'[15]

There is no answer, beyond the answer that the process of questioning itself provides. The question of the origin and location of selfhood is not solved. What preserves *Tristram Shandy* from a kind of monomaniac isolation and Swiftian – or Humean – scepticism is 'sensibility': the situation is comically benign, not threatening. The men might not understand each other, they may be trapped in the history of their own minds, but they feel instinctive sympathy for one another. Sentiment was the new guarantee of authenticity, lauded by Adam Smith as a physiological bond between people, the origin of social feeling.[16] There were problems: Sarah Fielding's *The Adventures of David Simple, in Search of a Real Friend* (1744) showed how the world could oppress someone who tried to live by the rules of sympathy and to follow the 'Mazes, Windings, and Labyrinths of the Heart' as her brother Henry put it in his Preface. In Henry Mackenzie's *The Man of Feeling* (1771), the central character, whose sensibility leads him to believe well of the world, is repeatedly cheated (on one occasion by the delusions of physiognomy). Joseph Surface, in Sheridan's comedy *The School for Scandal* (1777) offers the ready language of sensibility: but it is, precisely, surface and not interior, and he is exposed as a calculating cheat (while his brother's good-hearted fecklessness triumphs). In *Tristram Shandy* the warmth of sentiment is always preserved in comedy, and Sterne's own commitment to it was offset by sharp self-interest. Sterne's own life was transformed by the unexpected success of the novel, and he lived flamboyantly alongside its developing series. He was lionized in London society; and deliberately blurred the distinction between character and authorship, in a sense passing himself off as 'Parson Yorick', the clergyman of the novel, even publishing his own sermons under that authorship. Sterne's text focused intense and sceptical scrutiny on medical and psychological means to determine selfhood; the attendant obfuscations of the literary form passed into a social domain that appreciated the joke.

Notes

1 Locke, *Some Thoughts Concerning Education* (1693).
2 Anthony Ashley Cooper, 3rd Earl of Shaftesbury, *Soliloquy* (1710).

3 The period has several poems on spleen: Anne Finch, *The Spleen* (1713); Matthew Green, *The Spleen* (1737); and the 'cave of Spleen' in Canto IV of Pope's *Rape of the Lock*.
4 The words are from the title page of the second edition.
5 Pope, *Essay on Man*, II.1–2.
6 The text can be found in *Eighteenth-Century Poetry: An Annotated Anthology*, edited by David Fairer and Christine Gerrard (Oxford, 1999).
7 *Prose Works*, Vol. 2, 433–83.
8 Quotations are from the Everyman edition (London 1938).
9 Fielding also makes comic capital out of Cibber's indiscreet self-publication in *Shamela*.
10 Earlier postulations of the idea that private self-interest promotes public good can be found in Bernard Mandeville's *Fable of the Bees, or Private Vices, Public Benefits* (1714 and 1723) – and to some extent in Pope's *Epistle to Bathurst*.
11 The title also recalls Cibber's *Apology*: both are supreme fabricators of selfhood.
12 Boswell, *Life of Johnson*, II.249 and 174–5. Boswell disagreed.
13 Boswell, *Life of Johnson*, III.123.
14 Sterne, *The Life and Opinions of Tristram Shandy*, edited by Graham Petrie (Harmondsworth, 1978), p. 35.
15 Sterne, *Life and Opinions of Tristram Shandy*, p. 500.
16 Smith, *Theory of Moral Sentiments* (1759).

7

Sex and gender

The Incapacity, if there be any, is acquired not natural; and none of their Follies are so necessary, but that they might avoid them if they pleas'd themselves. Some disadvantages indeed they labour under, and what these are we shall see by and by and endeavour to surmount; but Women need not take up with mean things, since . . . they are capable of the best. Neither God nor Nature have excluded then from being Ornaments to their Families and useful in their Generation; there is therefore no reason they should be content to be Cyphers in the World, useless at the best, and in a little time a burden and nuisance to all about them. . . . The Cause therefore of the defects we labour under is, if not wholly, yet at least in the first place, to be ascribed to the mistakes of our Education, which like an Error in the first concoction, spreads its ill Influence throughout all our Lives. . . .

Women are from their very Infancy debar'd those Advantages, with the want of which they are afterwards reproached, and nursed up in those Vices which will hereafter be upbraided to them. So partial are Men as to expect Brick where they afford no Straw; and so abundantly civil as to take care we shou'd make good that obliging Epithet of Ignorant, which out of an excess of good Manners, they are pleas'd to bestow on us!

[Mary Astell, *A Serious Proposal to the Ladies for the Advancement of their True and Greatest Interest*, Part 1 (1694), pp. 8–9].

Power

We noted in Chapter 1 the unpromising political position of women in the period: no vote, no higher education, no real prospect of a career, no independent property within marriage, almost no possibility of initiating divorce. The maintenance of this oppressive divide between the sexes was explicit in the family conduct manuals that were published to regulate gendered behaviour; Lord Halifax's *The Lady's New Year's Gift; or, Advice to a Daughter*, published in 1688 and much reprinted, set out the categories (Religion, Husband, Family, Behaviour) which his twelve-year-old daughter was to study and unblushingly announced:

> You must first lay it down for a foundation in general, that there is inequality in the sexes, and that for the better economy of the world the men, who were to be the lawgivers, had the larger share of reason bestowed upon them; by which means your sex is the better prepared for the compliance that is necessary for the better performance of those duties which seemed to be most properly assigned to it.[1]

We have already seen how it was possible for political theorists to argue from the story of creation in the book of Genesis that Adam was granted an authority over the world, that Eve was secondary to him, and that therefore 'patriarchy' was the natural system of government as handed down by God. The subjection of women to their husbands could also be enforced using New Testament writings, notably the letters of St Paul. Milton looked for a marriage of minds, a positive companionship, but there is little challenge to the traditional ordering even in this most radical of poets: when the angel Raphael arrives to warn Adam and Eve, he talks to Adam while Eve gets a meal ready. When we first meet the couple in Eden, they appear equal:

> Two of far nobler shape erect and tall,
> Godlike erect, with native honour clad
> In naked majesty seemed lords of all . . . (IV.288–90)

They seem indistinguishable; but in fact they are

> Not equal, as their sex not equal seemed;
> For contemplation he and valour formed,
> For softness she and sweet attractive grace,
> He for God only, she for God in him. (IV.296–9)

We learn that Adam is first, that Eve is formed from his flesh. We also learn that her first instinct upon becoming conscious is narcissistic: she prefers her image in the lake to the actual body of Adam (VIII.452–510). Satan works on this, her false courage, her sense of aspiration. Nonetheless Milton also understands her frustration at her secondariness; in some sense her fall is more defensible than Adam's, since she is deceived because she lacks something, while he eats the fruit in full knowledge of what he is doing.

Women's speaking justified

Monolithic as the power of male literary culture to speak for and about women thus appears, women were scarcely quiet under the barrage of representation, and the sexual mythology of the male poets was strongly challenged by women writers. Quaker women justified female preaching and discipleship on religious grounds.[2] The period had in fact several different models of female authorship. One was aristocratic, personified in the person Margaret Cavendish, Duchess of Newcastle, *c.*1623–73, known as 'mad Madge' to her detractors for her complete disregard of social form. She wrote an autobiography, a series of *Sociable Letters* (1664), on topics such as science, literature, marriage, and war; and a science fiction fantasy, *The Description of a New World, called the Blazing World.*[3] Alternatively, there was Katherine Philips (1632–64), a merchant's daughter of Puritan background but Royalist sympathies whose poems were published in an unauthorized edition in 1664. She died of smallpox almost immediately afterwards, and her poems were republished in 1667, remaining popular into the eighteenth century. Much of the poetry celebrates non-sexual friendship between women, often identified by romance names such as Lucasia or Rosania. Marriage is sometimes a threat to these friendships but there is nothing politically radical in the poems and they served as a model of decorous women's writing against more ambiguous cases such as Aphra Behn (*d.*1689). Much myth, partly self-generated, surrounded Behn, but like male writers, she earned most from plays, producing some eighteen dramas from 1670 onwards, along with commendatory verses, prologues and epilogues for the work of established male dramatists like Dryden; the favour was returned. She contributed to Dryden's collective translation of Ovid's *Heroides* (a set of fictional letters from passionate heroines), winning his praise. 'A Letter to a brother of the pen in tribulation' enters the world of male satire. Like Philips she had a circle of admirers (she exchanged verses with Rochester's niece, Ann Wharton) and her work was much republished, usually with elegies by other women writers. For some, her gender was clearly a problem and she was accused of being a disgusting harlot. But for some she embodied the sexiness of the female author: 'But as she was mistress of uncommon charms of body, as well as mind, she gave infinite and raging desires, before she could know the least her self'.[4] There was, in short, a kind of sexual politics, if not a sex war, about the writing of the period.

Coupling

Very early in the period, there is a strong sense of sexual celebration. One of the more surprising aspects of *Paradise Lost* is Milton's fierce defence of sex *before* the Fall:

> Nor turned I ween
> Adam from his fair spouse, nor Eve the rites
> Mysterious of connubial love refused:
> Whatever hypocrites austerely talk
> Of purity and place and innocence,
> Defaming as impure what God declares
> Pure, and commands to some, leaves free to all. (IV.741–7)

After the Fall, however, the character of sex changes and becomes something violent and guilty (and something that causes arguments).[5]

Something of this contrast lies behind the polymorphous sexuality deployed in Rochester's poetry. In 'The Fall' Rochester writes wistfully of a time when sex was perfect and not troubled by physical failings. Elsewhere he experiments with a variety of sexual roles: he celebrates sexual expertise in 'The Song of a Young Lady to her Ancient Lover', he enjoys female masturbation in 'Fair Chloris in a pigsty lay', he dramatizes a mudslinging encounter between some of Charles's mistresses in 'Dialogue'; he writes as a pederast in 'Love a woman? You're an ass'; he even writes a scurrilous ballad on women's use of sex toys in 'Signior Dildo'. This exploratory role-play includes the more urbane verse epistle, 'A Letter from Artemisia in the Town to Chloe in the Country', which reflects interestingly on the position of the woman writer at the time. By and large, this sheer variety prevents Rochester from lapsing into misogyny, or even from adopting the regular sexual double standard. In 'Upon Leaving his Mistress' he commends 'Celia' to the sexual service of mankind in general as a kind of noble mission; in 'Against Constancy' he revels in serial sexual encounters; 'The Mistress' and 'Absent from thee, I languish still' offer more tender and stable lyrics of sexual partnership. There are nightmare visions, like the scene of 'A Ramble in St James's Park', where Rochester depicts a whole landscape of stomach-churning sexual excess before cursing an ex-mistress, Corinna, for her sexual choices (three men whom the poet-figure thinks are worthless). Even here, however, his criticism is that she is not doing sex properly, not that she is not doing it with him.

But to turn damned abandoned jade
When neither head nor tail persuade;
To be a whore in understanding,
A passive pot for fools to spend in! (99–102)

Rochester also situates himself in anxious relation to the female, as if masculinity is not something to be taken for granted but is always provisional. Rochester gives us a male sexuality which is essentially *fallible*. In 'The Imperfect Enjoyment' he recounts the experience of premature ejaculation. The sexual partners seem perfectly suited, but male failure ruins it, and the poet-figure curses himself, not 'Corinna'. Specifically, the poet-figure rants for 35 lines against his useless penis, apparently gaining some kind of secondary potency from verbal display, and concludes with the hope that 'ten thousand' other men will 'do the wrong'd Corinna right for thee'.

This poem was based on a number of literary archetypes, and was also imitated by Behn in 'The Disappointment'. Rochester's vocabulary was notoriously unrestrained, partly because of his status and partly because of the status of the work: it was not published, but circulated in manuscript. Behn, however, writing probably with some sense of female decorum and certainly with a sense of publication in mind, takes a contrasting view of the situation of sexual failure. She situates her lovers in the open air, in a kind of natural erotic landscape, and several stanzas are allotted to what might be called literary foreplay. Against the deliberately crude simplifications of Rochester's poem, Behn seeks a decorous eroticism:

His daring hand that altar seized,
Where gods of love do sacrifice:
That awful throne, that paradise
Where rage is calmed, and anger pleased,
That fountain where delight still flows,
And gives the universal world repose. (stanza V)

This is not how Rochester refers to the vagina. But Lysander's 'fabulous Priapas, / That potent god, as poets feign', simply fails, despite Cloris's touch, and the disastrous encounter ends with Cloris fleeing, frustrated, and Lysander in a misogynistic rage. Behn resembles Rochester (whom she much admired) in trying out a number of sexual ideas and roles in her poetry. In 'To the Fair Clarinda' Behn toys with androgynous hybrids of gender: 'Thou beauteous wonder of a different kind, / soft Cloris with the dear Alexis joined'. 'On her loving two equally' dramatizes a conflict of erotic choice; 'On Desire' does literary honour to sexual passion. 'On a Juniper-Tree' transforms a tree, witness to open-air sexual encounters, into the bones of a corset. She further resembles Rochester in saying almost nothing about marriage.

Couples

Rochester had a surprisingly stable marriage, though he also had a highly public affair with an actress, Elizabeth Barry. Charles II had not only reopened the theatres, closed by parliament, but had brought back from France the practice of using actresses rather than boys for female roles. There was something more than naturalism of representation in this, and the presence of women ensured that the theatre became a zone of special sexual frisson. The comedies of the period have a special concern with sex and marriage. William Wycherley's *The Country Wife* (1675) revels in the ability of Horner, the male lead, to gain access to the wives of others by putting it about that he is impotent; the scandal to his masculine reputation counts for nothing against the excess of sexual pleasure the rumour facilitates. Conversely, Sir George Etherege's *Man of Mode* (1676) takes a rake-figure, Dorimant, and reforms him sufficiently to offer marriage to the spirited heiress Harriet, who proves to be less of a pushover than women he has previously known. (The counterpart, heroic tragedy such as Thomas Otway's *Venice Preserved* of 1682, tends to contrast 'public' duty with 'private' affections.) William Congreve's *Love for Love* (1695) shows an economically dependent son fighting his father for the right to marry the woman of his choice. His *The Way of the World* (1700) brings together Mirabell and Millamant, an ambiguously named but intellectually well-matched couple, who fight it out wittily in difficult economic circumstances before agreeing to marry. Women dramatists of the Restoration characteristically gave these issues a feminized twist. Behn's *The Rover* (1677) presents a Rochesterian rake, Willmore, for whose wavering attentions two women vie: Angellica, a courtesan who charges (with justification, apparently) huge fees for her services, and Florinda, an intelligent and virtuous noblewoman. Florinda wins, though Angellica is allotted considerable dignity. Florinda's sister, Hellena, is supposed to be becoming a nun, but is having none of it, and woos and wins her own husband with a promising degree of sexual fervour. Of her successors, the most successful was Susannah Centlivre; the unexpected success of her play *The Busybody* (1709) led Steele to comment: 'the plot and incidents of the play are laid with that subtlety of spirit which is peculiar to females of wit, and is very seldom well performed by those of the other sex, in whom craft in love is an act of invention, and not, as with women, the effect of nature and instinct'.[6]

Debates about marriage and female intellect were also going on in pamphlets and poems written by women. In 1673 Bathsua Makin published an *Essay to Revive the Antient Education of Gentlewomen, in Religion, Manners, Arts & Tongues*, one of the earliest calls for women to take their education into their own hands. Behn addressed poems on high culture and literature to Thomas Creech and Gilbert Burnet, but like most other women writers had no formal education. Sarah Fyge (later Egerton) was banished by her father from London for writing *The Female Advocate* (1686), an answer to Robert Gould's misogynistic *Love given O're; Or, a Satire against the Pride, Lust and Inconstancy, &c, of Woman* (1682); she later endured an unhappy marriage, assuaging the unhappiness by commenting on it in verse. Mary Astell, who was instructed in some of the traditionally male areas of knowledge (logic, mathematics, philosophy) published in 1694 the treatise from which this chapter's Document is quoted: *A Serious Proposal to the Ladies*. Her arguments that women's disadvantages were cultural and not natural, and that they needed proper education in female seminaries, failed to attract finance, but were taken up into male culture by Defoe, in his *Essay on Projects* (1697), and to a lesser extent by Bernard Mandeville in *The Virgin Unmasked* (1709); Swift, however, mocked her proposal to educate women in 'Antient and Modern Amazonian Tactics' in *The Tatler*. Astell's *Reflections upon Marriage* (1700) again challenged the idea that women's subjection was natural rather than cultural and expressed profound scepticism about the condition of marriage as it then stood. Her arguments were enthusiastically endorsed by Mary, Lady Chudleigh, whose *The Ladies Defence* (1701) debates issues of female education and male prejudice. Her 'To the Ladies' is a bald injunction to women to avoid the subjection of marriage: 'Wife and servant are the same, / But differ only in the name'.

The fair sex

Despite advances in the recognition of female literary talent in the Restoration, the dominant literary culture after the accession of the Hanoverians was in many ways that of the unmarried Augustans, who assume the right to comment with authority on matters of gender. Neither Swift nor Pope married, though each had long-standing relationships of a slightly equivocal character with women friends. Johnson married a much older woman, and did not remarry after her death, though it was clear that he enjoyed the company of intelligent women, and equally clear that he was to some extent tormented by strong sexual feelings.[7] None of them had children, and Swift's depiction of the families of the Houyhnhnms, which are run along eugenic lines, with none of the usual emotional mess, suggests a strong resistance to the conventional dynamics of the nuclear family. After they have studied marriage in various contexts, the participants in *Rasselas* suggest that on balance marriage is better than its opposite: 'marriage has many pains, but celibacy has no pleasures'. It is notable that marriage is not the end in view for the characters in this novella, and that the quartet is arranged to provide gender contrasts (especially between Rasselas and his sister) but not romance.

Swift's verse satires shatter the polite fictions with which male–female relations were adorned in the period. In 'The Lady's Dressing Room' Strephon (the traditional pastoral lover) waits until Celia has finished dressing (it takes five hours) then takes a peek at her room, finding her dirty smock, filthy combs, smeared jars and bowls, disgusting towels and handkerchiefs, and the 'excremental Smell' of her chamber-pot. His imagination is poisoned, but, the poem argues, this is what you get for this kind of voyeurism: better to look at the 'prepared' Celia and be amazed to see 'Such Order from Confusion sprung, / Such gaudy Tulips rais'd from Dung' (140–1). 'Strephon and Chloe' recounts a similarly disastrous discovery made by a pair of pastoral lovers about the other's bodily habits.[8] In 'A Beautiful Young Nymph going to Bed' Swift tells the story of an unsuccessful prostitute ('Corinna, Pride of *Drury-Lane*, / For whom no Shepherd sighs in vain'), returning to her garret after failing to solicit a client. She is wasted by disease and malnutrition, and indeed is no longer a complete human being: the 'undressing' is a grim parody of erotic striptease as she takes off not only her clothes and make-up but her wig, false teeth, breasts, hips, and her glass eye. The black joke is once again the contrast between the self presented and the self as it actually is in the body; but there is unexpected sympathy in Swift's acknowledgement of 'the Anguish, Toil, and Pain, / Of gath'ring up herself again' (69–70), a feat she must perform every morning.

Pope is closer to the model of light satire of the 'fair sex', to be flattered and cajoled rather than given rights, provided by Addison's essays in *The Spectator*. In *The Rape of the Lock* he gives a mock-heroic account of a quasi-sexual frolic among his Catholic contacts in which a young nobleman had offended a woman by cutting off a lock of her hair. 'Belinda' is a society belle, addicted to the card-games, coffee rituals and social games of the young urban elite. Her self-presentation is, as in Swift, deeply laboured (the scene of her cosmetic rituals, in Canto I, is a mock-heroic miniaturization of the arming of Achilles from Homer's *Iliad*). But unlike Swift, dirt is carefully kept out of the picture. Belinda resists marriage: she is a 'coquet' who smiles on everyone but gives no favours, and in some ways what the baron who cuts off her hair does is to remind her, crudely, of her marriageable status: it is a symbolic 'possession' of her sexual allure. Belinda's will to power is clear enough in the card game, 'ombre' (meaning 'man'), which she wins; her hysterical womanhood is, however, also clear enough, in the 'Cave of Spleen' episode in Canto IV: after the 'rape' Belinda's depression is registered as a physical condition . . . In the last canto, Belinda and her women friends mount a spirited campaign for restoration of the lock, in another miniature Homeric epic – a literal battle of the sexes. But Pope will not determine the issue, preferring instead to extract the disputed lock and place it among the stars, offering Belinda instead 'this *Lock*', the poem itself, in literary compensation.

Pope plays games with sexual politics here: the mock-heroic fantasy involves a lot of ribald joking about chastity and a lot of playful mythologizing in the fairies or 'Sylphs' who (in a parody of the angels in *Paradise Lost*) stand between Belinda and her 'fall'. In 'Eloisa to Abelard', however, Pope gave full vent to the expressive feeling of a passionate medieval nun, in a verse letter describing her anguish on being separated from her lover, who had been castrated by her uncle. He also makes her look forward to a time when a poet of sufficient emotional literacy (such as Pope) might emerge to record her tragic love story in adequately sympathetic terms. He performed the same operation with the ending of the 'Elegy to the Memory of an Unfortunate Lady', apparently a story of thwarted, suicidal romance.

Pope was essentially protective, often to the point of officiousness, in his dealings with his women friends. He knew perfectly well that 'too much your sex is by forms confined', though this did not prevent him from producing misogynistic portraits of women writers in *The Dunciad* (indeed, the dominance of the smothering female Dulness in that poem is not an accident). The booksellers wage a pissing contest for possession of 'Yon Juno of Majestic size', with 'two babes of love, close clinging at her waist' – a cruel swipe at Eliza Haywood, whose sex life and illicit literary production (the 'babes of love') are here caricatured. 'Curl's Corinna', in whose urine Curll slips during the footrace, was the poet Elizabeth Thomas, a former mistress of Pope's friend Henry Cromwell and the woman who sold some of Pope's more embarrassing early letters to the bookseller. The collapse of Pope's relationship with Lady Mary issued in some fairly frank misogynistic comments on her lack of cleanliness and sexual continence.

In the *Epistle to a Lady* (1735) Pope contends that women do not have 'character' in the sense that men have it, they merely present a series of fronts, attitudes, roles, veering from virgin to whore and on to something else in the blink of an eye. It is the job of the painter-poet to 'catch, ere she fade, the Cynthia of this minute' and Pope provides a gallery of sketched female personae in demonstration of his own knack of representation. The poem (it is addressed to Martha Blount, his closest female friend, but she is not named in it) concludes with Pope's example of stable female character (Martha herself), but this proves to be in fact an androgynous blend of male and female characteristics, one of a kind, unreproducible except in Pope's poetic imagining.

The emergent novel had a different idea of the roles available to women. Behn's *The Fair Jilt* (1688) presents a heroine of extreme seductive power, morally corrupt but eternally fascinating, and this strain is evident in a number of Restoration fictions. Under Defoe, however, there is a distinct move towards the business of female economic survival. We have already noted Crusoe's reticence about family matters (the more notable since after his escape he supplies wives for his colonists). By contrast, Moll Flanders conceals nothing of this aspect of her life. Her title page (1722) proclaims that she was

> Born in *Newgate*, and during a Life of continu'd Variety for Threescore years, besides her Childhood, was Twelve Year a *Whore*, five times a *Wife* (whereof once to her own Brother) Twelve Year a *Thief*, Eight Year a Transported *Felon* in *Virginia*, at last grew *Rich*, liv'd *Honest*, and died a *Penitent*.

Sometimes, it may be added, she dressed as a man. Moll is an even greater economist than Crusoe, totting up gifts from admirers and her earnings from prostitution, theft, and marriage. She is also a superb economist with her narrative, turning it into a form of credit by releasing some of it and concealing other parts to the other characters; by this means she passes like a kind of counterfeit coin through the economy that surrounds her, gaining husbands and other partners. Her one real love is a male version of herself; they marry because they have each been deceived by the other's publicity. Defoe writes as a woman once more in *Roxana*, a character who once more prospers by using her body to gain advantage. Richardson's Pamela, however, is very clearly situated in a vulnerable, subject position, from which the only escape is virtuous marriage. In addition, *Pamela*'s insistence on the heartfelt moment of sexual fear leads inevitably to the possibility of a pornographic reading of the novel, and indeed a series of paintings of scenes from the novel, by Joseph Highmore in 1743–4, left little to the imagination: Pamela features in a variety of fetchingly half-dressed poses, making visually real the implied titillation of the letters. For Clarissa the economic situation is even worse, for she has been left an independent inheritance, and her family are out to remove this affront to the normal rules of primogeniture. Even before Lovelace (who, as a Rochesterian aristocrat, resents the Harlowe's for having made money in trade) comes on the scene, Clarissa is an economic victim.

The failing of the sex

As Dryden's *Absalom and Achitophel* reminds us, and as the poems of Behn and Rochester do not, the Restoration did not have effective means of contraception. Sex was likely to have consequences, whether in the spread of disease, or the production of children. This was of course another way in which women were disadvantaged, since they bore the children and ran the risks of childbirth. Because children, especially sons, would inherit property, sexual standards proscribed female adultery much more strongly than male. One of the few routes to divorce was through female adultery (though male impotence was another). Kings from Charles II to George II openly kept mistresses, as did Sir Robert Walpole; Anne was a domestic paragon, even if her children died young. Johnson listened quietly while Boswell (himself a serial adulterer with women of all classes) put the case that a certain woman, abandoned by her husband, was doing no harm if she took her own sexual freedoms; Johnson lightly retorted, 'the woman's a whore, and there's an end on't'. He claimed to have 'much more reverence for a common prostitute than for a woman who conceals her guilt'.[9] Tom Jones's sexual infidelities are criticized but in the end forgiven; Sophia must be virginal at marriage. In his final novel, *Amelia* (1751), Fielding has the hero, Booth, commit adultery while in prison with the seductive Miss Matthews. His wife cheerfully forgives him; but it is inconceivable that the reverse process could apply.[10]

Very little poetry of the later period approaches that of Rochester and Behn for sexual frankness. Sex did not go underground, though the Society for the Reformation of Manners tried to restrict obscenity, among other breaches of decorum; there were sex manuals, such as *Aristotle's Masterpiece*, and anti-masturbation manuals, such as the best-selling *Onania*. Prostitution, despite half-hearted attempts to suppress it, remained a constant feature of various areas of London; in *A Modest Defence of Public Stews* (1724), Mandeville actually recommended governmental oversight of licensed brothels. In the 1750s Sir Francis Dashwood had unemployed agricultural labourers contrive a series of tunnels and caves inside an old quarry on his estate at West Wycombe in Buckinghamshire, on the model of catacombs he had encountered on his Grand Tour of Europe and the East. Dashwood was leader of the 'Hell-Fire Club', a group of self-consciously rakish gentlemen who were alleged to meet in the caves for undisclosed and thus deeply suspect purposes, thought to involve drink and sex. Members included the poet Paul Whitehead and the radical MP John Wilkes, ever a thorn in the side of the government. His particular reputation for rakishness became crucial when the government needed to silence his attacks; his *Essay on Woman*, a cheerfully obscene parody of Pope's *Essay on Man*, was seized and used as evidence of his dissolute, unreliable character.

Pornography was not widespread, but Pope's crack at 'Curl's chaste press' in *The Dunciad* points to Curll's conviction for publishing *Venus in the Cloister; or, the Nun in her Smock* (1725), a tale packed with sexual activity of lesbian and heterosexual kinds.[11] Lesbianism was not an indictable offence and was often co-opted into the service of male-oriented pornography: John Cleland's notorious novel *Memoirs of a Woman of Pleasure* (1748–9) is an example of this. The only moral severity in the tale (in which sexual activity is wrapped up in lusciously euphemistic terms) is reserved for male homosexuality, then very much a criminal offence. A male homosexual brothel, known as a 'Molly House', had been broken up in the 1720s, and 'Sodomites' were regularly stoned and abused in the pillory. Pope's animus against Lord Hervey pits his own manliness against the effeminacy of 'Sporus'

> His wit all see-saw, between *that* and *this*,
> Now high, now low, now Master up, now Miss,
> And he himself one vile Antithesis.

Literary homosexuality is extremely quiet in the period: it is almost certain that Gray was homosexually inclined, and likely that Horace Walpole was, but there is little actual evidence.[12]

Female husbands

Gradually women's poetry was becoming less of a rarity. Anne Finch, Countess of Winchilsea, published a volume of her verse in 1713 and contributed a commendatory poem to Pope's *Works* of 1717: a kind of indication of status in itself. Finch wrote from a position of retirement, and in praise of that position, though some of the poetry is mildly satirical. More strident was Lady Mary Wortley Montagu, who could and did compete with the brittle satiric elegance of Gay and Pope. Elizabeth Thomas (1675–1731) wrote in praise of Mary Astell, condemned the state of marriage, and defended her right to write (in 'On Sir J— S— saying in a sarcastic manner, my books would make me mad'). Elizabeth Tollet (1694–1754), was also educated in the standard male way (in Tollet's case, with encouragement from no less a figure than Sir Isaac Newton). Her poem 'To my Brother at St John's College in Cambridge' cleverly expresses a wistful sense of absence from such a seat of learning even as it prescribes a course of study for him. Mary Barber, Swift's protégée, wittily opposed his 'Lady's Dressing Room' with her own 'The Gentleman's Study', and made poetry out of the very difficulties of her situation. Mary Leapor took on male literary models and standards in 'Man the Monarch' and 'An Essay on Woman'; her 'Crumble Hall' is a feminized critique of the country-house poem and 'The Epistle of Deborah Dough' makes fun of her own situation as a suspect woman poet. Mary Leapor was from the servant class, and there were a few labouring-class women poets: Mary Collier, a washer-woman from Petersfield, produced *The Woman's Labour* (1739), in answer to Duck's *Thresher's Labour*.

Women had their own ways of transgressing. Defoe is credited with the story of Christian Davies, a women who joined the army in male disguise, and with narratives of female pirates such as Anne Bonny. Fielding wrote a pamphlet, *The Female Husband* (1746), about a notorious case of sexual disguise and confusion. And women began to defend some of the sexual misdemeanours for which they were attacked. When Dryden died, in 1700, there was an outpouring of literary grief, this being one of the ways in which the publishing market organized itself. One of the collections of verse published on the occasion was ascribed to a woman dramatist of Tory sympathies, Delarivier Manley (1660–1724), daughter of a military governor. Manley's writing career, like Behn's before her, came to be viewed as subversive, and her biographical situation was investigated in support of the claim that she was in herself 'scandalous'. In 1689 she had married John Manley, who already had a wife living. Following this bigamous attachment she lived openly with another married man, and later in life lived with a Jacobite printer. She moved in Tory circles and in 1709 published *The New Atlantis*, a 'roman à clef' in which figures of the establishment could be identified under romance names. It was also a storehouse of erotic encounter, including a notorious description of a naked man, and contained a narrative of Manley's own misfortunes under the name 'Delia'. The book was considered to be a seditious libel (that is, it was offensive to the authorities) and she was arrested. Later she was one of the authors, with Swift, of *The Examiner*, a periodical in defence of the Tories. In 1714 she learned that a Whig author, Charles Gildon, was preparing a narrative of her life under the title *The Adventures of Rivella*, and she implored the publisher, Edmund Curll, to let her write her own story under the same title. This too cast itself in fictional form; the 'adventures' are told by a rejected but still amorous suitor of Rivella's, giving Manley the opportunity not only to put her conduct in a favourable light, but also to cast herself as perennially desirable in the masculine gaze. It takes the complaints against her concerning her comparatively free sexual conduct and her activities as a writer and meets them head-on by giving value to her writing, and her self, as erotic but not available. She makes her male narrator observe and second her own views of the sexual double standard unflinchingly:

> But the charter of that sex being much more confined than ours, what is not a crime in men is scandalous and unpardonable in woman, as she herself has very well observed in divers places, throughout her own writings. (47)

Swift, who sympathized with her, wrote to his friend 'Stella' in 1712: 'I am heartily sorry for her; she has very generous principles for one of her sort; and a great deal of good sense and invention: she is about forty, very homely and very fat'. In *Rivella*, the issue of weight becomes a positive asset: 'from her youth she was inclined to fat; whence I have often heard her flatterers liken her to the Grecian Venus' (47). It is a form of controlled display: the male narrator is scripted to discuss her in a kind of reverential, wistful version of locker-room gossip with his male friend, who asks for details:

> Her neck and breasts have an established reputation for beauty and colour: her feet small and pretty. Thus I have run thro' whatever custom suffers to be visible to us; and upon my word, Chevalier, I never saw any of Rivella's hidden charms' (48)

She is both desirable and inaccessible to the conventions of masculine narrative, sexy, powerful and unattainable. Some of the ensuing anecdotes of her life confirm this characterization by allotting Rivella an erotic power over men that she sometimes chooses not to consummate. Her various sexual adventures are given a literary gloss and novelistic explanations; the scandal against her is largely promoted by Whigs jealous of her literary activity on behalf of the Tories, or by fellow female authors (such as Catherine Trotter), jealous of her literary and amorous successes; and her conduct during the *Atalantis* prosecution is noble to the point of self-sacrifice.

The narrator is allowed some scope to criticize, even mock Rivella, and to advise her on her literary activity. Manley scripts her own acceptance of some of his critique of her transgressive past:

> When I would argue with her the folly of a woman's disobliging any one party, by a pen equally qualified to divert all, she agreed my reflection was just, and promised not to repeat her fault . . . She now agrees with me that politicks is not the business of a woman, especially of one that can so well delight and entertain her readers with more gentle pleasing theams. (112)

She shifts attention from her face (marked as so many were by smallpox) to her inner character: 'Few, who have only beheld her in publick, could be brought to like her; whereas none that became acquainted with her, could refrain from loving her' (47). The novel has been one way of converting the private into public: we eavesdrop on one man telling another about her. But something is always reserved or deferred – Rivella is perpetually to be desired. For Sir Charles, she still has a taste for love 'or whence is it that she daily writes of him with such fire and force? But whether she does love, is a question'. What is not a question is that others love her: 'I might have entertained you much more agreeably . . . with the songs, letters and adorations, innumerable from those who never could be happy.' Lovemore even advances in imagination to Rivella's bed,

> nicely sheeted and strowed with *roses*, *jessamins* or *orange-flowers*, suited to the variety of the season; her pillows neatly trimmed with lace or muslin, stuck round with *jonquils*, or other natural garden sweets, for she uses no perfumes, and there have given you leave to fancy your self the happy man, with whom she chose to repose her self, during the heat of the day, in a state of sweetness and tranquillity. (113)

D'Aumont interrupts by demanding to meet this woman, 'the only person of her sex that knows how to *live*'.

Other women were less successful at defending themselves. Hetty Wright, sister of the Methodist leaders John and Charles Wesley, had been educated to the same school standard as her brothers, but eloped, had an illegitimate child, and was forced into an intellectually unequal marriage she decried in poems such as 'Address to her Husband' and 'Wedlock. A Satire'. But around the middle of the century there was a small flowering of transgressive memoirs. Laetitia Pilkington (died 1750), was a precocious and more or less self-educated woman who married a clergyman, Matthew Pilkington, in 1725. The pair were introduced to Swift, who did his best to further the careers of the 'little poetical parson, who has a littler young poetical wife' by sending them to London with letters of recommendation to his friends, all of whom found Matthew shallow and conceited. The marriage fell apart and he divorced her on grounds of adultery in 1738; she wrote a poem about this event called *The Trial of Constancy* (1739). She attempted to survive in London by writing poetry, sometimes for hire, by running a print shop, and sometimes by straightforward appeals to the charity of the rich and influential. Her writing brought her to the attention of Colley Cibber and Samuel Richardson, both of whom helped her in her perennial struggle against destitution. In 1748 she began publishing her *Memoirs*, a lively and garrulous account of her life, containing a fund of anecdotes about Swift's eccentric domestic behaviour and a vigorous defence of her own conduct against the libels of her estranged (and by her account, depraved) husband. A second volume followed in 1749 and a third, posthumously, in 1754.

The *Memoirs* are irrepressible and unrepentant, vindicatory without being abject. At one point she declares, in defence of her unconventional narrative of selfhood, 'I am, in short, an heteroclite, or irregular verb, which can never be declined or conjugated'.[13] She names several of the men who made sexual advances to her and threatens to name others if they fail to subscribe to her poems; women involved in the sex industry are also named and shamed. She lavishes poetical praise on those who helped her and poetical scorn on those who didn't. Her own poems are liberally scattered through the text as specimens of her talent, points scored against the neglect of the world. But given her reputation it was inevitably the implied sexual content that drew most attention. The *Memoirs* mount a direct assault on the double standard, and ultimately express a complete disregard for a moral case against adultery, linking it instead with economic and political independence:

> As they tell us 'tis not lawful to separate on any cause, save that of adultery, a woman of spirit who is married to a sordid disagreeable wretch, has nothing to do but to make him a cuckold; and then welcome thrice dear liberty. Yet, methinks, the husbands should, in justice, return to the wives, when they abandon them, the dowry they brought with them.[14]

Some of her contemporaries, such as the novelist John Cleland, were sympathetic to her arguments; the strait-laced Richardson, however, classed her with other women autobiographers as 'a Set of Wretches, wishing to perpetuate their Infamy'.

A comparable text is 'Memoirs of a Lady of Quality', by Viscountess Vane (1713–88), shoe-horned into Smollett's *Adventures of Peregrine Pickle* (1751). A sort of miniature novel in itself, something between *Moll Flanders* and *Clarissa*, it is a self-justificatory narrative of her love-life from an idyllic marriage, initially opposed by her father but achieved through elopement, and ended by the death of the husband, through a disastrous second marriage to a man characterized as tyrannous, cowardly, temperamental and sexually both perverse and inadequate, from whom she separates but who will not leave her alone. Interspersed with his attempts to reclaim her, and her attempts to flee, come a series of clandestine affairs with a variety of amorous suitors. Giving full voice to her complaints about her legal and financial oppression, she narrates the attempts of her husband to control her (by abduction and imprisonment, on occasion). It makes no attempts at independence: the whole story revolves around attachment to one male or another.

A Narrative of the Life of Mrs Charlotte Charke appeared in 1755 with a tongue in cheek dedication to Charke herself. Charke (1713–60) was one of the numerous progeny mentioned but unnamed in Colley Cibber's own *Apology*. Her autobiography has some resemblance to Pilkington's; she settles scores, thanks sponsors and disputes rumours, such as the story that she hit her father with a flounder. Finally, the 'narrative' itself becomes her economic mainstay, 'the Staff of my Life', in her situation as a separated woman trying to maintain herself and child against the legal incursions of a profligate husband. In some ways it was a very radical narrative, giving full reign to anecdotal descriptions of her 'madness' as a child, when she hubristically donned her father's clothes and impersonated him at the age of four, a prophetic event. She later posed as a doctor. After a brief marriage to a man who (in her account) deserted her for the company of prostitutes, she takes to the stage (acting Hamlet on one occasion), runs a shop and a puppet theatre, and later cross-dressed habitually, partly as a disguise to avoid her creditors, and partly simply 'in Search of Adventures' (86). One of these was to have a young lady of fortune fall in love with her. She worked as a valet, as a sausage merchant, haggler, waiter, pastry cook, and proof-reader, but never 'prostituted my Person'. She has 'paid all due Regard to Decency wherever I have introduc'd the Passion of Love' and has avoided 'fulsomely inflaming the Minds of my young Readers, or shamefully offending those of riper Years' (p.16). She regrets over-educating herself and indicts her husband for failing to mould her character through affection. More particularly, in a repeatedly expressed desperation for reconciliation with her father: 'if strongest Compunction and uninterrupted Hours of Anguish, blended with Self-conviction and filial Love, can move his Hear to Pity and Forgiveness, I shall, with Pride and unutterable Transport, throw myself at his Feet, to implore the only Benefit I desire or expect, his BLESSING, and his PARDON' (p.17).

Bluestockings

Beyond these exceptional documents, however, women's writing was becoming respectable. In mid-century George Ballard celebrated female genius in *Memoirs of several Ladies of Great Britain, who have been celebrated for their Writings or Skill in the Learned Arts and Sciences* (1752); John Duncombe praised learned women in *The Feminiad* (1754) and an anthology of *Poems by Eminent Ladies* (1755) offered a canon of women writers from Behn onwards.[15] Mary Jones (*d.* 1778) was even offered a job as a reviewer in the otherwise exclusively male preserve of the *Monthly Review*. Eliza Haywood turned from the lubricious suggestions of her romance *Love in Excess* (1719), where the female characters come very close to free sexual activity, to the more domestic and moralistic concerns of *The History of Miss Betsy Thoughtless* (1751), though this retained a sharp edge of critique so far as marriage was concerned. Sarah Fielding's novels were indisputably educational and reformist. Charlotte Lennox's novel *The Female Quixote* presents a young heroine brought up in rural isolation with nothing but books of romance to educate her. As a consequence she interprets the world according to the conventions of heroic romance, causing havoc for herself and others. From this deluded state she is eventually reclaimed and made suitably marriageable.

The respectability of women's writing and intellectual status was incorporated in the literary salons of the 'bluestockings' in the later eighteenth century. Elizabeth Carter's exceptional scholarly talent, which produced a translation of an Italian treatise on the work of Newton 'for the use of the Ladies' in 1739, and a standard translation of Epictetus in 1758, was closely associated with the salon of Elizabeth Montagu (1720–1800) the hostess of the best-known group. Montagu was author of *An Essay on the Writings and Genius of Shakespear* (1769) and the patron of a number of other women writers. She quarrelled with Johnson over his treatment of some of her friends in his *Lives of the English Poets*. Johnson also quarrelled, this time on political grounds, with the historian, Catherine Macaulay (1731–91), whose radical *History of England* (1763–83) was far too democratically inclined for his taste. With Hannah More (1745–1833), a religious writer, he remained on good terms, praising her poem about the bluestockings, *Bas Bleu* (written 1782). He was impressed by *Evelina, or a Young Lady's Entrance into the World* (1778), Fanny Burney's first novel, an overnight success, recording in letters the passage of a young woman from innocent seclusion to social intelligence (and aristocratic marriage). Johnson was amused by the idea that Burney might knock Montagu off her perch as 'Queen of the Blues': under the banner of rivalry, women's writing might be said to have arrived.

Notes

1 George Savile, Marquis of Halifax, *Complete Works*, edited by J. P. Kenyon (Harmondsworth, 1969), p. 277. It is recorded that the daughter's eventual husband wrote the words 'Wasted effort!' on her copy. Jane Collier's *Essay on the Art of Ingeniously Tormenting* (1753) was a parody of such manuals.
2 Margaret Fell, *Women's Speaking Justified.*
3 She included 'A True Relation of my Birth, Breeding and Life' in a collection of her fantasy stories in 1656.
4 *Memoirs on the Life of Mrs Behn* (1696), unpaginated.
5 *Paradise Lost*, IX.1034–66.
6 *The Tatler*, no.19 (14 May 1709).
7 Boswell kept a collection of 'Tacenda' [things to be kept quiet] on Johnson's sex life.
8 Cassinus discovers the terrible fact that his beloved 'Caelia shits' in Swift's 'Cassinus and Peter: A Tragical Elegy'.
9 Boswell, *Journal of a Tour to the Hebrides*, 14 September 1773. Politically, however, Johnson was adamantly opposed to the light waiving of women's civil rights, and firmly opposed Boswell's plan to entail his estate to exclude the female line.
10 The double standard in sexual matters was explicitly formulated in Halifax's *Letter to a Daughter*; *Complete Works*, p. 279.
11 Curll also published a series he called *Cases of Impotency and Divorce*, as well as a number of trials for sex offences.
12 See Robert Mack, *Thomas Gray: A Life* (New Haven, 2000) and Timothy Mowl, *Horace Walpole: The Great Outsider* (London, 1996).
13 *Memoirs of Mrs Laetitia Pilkington 1712–1750 Written by Herself*, with an introduction by Iris Berry (London: George Routledge & Sons, 1928), p. 359.
14 Ibid. p. 396.
15 It was edited by George Colman and Bonnell Thornton, the latter a friend of Johnson's.

8

Forward into the past

But though Richard's son did not walk at his father's coronation, Edward the Fifth probably did, and this is my third proof. I conceive all the astonishment of my readers at this assertion, and yet it is founded on strongly presumptive evidence. In the coronation roll itself is this amazing entry; 'To Lord Edward, son of late king Edward the Fourth, for his apparel and array, that is to say, a short gowne made of two yards and three quarters of crymsy clothe of golde [. . .] besides two foot cloths, a bonet of purple velvet, nine horse harness, and nine saddle houses (housings of blue velvet), gilt spurs, with many other rich articles, and magnificent apparel for his henchmen or pages.'

Let no body tell me that these robes, this magnificence, these trappings for a cavalcade, were for the use of a prisoner. Marvellous as the fact is, there can no longer be any doubt but the deposed young king walked, or it was intended should walk, at his uncle's coronation. This precious monument, a terrible reproach to Sir Thomas More and his copyists, who have been silent on so public an event, exists in the great wardrobe; and is in the highest preservation; it is written on vellom, and is bound with the coronation rolls of Henry the Seventh and Eighth. These are written on paper, and are in worse condition; but that of king Richard is uncommonly fair, accurate and ample. [. . .] The whole is couched in the most minute and regular manner, and is preferable to a thousand vague and interested histories. The concourse of nobility at that ceremony was extraordinarily great: there were present no fewer than three duchesses of Norfolk. Has this the air of a forced and precipitate election? Or does it not indicate a voluntary concurrence of the nobility? No mention being made in the roll of the young duke of York, no robes being ordered for him, it looks extremely as if he was not in Richard's custody; and strengthens the probability that will appear hereafter, of his having been conveyed away.

[Horace Walpole, *Historic Doubts on the Life and Reign of Richard the Third* (1768)]

Horace Walpole had little of the bluff public confidence of his father, the political strongman Sir Robert Walpole, though he sat as a Whig MP until 1768. He did have considerably more literary tastes and ambitions, together with the financial means to develop them, and he produced a bibliography of *Royal and Noble Authors* (1758) and *Anecdotes of Painting in England* (1762–5). His *Historic Doubts* was a challenge to the accepted wisdom that Richard III was an evil usurper who had murdered his way to the throne. Walpole argued that the historical view had been extensively biased by the political allegiances of the followers of Henry VII, who ousted Richard in 1483. This 'Lancastrian' tendency, affecting writers as disparate as Sir Thomas More and William Shakespeare, had produced the sneering, hunchbacked Mafioso of popular mythology. Walpole's point was not to whitewash Richard, though he clearly thinks him a better politician than normally allowed, nor even to claim necessarily that he was innocent of the seven separate counts of murder laid against him in the historical record. It was that these accounts were founded on little or no evidence, and simply recycled from one writer to another. In place of historical fiction, therefore, Walpole proposed a model of historical imagining based on archives. Chief among his new sources was what he called the 'coronation roll' of Richard III, which appeared to show that Edward V, popularly supposed to have been murdered in the Tower at Richard's instigation, actually appeared at his uncle's coronation. He also used his own imagination, in spite of his caveat against it, to a considerable degree and much of the argument is based on a reconstruction of Richard's supposed state of mind and what might be called the psychology of government: to that extent it is a kind of historical fiction in itself.

The book was controversial and sold out within twenty-four hours, a mark of the popularity of the genre of historical writing in the period. Other antiquaries got to work on the evidence and showed that the main contention was in fact a mistake: the 'coronation roll' was actually the wardrobe account for that year and the key entry on Edward V was made before he had been deposed. This is an important moment in literary history, when history itself is recognized as a literary genre, when it is popular enough to stir controversy both political and methodological, and when 'imagination' becomes a key part of writers' perceptions of how the past could or should (or should not) be envisaged.

New classicism

For the poets of the period 1660–1750, 'the past' meant initially the classical past of imperial Greece and Rome, recorded in the writings rediscovered and reprinted in the Italian Renaissance. This offered a stable canon of familiar literature, especially in Latin: Virgil, the poet of pastoral, georgic and epic; Horace, the engaging lyrist and conversational satirist; Ovid, the poet of exile and desire; and Juvenal, the satirist who ranted against the corruptions of Rome. The orator and letter-writer Cicero was a model of prose style. Greek was less familiar, but the philosopher and literary theorist Aristotle, and above all, the ancient epic poet Homer, were touchstones of authority in all literary matters.

The traces of this inheritance are not hard to find in Restoration culture. In 1678 Thomas Rymer attacked the Restoration stage for failing to follow 'the practice of the ancients', though the fact that he had to do this suggests that classical practice was already far from dominant.[1] Dryden's more measured and practised theatrical criticism continued to ascribe great weight to Aristotle's *Poetics*. Milton's epics aim to splice an English version of Homeric diction and mythology with biblical narrative; mock-heroic, the favoured vehicle of satire for Dryden and Pope, depends on a knowledge of Homer and Virgil; pastorals all have Virgil somewhere in mind, as do georgics. Dryden translated the satires of Juvenal (with an influential 'Essay on Satire') and the complete works of Virgil. Many poets, including John Oldham, Rochester, Pope and Johnson, produced 'Imitations' of Horace or Juvenal in which the classical source was the springboard for observations on a very different contemporary situation. Some poets, such as Addison and Johnson, wrote verse in Latin as easily, even more easily, than they did in English.

This position was far from pure or stable, however. Towards the end of the seventeenth century, a bitter quarrel developed among the intelligentsia in France and Britain as to the relative merits of ancient and modern learning. The dominance of the classical Greece and Rome as models of achievement in government, literature, criticism, architecture and science was seriously challenged by adherents of modern thinking, especially in the area of empiricist philosophy (represented by Locke) and practical science (in the tradition embodied in the Royal Society). Champions of the Ancients included Swift, whose *Battle of the Books* (1704) dramatizes the quarrel in the form of an allegorical contest between books, figured as the physical presences of their authors in the Royal Library. The 'Battle' overshadows Swift's *The Tale of a Tub* as well, and there was a fairly clear political element in the split, with Tories siding with the old and Whigs with the new. However, few people of any intelligence took up extreme positions. For all his moral reliance on stable classicism, Swift's own writing has little formal classical precedent, engaging and feeding off contemporary situations and pamphlets and freely inventing bizarre new forms.

Something similar might be said of Pope, though his commitment to classicism was much stronger than Swift's. In 1711 he published *An Essay on Criticism*, a breezy, confident discussion of poetry and literary criticism that was immediately recognized as a contemporary rival to Horace's 'Art of Poetry' (as his 'Epistola ad Pisones' was conventionally known). Like Horace's poem, it was a form of criticism in verse. The poem celebrated Homer, imagined Virgil reading Homer, and counselled a wise adherence to 'Ancient *Rules*' (the practice of these epic poets, and the theory of Aristotle and Horace) as a means to keep close to nature. But Pope also stressed the need for poets occasionally to exceed the rules, and cited Longinus (a later Greek text, familiar to his readers through late seventeenth-century translations), who was more prone to celebrate noble flights of the imagination than dull adherence to precept. Pope saw these classical aspects as stable beneath the corruptions (politics, envy, scandal) that attended literature in the modern world; he concluded with a brief and suggestive history of criticism from the fall of Rome through to British examples that might carry on the good work: the *Essay* comes close to offering itself as the next authoritative statement.

Longinus was to become an increasingly 'modern' sort of critic through the century, as his concept of 'the sublime' gained critical ground. Pope's other great use of him came in his mock-treatise *Peri Bathous: or the Art of Sinking in Poetry* (1728), a collection of bellyfloppers from contemporary verse put together as a pseudo-Longinian essay on how to write badly.[2] *The Dunciad*, of course, used a Virgilian epic frame, classical-sounding gods and goddesses, and a largely epic language to condense a mock-epic contrast between the low, filthy and stupid world of London literature with the high aspirations of the classical past, just as *The Rape of the Lock* had adapted famous battle scenes from Homer to take a rise out of the contemporary battle of the sexes. Between 1733 and 1738 Pope issued his slow-burning series of 'Imitations of Horace'. The poems could encompass considerable variety of tone, from comic self-deprecation to fevered denunciations of vice and careful defences of the role of satire and writing generally: the slyness of Horatian wit allowed Pope to pretend he was saying less than he was saying, as well as allowing him to adopt a position of literary authority.

The extent of Pope's classicism can be overstated. He wanted to be the Horace of his day, but he did not pine to be the Horace of Horace's day. Not particularly skilled in Greek himself, Pope translated Homer into modern verse for an audience that, largely, had no Greek at all; Dryden's translations show that contemporary poetry needed classical content, but also that classical poetry now had to be marketed for a reading audience that could not be relied upon to read the Latin original. Translation continued to flourish because classical literature retained high status but the actual reading public was bigger than the public educated in the languages of Greece and Rome. Pope wrote with classicism at his fingertips, but he could not have written as he did without a thorough sense of engagement with his time. Though the neoclassical eighteenth century is often associated with clarity, rationality, symmetry, and above all light (the 'enlightenment'), there was a nearly equal, and perhaps corresponding, search for darkness. The *Rape of the Lock* celebrates glitter and sparkle; it also makes poetic capital out of melancholy interiors. Soon after that poem Pope was writing the gothic fantasy 'Eloisa to Abelard', with its craggy, dark, tomb-laden landscapes and psychological traumas; this took from Ovid's *Heroides* the form of a love-letter from a woman to her absent lover, and fused it with a powerful medieval history. Pope's house was rectilinear and symmetrical above; beneath it was a carefully constructed grotto, full of dark corners and mysterious lighting effects.

Classicism was implicitly challenged by the working-class and mercantile fictions of Defoe, which had little concern with classical precedent; those of Richardson (like Defoe, not educated at university), tended to regard classical learning as the faintly suspect preserve of corrupt Lovelaces. Fielding's novels, by contrast, are saturated with classical reference and analogy: he refounds the new genre as a 'comic epic in prose', infusing it with aspects of classical epic and satire, from structure to simile. His lead was followed by Smollett; but as a whole the genre moves away from classical norms. Johnson was a better classicist than Pope, but his dream of high European culture founded on the Latinate values of humanism was giving way before the practical, empirical, secular and democratic culture of the Enlightenment, which he also embraced in part.

Moreover, the sense of how classical civilization could be apprehended began to change. The reputation of Augustus, the emperor who supposedly presided over the golden age of Latin poetry, came under attack and his image as benign despot was extensively tarnished by historians. Poets such as Thomson (in *Liberty*, 1735–6) or Richard Glover (*Leonidas*, 1737) could align British destinies with classical models; but the great historical book of the latter half of the century is Edward Gibbon's *History of the Decline and Fall of the Roman Empire* (1776–88), a story of descent into ruination from classical heights, a process to some extent already noted in John Dyer's poem *The Ruins of Rome* (1740). There are links here with early forms of archaeology: Herculaneum was being excavated through the century, and Grand Tourists collected ancient statues and vases as well as paintings. Architects and artists brought back new specimens of picturesque decay in heavily illustrated volumes such as Robert Wood's *Ruins of Palmyra* (1753) and Robert Adam's *Ruins of the Palace of the Emperor Diocletian* (1764). Britain, as part of the Roman empire, had its own visible reminders of Roman decay and a number of sites began to be excavated; Roman finds were collected and mosaics uncovered. These discoveries and relics opened a new scene of melancholy imaginative pleasures.

Bards of Britain

As England metamorphosed into the world power, 'Britain', so its sense of history and historical destiny deepened. The nationalism that went with empire challenged the supremacy of Rome (Pope himself says as much in his 'Epistle to Addison'). History became a popular genre, and it is noteworthy that the most popular history of Britain was written not by a specialist historian but by the philosopher Hume, and its continuation was written by the novelist Smollett. Walpole's *Historic Doubts* opposed Hume's account of Richard III's reign and his response to Walpole's objections. To be sure, some of this was politics under yet another guise. The history of the seventeenth century, particularly of the Civil War, Protectorate, and Revolution, could scarcely be written about other than from Whig, Tory, or Jacobite perspectives, and judgements on Elizabeth I and Mary Queen of Scots also tended to divide along party lines. In *Historic Doubts* Walpole several times nails his Whig credentials to the mast by pouring scorn on defenders of the reigns of the Stuarts. While more remote history was in general safer, accounts of Magna Carta (with its implications for the status of sovereignty) could still stir up a political storm.

Antiquarian studies and local history, which had originally had a strong link to political need, giving legitimacy to certain forms of political organization or conserving the monuments of the past against the threat of revolution, produced sufficient materials to become fascinating as a study of a lost world of feudal power and romance: 'orientalism' could mutate into 'medievalism'. In 1718 the Society of Antiquaries was formed, dedicating itself to a new science of archaeology. Walpole was a member and it was in the society's journal, *Archaeologia*, that the two most damaging criticisms of *Historic Doubts* were published, causing him to resign shortly afterwards. The British Museum was opened in 1759, incorporating a number of private collections (some of the documents Walpole reprinted in *Historic Doubts* had been discovered here). Pre-Roman barrows began to be excavated; Saxon finds were hoarded in private museums. Even Defoe, whose primary interest was in models of economic organization, spent time in the *Tour* giving detail (mostly plagiarized) on local antiquities.

Stonehenge, which the Jacobean architect Inigo Jones had conceived of as a Roman building, was radically reassigned to a wild Celtic past by the archaeologist William Stukeley. He took the first proper geometrical survey of the monument and surrounding antiquities and excavated some of the associated barrows, publishing the results in an illustrated book that advanced the view not only that Stonehenge was an ancient British temple but that it corresponded to a Druid monument. Stonehenge became a tourist attraction (even Johnson visited it) and the subject of many a watercolour, as fantastic schemes of primitive religion were constructed around it. Avebury, which had not been noticed at all until John Aubrey made notes on it – and guided Charles II round it – was co-opted into this network of Druid mythology.

There were corresponding changes in the literary map. Shakespeare, whose plays were still popular on the stage (though often in forms adapted to neo-classical concepts of moral efficacy and poetic justice), was seized on as the poet of uneducated nature and edited again and again. Edmund Spenser was a favourite of Pope's; he read *The Faerie Queene* at the age of 12 and continued to read it until his death, providing himself with a source of deliberately antiquated romance and wonder. The *Observations on the Faery Queen of Spenser* (1754), by the medievalizing poet and academic Thomas Warton, took the poem still more seriously. Richard Hurd's *Letters on Chivalry and Romance* (1762) argued strongly for the value of medieval fabling. Chaucer was 'translated' by Dryden, imitated by Pope (sometimes in smutty squibs, but also in sober reflections on his own authorial position, as in *The Temple of Fame* of 1715), and formally edited by a number of scholars. As poets looked away from the contemporary London scene towards remoter areas of Britain, they fastened especially on the 'pre-civilized' enclaves of Celtic language: Ireland, Wales, the Highlands of Scotland. The past represented a foreign country in which all kinds of contemporary restraint could be jettisoned, and onto which any manner of fantasy could be projected. This process was strengthened by critical work that combined ancientness with exotic location: Robert Lowth gave an influential series of lectures on Hebrew poetry in the 1750s at Oxford (in Latin).[3] Poets like Gray began to seek something even more natural and primordial than Shakespeare.

It is not that Gray was not an extremely competent classicist: 24 of his 72 surviving poems are in Latin. But he added to this a strong fascination with remote, non-classical writing. Shortly after his definitively 'English' poem, the *Elegy*, he projected a history of English poetry, and began writing *The Progress of Poesy*, which he completed in 1754. (The never-completed *History* was, in one sense, taken up by Thomas Warton, who from 1774 to 1781 produced three volumes of a *History of English Poetry*.) *The Progress of Poesy* was a 'Pindaric Ode', so called after the Greek poet Pindar, who was renowned for lyric poetry of a wild and passionate character and thus often the model for 'irregular' verse of the period. It was a kind of recognized and conventional licence for overstepping more strictly formal versification. Thus Gray's poem invokes the 'Aeolian lyre', summoning it to 'give to rapture all thy trembling strings'; he imagines the streams of Helicon (in Greek mythology, home of the Muses) gathering force into an 'impetuous' torrent. Poetry figures as a powerful force, able to overcome the ancient gods of Greece and to comfort the inhabitants of desolate regions the world over, from the frozen north to the forests of Chile. The Muses are imagined leaving the failing empire of Greece for that of Rome, and upon Rome's speedy demise searching out the 'sea-encircled coast' of Albion, a poetic name for Britain, where Shakespeare ('Nature's Darling'), Milton ('that rode sublime / Upon the seraph-wings of Extasy') and Dryden are their favoured sons. The poem's last stanza asks 'Oh! lyre divine, what daring spirit / Wakes thee now?', inviting a contemporary successor to the mantle of the 'Theban eagle' (Pindar).[4]

Gray's answer is somewhat surprising. *The Progress of Poesy* was first published in 1757 alongside another Pindaric ode, *The Bard*, written somewhere between 1755 and 1757 and later one of his most influential poems (it also became a popular subject for painting and was later illustrated by William Blake). The 'bard' of the title is Welsh, and the poem is largely his denunciation of the English king, Edward I, declaimed from a precipice above a 'foaming flood' in Snowdonia as Edward returns from his suppression of the Welsh in 1238. The voice of the poem is thus strongly identified with a poetry of resistance to modernity: ancient, 'primitive', remote, and marginal. The bard has the requisite lyre, wild hair, flowing robes and impassioned demeanour and his poetry is, from the bard's point of view, extempore, unstudied, passionate, all aspects of poetry Gray was giving himself the opportunity to imitate. But the bard does more than complain and curse ('Ruin seize thee, ruthless King!'). As the poem develops, so it gradually turns into a form of magic incantation. The bard summons the ghosts of his poetic predecessors to join him in his work:

> On yonder cliffs, a griesly band,
> I see them sit, they linger yet,
> Avengers of their native land:
> With me in dreadful harmony they join,
> And weave with bloody hands the tissue of thy line. (44–8)

Though defeated in battle, in their supernatural power they 'weave' Edward's fate, envisaging a series of sticky ends for Edward's Plantagenet descendants (recognizable to the actual, contemporary modern, historically minded audience of Gray's poem, which knows that these 'prophecies' were fulfilled). These included the 'Bristled Boar', or Richard III, subject of Walpole's ingenious defence. As the vision of past poets fades ('The web is wove. The work is done'), it is replaced by a vision of future political and poetic glories, exemplified in the reign of Elizabeth I; again, the bard's visionary power discovers in the future what we recognize as true in the past. Optimistically aligning Elizabeth with a Welsh version of Britishness, the bard celebrates what he can see of Spenser, Shakespeare, and Milton, and with the comfort of this poetic future, he throws himself off the mountain and into the river. After Milton, the bard can only catch glimpses: 'distant warblings lessen on my ear, / That lost in long futurity expire'. Whether or not Gray sees himself (or perhaps Pope) as a distant warbler in this line of succession, the poem is immensely significant for its sense of poetic history. Gray's poetic energy, his answer to the query raised in *The Progress of Poesy*, goes into the creation of an imaginary bard whose power is greater than kings and whose vision is so accurate as to predict exactly the same British poetic glories as Gray had himself celebrated in the earlier poem. Poetry looks backwards in order to 'progress'.

The moment was right for such perspectives. In 1760 a young man from the Scottish Highlands, James Macpherson, published what he called *Fragments of Ancient Poetry, Collected in the Highlands of Scotland* and translated from Gaelic into English poetic prose. Brief wisps of elegy, they appeared to offer a glimpse of a vanished poetic culture, and Macpherson was funded to go on tour round the Highlands to see what else he could recover from oral tradition. He came back with a six-book epic, *Fingal* (1762), followed by another, *Temora* (1763), narrating the adventures of the Gaelic superhero Fingal. The poet of the epics is supposed to be Ossian, Fingal's son, himself a noble warrior, now blind (like Homer was supposed to be) and nearing death. The Ossianic epic thus fits the kind of primitive bardic nobility embodied in Gray's *The Bard*, located in much the same kind of elemental landscape and with some of the same quality of lament about it (though it was more feminine in character than Gray's poem, giving it cross-gender appeal). Macpherson had produced exactly the right text at the right time; it was enthusiastically taken up by proponents of primitive culture in the Scottish universities and had a major influence on theories of folk poetry throughout Europe: it is celebrated in Smollett's *Humphry Clinker*. That it came from Scotland was in one sense an advantage, since that region had already been identified as backward and superstitious, and thus in a new sense 'poetic', before Macpherson's work appeared. It was controversial, since it envisaged a noble and victorious Scottish army within fifteen years of the disaster at Culloden, and several English writers denounced it as a kind of backdoor Jacobite literary invasion. Others merely doubted that poetry of this length could remain preserved in oral culture for the fourteen hundred years Macpherson was claiming: Johnson went out of his way to be rude about Ossian on his tour in Scotland and denounced it as an absolute fraud in the published *Journey*. Controversy about the texts was buoyant for half a century and has never entirely died down, though it is generally accepted that Macpherson embroidered and padded out his sources in Gaelic ballads very considerably in order to produce what he thought the Gaelic epic ought to sound like.[5] Something similar happened when Bishop Thomas Percy (who had directed Walpole to his 'coronation roll') put together an influential anthology of early British folk-poetry, *Reliques of Ancient English Poetry* in 1765: he too had sources, printed and manuscript, and he too tidied them up in order to meet the expectations of his audience. Nonetheless these texts were the first monuments of an interest in the origins of regional and national poetry which became a major feature of the Romantic movement across Europe.

Gray was very excited by Macpherson's 'discoveries' (though occasionally he doubted their authenticity) and also by the publication by Evan Evans of specimens of Welsh poetry.[6] In their wake he produced 'The Triumphs of Owen', based on a Welsh source, 'The Fatal Sisters' and 'The Descent of Odin', imitations of old 'Norse' poetry. These pieces once again revelled in the dark elemental landscapes and magic or prophetic forces Gray had tapped in 'The Bard'. Gray had refused the post of poet laureate in 1757, but after several years reading in the newly founded British Museum library he was elected Regius Professor of Modern History at Cambridge in 1768, an indication of how literary the discipline of history was. Though Gray's duties did not take up much of his time (he was scarcely called upon to teach or lecture), the appointment was not inappropriate in that Gray, now enshrined as the major mid-century poet and precursor of the Romantics, was profoundly historically minded.

One of Gray's correspondents on the matter of Ossian was Walpole, who was considerably less impressed by Macpherson. Gray, in fact, helped Walpole out with some queries about another document for his *Historic Doubts*. But Walpole, though classically educated in the conventional way, was himself the proponent of an anti-classical mode of writing – and building. Whereas his father, Sir Robert Walpole, had followed the usual route of successful landed gentry by tearing down an old house and shifting an old village to create a monumental neo-classical mansion for himself at Houghton in Norfolk (it is one of many candidates for the original of 'Timon's Villa'), Horace bought a tumbledown cottage in Twickenham, not far from Pope's villa, and set about creating a fantasy gothic castle later known as Strawberry Hill. This 'gothic revival' had an important literary consequence.[7]

On Christmas Eve, 1764, a small book appeared in London with the title: *The Castle of Otranto, A Story, translated by William Marshall, Gent. From the original Italian of Onuphrio Muralto, Canon of the Church of St Nicholas at Otranto*. The Preface explained that the book, which had been printed in black letter at Naples in 1529, had been found 'in the library of an ancient catholic family in the north of England'. The events were dated to the period of the crusades but the Italian was of a kind current in about 1500, and it was suggested that it had been published as a Catholic riposte to the attack on superstition mounted by the proponents of the Reformation.

This much was obfuscation; the story was actually written by Walpole. In a Preface to the second edition (1765), in which the explanation 'A Gothic Story' is added to the title page, Walpole accounts for his ruse as the effect of diffidence and explains the story as an attempt to blend the ancient style of romance, where 'all was imagination and improbability', with the modern style in which 'nature is always intended to be . . . copied with success'. The return to a period of superstitious belief in the miraculous, as outlined in the first Preface, was clearly a source of novelistic pleasure to Walpole. In private correspondence he was still more keen to stress how the story represented his own free imaginative play. In one letter, to his fellow antiquary William Cole, he points out the origin of some of the details of the setting in aspects of his own house, and describes the origin of the novel as an unconscious imaginative stimulus:

> I waked one morning . . . from a dream, of which all I could recover was, that I had thought myself in an ancient castle (a very natural dream for a head like mine filled with Gothic story) and that on the uppermost bannister of a great staircase I saw a gigantic hand in armour. In the evening I sat down and began to write, without knowing in the least what I intended to say or relate.[8]

The result was a plot of extreme melodrama. Manfred, prince of Otranto, is desperate to avoid the effects of a prophecy which warns that the lordship of Otranto will pass from his family when there are no more male heirs and 'whenever the real owner should be grown too large to inhabit it'. He attempts to marry his son, Conrad, to the unenthusiastic Isabella, in order to prolong the line, but Conrad is killed by the fall of an immense helmet. A peasant, Theodore, who recognizes the helmet as resembling that of Alfonso, a former prince of Otranto, is suspected of sorcery and imprisoned under it. A gigantic foot and leg also appear in the castle. Theodore escapes into an underground passage and helps Isabella to escape to the neighbouring monastery where she claims sanctuary; he is recaptured. Manfred, who has seen the ghost of his grandfather walk out of a picture to admonish him, tries to enlist the help of the priest, Jerome, to dissolve his marriage to Hippolita so that he can marry Isabella himself and thus produce heirs. Manfred's daughter, Matilda, falls in love with Theodore, whom Jerome recognizes as his own son. Isabella's father (Frederic) arrives, with an improbably enormous sword, to reclaim both her and the seat of Otranto, which Manfred is alleged to have usurped. Theodore escapes with Matilda's help and discovers Isabella in a cave in a gloomy forest; he protects her from a masked knight, who turns out to be her father. Manfred then offers Matilda to Frederic if he will agree to his own marriage to Isabella. These events are accompanied by further portents: dreams, thunder, unearthly groans, drops of blood falling from statues. A giant hand interrupts proposals for furthering the marriages, and Frederic is warned off by a spectral skeleton. Enraged, Manfred follows Theodore and stabs the woman with him, thinking she is Isabella; but she turns out to be his own daughter, who then dies. A final apparition unites the scattered members of the phantasmal body and indicates something of the aspirations of Walpole's gothic imagination: the form of Alfonso, 'dilated to an immense magnitude', declares Theodore the true heir of Otranto before ascending to heaven. Manfred finally confesses that Alfonso was poisoned by Manfred's grandfather and that the will declaring him heir was a forgery. He and Hippolita retire to neighbouring monasteries. Theodore turns out to be the grandson of Alfonso and becomes lord of Otranto, eventually marrying Isabella, but the gothic mood is maintained to a surprisingly sombre conclusion: 'It was not until after frequent discourses with Isabella, of his dear Matilda, that he was persuaded he could know no happiness but in the society of one with whom he could forever indulge the melancholy that had taken possession of his soul.'[9]

The main feature of the novel is thus its open use of supernatural events as indicators of human crimes and psychological states in an exotic premodern setting. The story narrates the interweaving of dynastic struggles with personal emotions; it is fascinated with lineage (both in the story itself and in the first, obfuscatory Preface, that projects a fictional provenance for the story); it is permeated by a strong sense of guilt. A strongly defended family home is blown apart by the sins of the past. The sexual tyranny exerted by the powerful father over the weak son and all the women within his circle has led to suggestions that Walpole was drawing on some suppressed elements of his family background (in public he was staunchly defensive of Sir Robert Walpole). In his political life Walpole was an unvarying Whig, but in *Otranto* he was fascinated by images of (almost) unlimited power and the authority of the Catholic church; in the first Preface he also impersonates a Catholic nobleman and crypto-Jacobite. A story in which the tyrannical grandson of a usurper is replaced by the noble grandson of the rightful ruler has a disconcerting fit with Jacobite views of George III. The book thus allows Walpole to identify with fantasies of power and restoration fundamentally at odds with his normal political position.

Otranto was outrageously innovative and influential. It was universally read, and though it provided, more in less in kit form, a standard apparatus for the shilling shocker of the early nineteenth century (castle, subterranean passage, mysterious noises, apparitions, skeletons, tyranny, guilt, predatory sexuality, and so on) it also had the more serious effect of making it possible to cast 'the novel' in non-realist guises, with exotic and historical settings and overt psychological symbolism. Three years after his novel, Walpole published the *Historic Doubts* discussed above: a sort of anti-gothic history that ascribed to a late medieval monarch something more like eighteenth-century norms of psychology and action. In the same year Walpole finished but did not formally publish a gothic tragedy, *The Mysterious Mother* (1768), an even more shocking version of dysfunctional family sexuality involving the complicated ramifications of an act of incest. This, however, he kept under wraps, though it was known to the Romantic poets, who found it horrifying and inspirational by turns.

Shortly after this, in March 1769, Walpole was approached by Thomas Chatterton, a Bristol youth who claimed to have discovered a cache of late medieval poetry and other documents relating to the activities of a fictional poet-priest, Thomas Rowley, and a historical merchant, William Canynge, and forming a rich archive of life in medieval Bristol. Gray advised him that the pieces were forgeries and Walpole rejected them. Chatterton went to London, wrote a variety of topical and satirical verse, and died in 1770, at the age of 18, apparently of an overdose. The poetry, about which there was much debate, was published in 1777 by Thomas Tyrwhitt, who had edited a fine edition of Chaucer's *Canterbury Tales* in 1774–5. He decided, apparently quite late in the editorial process, that the poems were not what they claimed to be, but published them anyway to great public curiosity (Goldsmith and Johnson were among those who took an interest). Most scholars argued that the documents were forgeries, but no less a figure than Dean Milles, Walpole's antagonist over Richard III, took up the cudgels on behalf of the poems, issuing a massive dissertation in favour of their authenticity. The issue was more quickly decided than in the case of Ossian, for interest rapidly shifted from the poems themselves to the youth who had produced them so astonishingly and died so young. While the poetry is further evidence of the prevalent late eighteenth-century need to imagination pre-modern life, and the attendant tendency to imagine it in modern terms, the death of Chatterton became a stock instance of the oppression of genius by a Philistine society. Satirist and journalist though he was, Chatterton was made to represent youthful poetic fire, a talent now easily mapped onto the early poetry he had (re-)created.

1777 also saw another event of relevance to Walpole, which was Clara Reeve's *The Champion of Virtue* (1777; retitled *The Old English Baron: A Gothic Story*, 1778). This was a new version of *The Castle of Otranto* that transposed the events to England and a more rationalistic and legalistic context. Edmund, in the role of Walpole's Theodore, is the son of aristocratic parents who have been killed by the villainous Baron Lovel, occupying the role of Manfred; he is brought up as a peasant but is evidently of noble character, and distinguishes himself in the service of the current occupant of his family home, the Baron Fitz-Owen (Baron Lovel, finding the castle he has obtained by murder to be haunted, has sold it). Despite the machinations of Fitz-Owen's sons, Edmund is revealed as the rightful heir fairly early on the story, and the rest of it is devoted to the drawn-out process of discovering proofs of his story (*Otranto* scarcely bothers with such social niceties). Having moved the action to England 'in the minority of Henry the Sixth' (that is, somewhere between 1422 and 1437), Reeve imagines it as a place of sentimental nobility in which the lords of the realm uphold strict justice. A friend of Edmund's, Sir Philip Harclay, takes the case to trial by combat against Baron Lovel, and defeats him; he obtains witnessed confession of the murder, arranges for appropriate documents to be drawn up, for the evidence to be formally and publicly displayed, for all aspects of the narrative to be publicly affirmed, and for the exact disposition of all the money and property in case. Walpole's dramatic 'jigsaw' narrative becomes a court-case in which social assent and legal authentication takes over from the force of the supernatural. Finally, the breach between Edmund and Baron Fitz-Owen is healed by marriage to his daughter, a marriage which was in any case desired. We learn that everything has been formally written up and circulated, and indeed the story comes to us in the romance form of a discovered manuscript.

In her Preface to the second edition, Reeve objects to the excess of the supernatural in Walpole's story, on the grounds that it is 'so violent, that it destroys the effect it is intended to excite'; by exceeding the 'utmost *verge* of probability' Walpole prompts laughter rather than enchantment. Reeve is trying to offer 'a picture of Gothic times and manners', a genuine historical fiction.[10] Accordingly she strips out everything from Walpole's apparatus except a couple of ghosts, some ghostly noises and some supernatural dreams, mostly confined to a chamber where a murder victim has been buried and thus in line with a quasi-rational explanation. Reeve also deletes the bundles of sexual tension pervading *Otranto*, substituting instead a simplified and scarcely challenged version of romance ending in happy and fruitful marriage. By shifting the Manfred figure out of the main sequence to the margin of the story, she greatly diminishes the head-on collision between the rightful heir of the castle and the current occupant; by adding in the figure of Harclay, who adopts Edmund as his son, retribution is achieved almost without the involvement of the central character. The 'Old English' Baron does things in accordance with a supposed ancient version of noble justice, though common-law prosecution is from time to time threatened; the sentimental attachments formed by everyone except the villain project back into English history a form of emotional bonding. There is however a supplementary trace of exoticism in the figure of Zadisky, a friend of Harclay's, who returns to Palestine in quest of his own son.

Reeve's version of gothic was popular (though not with Walpole) and it marked the tendency of gothic fiction to become a female domain: Sophia Lee's historical fiction *The Recess: or, a Tale of Other Times* (1783) invented a pair of daughters for Mary Queen of Scots and brought them up in a decaying Catholic convent, while the work of Ann Radcliffe, populated with virtuous heroines in distress, would dominate the genre in the 1790s. Reeve followed up her novel with several others, and with an extensive critical treatise, in some ways more radical than the novels. The format of *The Progress of Romance* (1785) is, like Dryden's essay *Of Dramatick Poesie* (1668), a dialogue; but it is much less ambiguous than its model. An educated woman writer, Euphrasia, representing Reeve, challenges an educated but prejudiced male reader, Hortensius, to a debate of the virtues of romance writing, which he professes to scorn as feminine and fanciful. The debate takes place before a female 'moderator', Sophronia, and Euphrasia wins hands down. She takes a scholarly cue from Percy, with occasional references to the poet James Beattie's dissertation 'on Fable and Romance' and Warton's *History of English Poetry*.[11] But in the main relying upon her own primary reading, Euphrasia boldly asserts that there is no fundamental difference between the 'male' domain of epic and the 'female' one of romance. In a wide historical and geographical survey, Euphrasia finds high moral worth and imaginative content in romances of all periods, and faults traditionally ascribed to romance in epic. Homer is full of romance elements and the tale of Sinbad from the *Arabian Nights* is comparable with the travails of Odysseus. Romance is unimpeachably 'polite'. Chaucer's *Knight's Tale* is virtually an epic; Reeve quotes the opinion of Dryden, who modernized it, to the effect that it could well stand alongside Homer. Spenser, and even Milton, could not have written as they did without a thorough grounding in Romance. *Rasselas* is highly regarded among the 'Eastern Tales'. But Reeve also ventures to analyse Ossian alongside Virgil and to commend the 'oriental' love of pure story-telling.

We began this book with Johnson's farewell, in the *Lives of the English Poets*, to the long eighteenth century: a biographical understanding of what male poetry was and could be. Reeve offers an alternative, feminized literary history, where Romance progresses to the verge of Romanticism (even if the events of 1789–94 across the Channel would show that literary history is never simply a matter of 'progress'). She has strong opinions on modern women novelists: she rates Behn highly, despite moral qualms, thinks Manley too scandalous, and likes the later 'domestic' Haywood better than the early amorous fictions. Sarah Fielding and Charlotte Lennox are compared with Defoe, Fielding, Smollett and Sterne. Ultimately, Reeve opens a window on the future by looking to the past. The volume ends with Reeve's own contribution to the genre of the Oriental Tale, 'The History of Charoba, Queen of Ægypt', a short story fusing biblical chronology (the story of Abraham and Sarah), romance, antiquity and exoticism. Charoba succeeds to the throne, despite being female, and remains a virgin queen; she murders the giant ruler who attempts to marry her by force, and on her own death (from a snakebite) the throne passes to a kinswoman. In a small, supplementary way, matriarchy was back in literary fashion.

Notes

1 Rymer, *The Tragedies of the Last Age Consider'd and Examin'd by the Practice of the Ancients* (1678).
2 For a modern text see *Prose Works of Alexander Pope*, Vol. 2, *The Major Works 1725–1744*, edited by Rosemary Cowler (Oxford, 1986).
3 Lowth, *De Sacra Poesi Hebræorum* (1753); translated into English, 1787.
4 Quotations from Gray's poems are from *The Poems of Thomas Gray, William Collins, Oliver Goldsmith*, edited by Roger Lonsdale (Harlow, 1969).
5 See James Macpherson, *The Poems of Ossian*, edited by Howard Gaskill (Edinburgh, 1996).
6 Evans, *Some Specimens of the Poetry of the Antient Welsh Bards* (1764).
7 The building of Strawberry Hill is described in Timothy Mowl, *Horace Walpole: the Great Outsider* (London, 1996).
8 Walpole to Cole, 9 March 1765; *Yale Edition of Horace Walpole's Correspondence*, edited by W. S. Lewis, 48 vols (New Haven and London, 1937–83), I.88.
9 Walpole, *The Castle of Otranto*, edited by Michael Gamer (London, 2001), pp. 100–01.

10 Clara Reeve, *The Old English Baron*, edited by James Trainer (Oxford, 1977), pp. 3–5.
11 Beattie's *Dissertations Moral and Critical* were published in 1783. Beattie also produced a notable Spenserian poem, *The Minstrel* (1771–4), recounting the poetic education of a shepherd boy.

Chronology of authors of the long 18th century

1660 Restoration of King Charles II
Royal Society founded
Theatres reopen
Milton, *Ready and Easy Way*
Dryden, *Astraea Redux*
Cotton, *Panegyrick*
Pepys begins *Diary*

1661 Defoe born (?)

1662 Charles II marries Catherine of Braganza

1663 Butler, *Hudibras* (Book I)
Delarivier Manley born

1664 Butler, *Hudibras* (Book II)
Katherine Philips dies

1665 Plague in London
War with Holland
Marvell, *Character of Holland*

1666 Centre of London burned down in Great Fire
Bunyan, *Grace Abounding*

1667 War with Holland concluded
Cowley dies

Swift born
Arbuthnot born
Milton, *Paradise Lost* (ten books)
Katherine Philips, *Poems*
Dryden, *Annus Mirabilis*
Marvell, *Last Instructions to a Painter* written (published 1689)

1668 Dryden made Poet Laureate
Essay of Dramatic Poesy

1669 Pepys ceases writing *Diary*

1670 Congreve born

1671 Milton, *Paradise Regained* and *Samson Agonistes*

1672 Dryden, *Marriage a la Mode*
Addison born
Steele born

1673 Test Act

1674 Herrick, Milton and Traherne die
Marvell, 'On Milton's *Paradise Lost*'

1675 Wycherley, *The Country Wife*

1676 Etherege, *The Man of Mode*

1677 Dryden, *All for Love*
Wycherley, *Plain Dealer*
Behn, *The Rover*
Marvell, *Growth of Popery*

1678 Popish Plot begins
Marvell dies
Bolingbroke born
Dryden writes *Mac Flecknoe* (published 1682)
Butler, *Hudibras* (III)
Bunyan, *Pilgrim's Progress* (I)
Rymer, *Tragedies of the Last Age Consider'd*

1679 Exclusion Bill

1680 Butler dies
Rochester dies; *Poems*
Filmer, *Patriarcha*
Bunyan, *Mr Badman*

1681 Exclusion Bill reintroduced
Otway, *Venice Preserv'd*
Oldham, *Satires upon the Jesuits*
Dryden, *Absalom and Achitophel*
Marvell, *Miscellaneous Poems*
Cotton, *Wonders of the Peak*

1682 Dryden, *The Medal*, *Religio Laici*
Behn, *City Heiress*
Bunyan, *Holy War*

1683 Rye House Plot
Oldham dies
Poems and Translations

1684 Bunyan, *Pilgrims's Progress* (2)

1685 Charles II dies
James II succeeds
Monmouth rebellion
Dryden, *Threnodia Augustalis*
Dryden becomes Roman Catholic
Otway dies
Gay born

1686 Anne Killigrew, *Poems*

1687 Declaration of Indulgence
Cotton dies
Newton, *Principia*
Dryden, *The Hind and the Panther*

1688 Second Declaration of Indulgence
James II's son born

William of Orange lands at Torbay
James II flees to France
'Glorious Revolution'
Dryden deprived of court posts
Pope born
Behn, *Oroonoko*

1689 Accession of William and Mary
Bill of Rights and Toleration Act
Convention Parliament
War with France
James II lands in Ireland
Richardson born
Behn dies

1690 William defeats James at Battle of Boyne
Locke, *Two Treatises of Government*; *Essay concerning Human Understanding*

1692 Congreve, *Incognita*

1693 Dryden, *Satires of Juvenal and Persius*
Congreve, *The Old Bachelor*

1694 Death of Queen Mary
Foundation of Bank of England
Congreve, *The Double Dealer*

1695 Vaughan dies
Congreve, *Love for Love*
Licensing Act lapses

1696 Jacobite Rising

1697 Treaty of Ryswick ends European war
Dryden, translation of Virgil's *Aeneid*
Defoe, *Essay on Projects*

1698 Collier, *Short View of the Immorality and Prophaneness of the Stage*

1699 Garth, *The Dispensary*

1700 Second Partition Treaty
Dryden, *Fables*
Dryden dies (1 May)
Dyer born
Thomson born
Congreve, *Way of the World*

1701 War of Spanish Succession commences
Act of Settlement to secure Protestant rule in England
Society for Propagation of the Gospel founded

1702 Death of William III
Accession of Queen Anne
Daily Courant inaugurates daily newspaper
Defoe, *Shortest Way with Dissenters*

1703 Great Storm
Pepys dies
John Wesley born
Defoe in the pillory
Hymn to the Pillory

1704 Battle of Blenheim
Newton, *Opticks*
Locke dies
Swift, *Tale of a Tub* and *Battle of the Books*
Defoe begins *Review*

1705 Newcomen's steam engine

1706 Battle of Ramillies

1707 Union of England and Scotland
Fielding born
Watts, *Hymns and Spiritual Songs*
Charles Wesley born

1708 Battle of Oudenarde
Swift, *Argument against abolishing Christianity*
Philips, *Cyder*
Shaftesbury, *Letter Concerning Enthusiasm*

1709 Battle of Malplaquet
'Copyright Act'
Johnson born
Addison and Steele commence *The Tatler*
Pope, *Pastorals*
Rowe's edition of Shakespeare
Manley, *New Atalantis*

1710 Sacheverell crisis, fall of Whig ministry
Tory ministry run by Robert Harley and Henry St John
Berkeley, *Principles of Human Knowledge*

1711 Addison and Steele end *Tatler* and begin *The Spectator*
Pope, *An Essay on Criticism*
Shaftesbury, *Characteristics*
Hume born

1712 Pope, *Rape of the Locke* (two-canto version)
Swift, *Proposal for Correcting the English Language*
Arbuthnot, *History of John Bull*

1713 Treaty of Utrecht ends War of Spanish Succession
Sterne born. Shaftesbury dies
Pope, *Windsor-Forest*. Meetings of Scriblerus club
Addison, *Cato*
Gay, *Rural Sports*
Finch, *Miscellany Poems*
Defoe's *Review* ceases publication
Collins, *Discourse of Freethinking*

1714 Death of Queen Anne
Accession of George I
Fall of Tory ministry
Whigs take power
Shenstone born
Pope, *Rape of the Lock* (five-canto version)
Gay, *Shepherd's Week*
Manley, *Adventures of Rivella*
Swift returns to Dublin

1715 Abortive Jacobite Rising; Bolingbroke flees to France
Pope, *Temple of Fame* and first volume of translation of Homer's *Iliad*
Watts, *Divine Songs*

1716 Septennial Act (seven-year parliaments)
Sinking Fund to reduce national debt
Lady Mary Wortley Montagu leaves for Constantinople
Gray born
Wycherley dies
Gay, *Trivia*

1717 Pope, *Works*
Horace Walpole born

1718 Return of Lady Mary
Rowe dies
Society of Antiquaries founded

1719 Addison dies
Pope leases villa at Twickenham
Defoe, *Robinson Crusoe*
Haywood, *Love in Excess*
Watts, *Psalms of David*

1720 South Sea Bubble
Gilbert White born
Last volumes of Pope's *Iliad* published

1721 Sir Robert Walpole assumes main role in government
Akenside, Collins and Smollett born

1722 Francis Atterbury implicated in Jacobite plotting and exiled
Smart born
Joseph Warton born
Defoe, *Moll Flanders*, *Colonel Jack*, *Journal of the Plague Year*

1723 Bolingbroke pardoned and returns
Adam Smith and Joshua Reynolds born
Centlivre dies

1724 Manley dies
Swift, *Drapier's Letters*
Defoe, *Roxana*; begins *Tour*; Ramsay, *Ever-Green*

1725 Pope's edition of Shakespeare
First volumes of his translation of Homer's *Odyssey*
Ramsay, *Gentle Shepherd*

1726 Swift, *Gulliver's Travels*
Pope's edition of Shakespeare attacked by Lewis Theobald
Odyssey translation completed
Defoe's *Tour* completed
Thomson begins *Seasons*
Dyer, *Grongar Hill*

1727 Death of George I
Accession of George II
Newton dies
Gay, *Fables*

1728 Gay, *The Beggar's Opera*
Pope, *The Dunciad* (three-book version)
Thomas Warton Jr born

1729 Treaty of Seville ends war with Spain
Wesley brothers found Methodist Society
Congreve and Steele die
Burke born
Percy born
Pope, *The Dunciad Variorum* (three-book version with notes)
Swift, *Modest Proposal*

1730 Walpole splits from Townshend
Colley Cibber appointed Poet Laureate
Duck, *Poems*
Fielding, *Tom Thumb*
Thomson completes *Seasons*
Goldsmith born (?)

1731 Defoe dies
Cowper and Churchill born

Lillo, *London Merchant*
Pope, *Epistle to Burlington* (first version)
The Gentleman's Magazine begins
Jethro Tull, *Horse-hoeing Husbandry*

1732 Gay dies
Academy of Ancient Music founded
Fielding, *Covent Garden Tragedy*

1733 Excise crisis
Walpole defeated
Pope, *Epistle to Bathurst* and *Essay on Man* (I–III)
Pope begins series of *Imitations of Horace*; attacked by Lord Hervey and Lady Mary Wortley Montagu

1734 John Dennis dies
Pope, *Essay on Man* (IV) and *Epistle to Cobham*

1735 Arbuthnot dies
Pope, *Epistle to Dr Arbuthnot*, *Epistle to a Lady* and *Works*, Vol. II; Pope begins publishing letters
Johnson, *Voyage to Abyssinia*
Thomson, *Liberty* (completed 1736)
Somervile, *The Chace*

1736 Haywood, *Adventures of Eovaai*
Macpherson born

1737 Death of Queen Caroline
Theatre Licensing Act
Gibbon born
Pope, *Epistle to Augustus*
Shenstone, *Poems*

1738 Excavations at Herculaneum
Pope, *Epilogue to the Satires*, completing Horace series
Johnson, *London*
John Wesley experiences 'conversion'

1739 War of Jenkin's Ear against Spain
Walpole and Gray on Grand Tour (to 1741)

	Hume, *Treatise of Human Nature* (completed 1740)
	Wesley brothers, *Hymns and Sacred Poems*
	Swift, *Verses on the Death of Dr Swift*
1740	War of Austrian Succession
	Anson circumnavigates globe
	Boswell born
	Richardson begins *Pamela*
	Cibber, *Apology for the Life of Colley Cibber*
	Dyer, *Ruins of Rome*
1741	Fielding, *Shamela*
	Scriblerians, *Memoirs of Martinus Scriblerus*
1742	Walpole resigns
	Richardson completes *Pamela*
	Pope, *The New Dunciad*
	Fielding, *Joseph Andrews*
	Collins, *Persian Eclogues*
	Young begins *Night Thoughts*
1743	Pelham ministry
	Battle of Dettingen
	Pope, *The Dunciad in Four Books* (with Cibber as hero)
	Fielding, *Jonathan Wild*
1744	Pope dies
	Johnson, *Life of Savage*
	Akenside, *Pleasures of the Imagination*
1745	Robert Walpole dies
	Battle of Fontenoy; Jacobite Rising
	Swift dies
	Young completes *Night Thoughts*
1746	Jacobite armies heavily defeated at Culloden
	Collins, *Odes*
	J. Warton, *Odes*
1747	Gray, *Ode on Eton College*
	Richardson begins *Clarissa* (completed 1748)

1748 Discovery of Pompeii ruins
Peace of Aix-la-Chapelle concludes war
Thomson dies
Castle of Indolence
Smollett, *Roderick Random*

1749 Horace Walpole takes lease on Strawberry Hill, Twickenham
Fielding, *Tom Jones*
Johnson, *Vanity of Human Wishes*; his *Irene* performed
Cleland, *Memoirs of a Woman of Pleasure*
Hartley, *Observations on Man*

1750 Johnson begins *Rambler*

1751 Gray, *Elegy*
Fielding, *Amelia*
Smollett, *Peregrine Pickle*
Haywood, *Betsy Thoughtless*

1752 Gregorian calendar adopted
Chatterton born
Fanny Burney born
Charlotte Lennox, *Female Quixote*
Johnson ends *Rambler*
Smart, *Poems*

1753 Abortive Jewish naturalization Bill
Richardson, *Sir Charles Grandison* (completed 1754)
Wesley brothers, *Hymns and Spiritual Songs*

1754 Pelham dies
Newcastle ministry
Crabbe born
Fielding dies
Hume begins *History of England*

1755 Johnson's *Dictionary*
Fielding, *Voyage to Lisbon*

1756 Seven Years' War (Britain and Prussia against France, Russia and Austria)

Black Hole of Calcutta
J. Warton, *Essay on Pope* (I)

1757 British ascendancy in India confirmed
Pitt–Newcastle ministry
Horace Walpole starts private press
Cibber dies
Blake born
Gray, *Odes*
Dyer, *The Fleece*
Burke, *Sublime and Beautiful*

1758 Dyer dies
Johnson begins *Idler*

1759 Capture of Quebec
British Museum opened
Collins dies
Burns born
Johnson, *Rasselas*
Young, *Conjectures on Original Composition*

1760 George II dies; accession of George III
Johnson ends *Idler*
Sterne begins *Tristram Shandy*
Macpherson, *Fragments*
Beckford born

1761 Pitt resigns
Richardson dies
Hume completes *History of England*

1762 Bute ministry
Macpherson, *Fingal*
Goldsmith, *Citizen of the World*
Hurd, *Letters on Chivalry and Romance*
Mary Collier, *Poems*

1763 Peace of Paris ends war with France
Grenville ministry
John Wilkes arrested

	Shenstone dies
	Johnson meets Boswell
	Macpherson, *Temora*
	Smart, *Song to David*
1764	Walpole, *The Castle of Otranto*
	Goldsmith, *Traveller*
1765	Rockingham ministry
	Young dies
	Johnson's edition of Shakespeare
	Percy, *Reliques*
	Smart, *Psalms of David*
1766	Chatham ministry
	Smollett, *Travels*
	Goldsmith, *Vicar of Wakefield*
1767	Revenue Bill (America)
	Sterne completes *Tristram Shandy*
1768	Grafton ministry
	Cook's first voyage begun
	Sterne, *Sentimental Journey*
	Sterne dies
	Walpole, *The Mysterious Mother*
	Royal Academy opened
1769	Wilkes's political agitation continues
	Arkwright's spinning frame
	Watts steam engine patented
	Reynolds, *Discourses* begun
	Garrick's Shakespeare jubilee
1770	North ministry
	Falkland islands crisis
	American tea duty
	Akenside dies
	Chatterton dies
	Wordsworth born
	Goldsmith, *Deserted Village*

1771	Cook returns from first voyage Smollett, *Humphry Clinker* Smollett dies Gray dies Smart dies Mackenzie, *Man of Feeling* Walpole, *Modern Gardening*
1772	Cook's second voyage begun Coleridge born Slavery declared unsustainable in England
1773	Boston Tea Party Johnson tours Scotland Goldsmith, *She Stoops to Conquer*
1774	American Declaration of Rights Omai in London Goldsmith dies Warton begins *History of English Poetry*
1775	Cook's second voyage concluded American War of Independence begins Austen born Johnson, *Journey* Sheridan, *The Rivals*
1776	American Declaration of Independence Cook's third voyage begun Hume dies Gibbon begins *Decline and Fall* Smith, *Wealth of Nations*
1777	Sheridan, *School for Scandal* Chatterton's 'Rowley Poems' published
1778	Burney, *Evelina*
1779	Cook killed Johnson begins *Lives of the English Poets* Cowper, *Olney Hymns*

1780 Gordon Riots in London against liberation of Catholics

1781 Johnson completes *Lives of the English Poets*

1782 Allan Ramsay dies
J. Warton, *Essay on Pope* (II)

1783 Treaty of Versailles ends American war
Pitt the Younger in power
Crabbe, *The Village*
Blake, *Poetical Sketches*

1784 First balloon flights
Cook, *Voyage to the Pacific Ocean*
Clara Reeve, *Progress of Romance*
Johnson dies

1785 Boswell, *Journal of a Tour in the Hebrides*
Cowper, *The Task*

1786 Burns, *Poems, chiefly in the Scottish Dialect*
Beckford, *Vathek*

1787 Charlotte Smith, *Elegiac Sonnets*

1788 Colonization of Australia by British
Wilberforce's first motion to abolish slave trade
Gibbon completes *Decline and Fall*

1789 Fall of the Bastille begins French Revolution
Mutiny on the Bounty
Equiano, *Interesting Narrative*
Blake, *Songs of Innocence*, *Book of Thel*
Radcliffe, *Castles of Athlin and Dunbayne*
White, *Natural History of Selborne*
Warton concludes *History of English Poetry*

1790 Burke, *Reflections on the Revolution in France*
Blake, *Marriage of Heaven and Hell*

1791 Boswell, *Life of Johnson*

Suggestions for further reading

Primary works

Anthologies

Demaria, Jr, Robert, (ed., *British Literature 1640–1789*, second edn (Oxford, 2001).

Copley, Stephen, ed., *Literature and the Social Order in Eighteenth-Century England* (London, 1984).

Denvir, Bernard, ed., *The Eighteenth Century: Art, Design and Society 1689–1789* (Harlow, 1983).

Fairer, David and Gerrard, Christine, eds, *Eighteenth-Century Poetry: An Annotated Anthology* (Oxford, 1999).

Finberg, Melinda, ed., *Eighteenth-Century Women Dramatists* (Oxford, 2001).

Greer, Germaine; Medoff, Jeslyn; Sansone, Melinda and Hastings, Susan, eds, *Kissing the Rod: An Anthology of Seventeenth-Century Women's Verse* (London, 1988).

Lonsdale, Roger, ed., *Eighteenth-Century Women Poets: An Oxford Anthology* (Oxford, 1989).

Lyons, Paddy and Morgan, Fidelis, eds, *Female Playwrights of the Restoration: Five Comedies* (London, 1991).

Mack, Robert L., ed., *Oriental Tales* (Oxford, 1992).

Mullan, John and Reid, Christopher, eds, *Eighteenth-Century Popular Culture* (Oxford, 2000).

Womersley, David, ed., *Restoration Drama: An Anthology* (Oxford, 2000).

Womersley, David, ed., *Augustan Critical Writing* (London, 1997).

Major works of individual authors

Astell, Mary, *The First English Feminist: Reflections upon Marriage and other Writings*, ed. Bridget Hill (Aldershot, 1986).

Behn, Aphra, *Oroonoko, The Rover and Other Works*, ed. Janet Todd (London, 1992).

Boswell, James, *Boswell's Life of Johnson*, ed. G. B. Hill and L. F. Powell, 6 vols (Oxford, 1950).

Burney, Fanny, *Evelina*, ed. Steward Cooke (New York, 1998).

Cleland, John, *Memoirs of a Woman of Pleasure*, ed. Peter Sabor (Oxford, 1985).

Collins, William, *The Poems of Thomas Gray, William Collins, Oliver Goldsmith*, ed. Roger Lonsdale (London, 1969).

Cowper, William, *The Task and Selected Other Poems*, ed. James Sambrook (London, 1994).

Defoe, Daniel, *Robinson Crusoe*, ed. Angus Ross (Harmondsworth, 1965).

Defoe, Daniel, *Moll Flanders*, ed. Edward Kelly (New York, 1973).

Defoe, Daniel, *Colonel Jack*, ed. S. H. Monk (Oxford, 1965).

Defoe, Daniel, *Roxana*, ed. Jane Jack (Oxford, 1981).

Dryden, John, *Dryden: Poems and Prose*, ed. William Grant (London, 1985).

Equiano, Olaudah, *The Interesting Narrative and Other Writings*, ed. Vincent Caretta (London, 1995).

Fielding, Henry, *Joseph Andrews with Shamela and Related Writings*, ed. Homer Goldber (New York, 1981).

Fielding, Henry, *Tom Jones*, ed. R. P. C. Mutter (Harmondsworth, 1966).

Fielding, Henry, *Amelia*, ed. David Blewett (Harmondsworth, 1987).

Fielding, Sarah, *The Adventures of David Simple*, ed. Malcolm Kelsall (Oxford, 1969).

Gibbon, Edward, *The Decline and Fall of the Roman Empire*, abridged edition, ed. David Womersley (London, 2000).

Goldsmith, Oliver, *The Vicar of Wakefield*, ed. Arthur Friedman (Oxford, 1981): see also Collins, William.

Gray, Thomas: see Collins, William.

Haywood, Eliza, *Love in Excess*, ed. David Oakleaf (Peterborough, Ontario, 2000).

Haywood, Eliza, *The Adventures of Eovaai*, ed. E. A. Wilputte (Peterborough, Ontario, 1999).

Haywood, Eliza, *The History of Miss Betsy Thoughtless*, ed. Christine Blough (Peterborough, Ontario, 1998).

Johnson, Samuel, *The Complete English Poems*, ed. J. D. Fleeman (Harmondsworth, 1971).

Johnson, Samuel, *The History of Rasselas, Prince of Abissinia*, ed. D. J. Enright (Harmondsworth, 1976).
Samuel Johnson, ed. Donald Greene (Oxford, 1986).
Lennox, Charlotte, *The Female Quixote*, ed. Margaret Dalziel (Oxford, 1970).
Mackenzie, Henry, *The Man of Feeling*, ed. Brian Vickers (Oxford, 1967).
Macpherson, James, *The Poems of Ossian*, ed. Howard Gaskill (Edinburgh, 1996).
Mandeville, Bernard, *The Fable of the Bees*, ed. Philip Harth (Harmondsworth, 1970).
Manley, Delarivier, *The New Atalantis*, ed. Rosalind Ballaster (Harmondsworth, 1992).
Manley, Delarivier, *The Adventures of Rivella*, ed. Katherine Zelinsky (Peterborough, Ontario, 1999).
Milton, John, *Complete Shorter Poems*, ed. John Carey (Harlow, 1971).
Milton, John, *Paradise Lost*, ed. Alastair Fowler (Harlow, 1971).
Montagu, Lady Mary Wortley, *Essays, Poems, and Simplicity, A Comedy*, ed. Robert Halsband and Isobel Grundy (Oxford, 1977).
Pope, Alexander, *Poetical Works*, ed. Herbert Davis (Oxford, 1978).
The Prose Works of Alexander Pope: Vol. I. The Earlier Works, 1711–1720, ed. Norman Ault (Oxford, 1936).
The Prose Works of Alexander Pope: Vol. 2. The Major Works, 1725–1744, ed. Rosemary Cowler (Oxford, 1986).
Reeve, Charlotte, *The Old English Baron*, ed. James Trainer (Oxford, 1977).
Richardson, Samuel, *Pamela*, ed. Tom Keymer (Oxford, 2001).
Richardson, Samuel, *Clarissa*, ed. Angus Ross (Harmondsworth, 1985).
Smollett, Tobias, *Humphry Clinker*, ed. James L. Thorson (New York, 1983).
Smollett, Tobias, *Travels through France and Italy*, ed. Frank Felsenstein (Oxford, 1979).
Sterne, Laurence, *The Life and Opinions of Tristram Shandy*, ed. Graham Petrie (Harmondsworth, 1967).
Sterne, Laurence, *A Sentimental Journey Through France and Italy*, ed. Ian Jack (Oxford, 1968).
Swift, Jonathan, *Gulliver's Travels*, ed. Paul Turner (Oxford, 1994).
Swift, Jonathan, *A Tale of a Tub and other Works*, ed. Angus Ross and David Woolley (Oxford, 1986).
Thomson, James, *The Seasons and the Castle of Indolence*, ed. J. A. Sambrook (Oxford, 1972).
Walpole, Horace, *The Castle of Otranto*, ed. Michael Gamer (London, 2001).

Wilmot, John, Earl of Rochester, *The Complete Poems*, ed. D. M. Vieth (New Haven, 1968).

Secondary reading, by chapter

1 Situations

Brewer, John, *The Pleasures of the Imagination: English Culture in the Eighteenth Century* (London, 1997).

Gallagher, Catherine, *Nobody's Story: The Vanishing Acts of Women Writers in the Market Place, 1670–1820* (Oxford, 1994).

Griffin, Dustin, *Literary Patronage in England, 1650–1800* (Cambridge, 1996).

Hammond, Brean, *Professional Imaginative Writing in England, 1670–1740: Hackney for Bread* (Oxford, 1997).

Holmes, Richard, *Dr Johnson and Mr Savage* (London, 1993).

Kernan, Alvin, *Printing Technology, Letters and Samuel Johnson* (Princeton, 1987).

Love, Harold, *Scribal Publication in Seventeenth-Century England* (Oxford, 1993).

McDowell, Paula, *The Women of Grub Street: Press, Politics, and Gender in the London Literary Marketplace, 1678–1730* (Oxford, 1998).

McLaverty, James, *Pope, Print and Meaning* (Oxford, 2001).

Rogers, Pat, *Grub Street: Studies in a Subculture* (London, 1972).

2 Writing and belief

Clark, J. C. D., *Samuel Johnson: Literature, Religion and English Cultural Politics from the Restoration to Romanticism* (Cambridge, 1994).

Cohen, I. Bernard and Smith, George E., eds, *The Cambridge Companion to Newton* (Cambridge, 2002).

Dunn, John, *The British Empiricists: Locke, Berkeley, Hume* (Oxford, 1992).

Hempton, David, *Religion and Political Culture in Britain and Ireland: From the Glorious Revolution to the Decline of Empire* (Cambridge, 1996).

Nicolson, Marjorie Hope, *Newton Demands the Muse: Newton's Opticks and the Eighteenth Century Poets* (Princeton, 1946).

Rack, H. D., *Reasonable Enthusiast: John Wesley and the Rise of Methodism* (Oxford, 1989).

Rivers, Isabel, *Reason, Grace, and Sentiment: A Study of the Language of Religion and Ethics in England, 1660–1780*, 2 vols (Cambridge, 1991–2000).
Rupp, E. G., *Religion in England, 1688–1791* (Oxford, 1986).

3 Court and parliament

Brewer, John, *The Sinews of Power: War, Money and the English State, 1688–1783* (London, 1989).
Brooks-Davies, Douglas, *Pope's Dunciad and the Queen of the Night: A Study in Emotional Jacobitism* (Manchester, 1985).
Bucholz, R. O., *The Augustan Court: Queen Anne and the Decline of Court Culture* (Stanford, 1993).
Cannon, John, *Samuel Johnson and the Politics of Hanoverian England* (Oxford, 1994).
Clark, J. C. D., *English Society 1688–1832: Ideology, Social Structure and Political Practices during the Ancien Regime* (Cambridge, 1985).
Clark, J. C. D., and Howard Erskine-Hill, eds, *Samuel Johnson in Historical Context* (London, 2002).
Dickinson, H. T., *Liberty and Property: Political Ideology in Eighteenth-Century England* (London, 1977).
Erskine-Hill, Howard, *Poetry of Opposition and Revolution: Dryden to Wordsworth* (Oxford, 1996).
Hill, Christopher, *Milton and the English Revolution* (London, 1977).
Hutton, Ronald, *The Restoration: A Political and Religious History of England and Wales 1658–1667* (Oxford, 1985).
Langford, Paul, *A Polite and Commercial History: England 1727–1783* (Oxford, 1989).
Monod, Paul, *Jacobitism and the English People, 1688–1788* (Cambridge, 1989).
O'Gorman, Frank, *The Long Eighteenth Century: British Political and Social History 1688–1832* (London, 1997).
Sim, Stuart, and Walker, David, *The Discourse of Sovereignty, Hobbes to Fielding* (Aldershot, 2003).
Thomas, P. D.G., *John Wilkes: A Friend to Liberty* (Oxford, 1996).

4 Town, country, nation

Andrews, Malcolm, *The Search for the Picturesque: Landscape Aesthetics and Tourism in Britain, 1760–1800* (Aldershot, 1989).

Barrell, Barrell, *The Dark Side of the Landscape: The Rural Poor in English Painting, 1730–1840* (Cambridge, 1980).
Borsay, Peter, *The English Urban Renaissance: Culture and Society in the Eighteenth-Century Provincial Town, 1660–1770* (London, 1989).
Colley, Linda, *Britons: Forging the Nation, 1707–1837* (New Haven, 1992).
Faller, Lincoln B., *Crime and Defoe: A New Kind of Writing* (Cambridge, 1993).
George, M. Dorothy, *London Life in the Eighteenth Century* (Harmondsworth, 1976).
Hudson, P., *The Industrial Revolution* (London, 1992).
Hunt, John Dixon, *The Figure in the Landscape: Poetry, Painting, and Gardening During the Eighteenth Century* (Baltimore, Maryland, 1976).
Hunt, John Dixon, *The Genius of the Place: The English Landscape Garden, 1670–1820* (Cambridge, Mass., 1988).
Martin, Peter, *Pursuing Innocent Pleasures: The Gardening World of Alexander Pope* (Hamden, 1984).
Sharpe, J. A., *Crime in Early Modern England 1550–1750* (Harlow, 1984).
Sean Shesgreen, *Engravings by Hogarth* (New York, 1973).
Summerson, John, *Georgian London* (Harmondsworth, 1978).
Sweet, Rosemary, *The English Town, 1680–1740: Government, Society and Culture* (Harlow, 1999).
Weinbrot, Howard, *Britannia's Issue: The Rise of British Literature from Dryden to Ossian* (Cambridge, 1993).

5 World views

Black, Jeremy, *A System of Ambition: British Foreign Policy, 1660–1793* (London, 1991).
Black, Jeremy, *The British Abroad: The Grand Tour in the Eighteenth Century* (New York, 1992).
Bohls, Elizabeth, *Women Travel Writers and the Language of Aesthetics, 1716–1818* (Cambridge, 1995).
Curley, Thomas, *Samuel Johnson and the Age of Travel* (Athens, Ga, 1976).
Edwards, Philip, *The Story of the Voyage: Sea-Narratives in Eighteenth-Century England* (Cambridge, 1994).
Jones, J. R., *Britain and the World 1649–1815* (London, 1980).
Marshall, P. J., *The Great Map of Mankind: British Perceptions of the World in the Age of Enlightenment* (London, 1982).
Richardson, John, *Slavery and Augustan Literature: Swift, Pope, Gay* (London, 2004).

Thomas, P. D. G., *Revolution in America: Britain and the Colonies, 1763–1776* (Oxford, 1992).
Viviès, Jean, *English Travel Narratives in the Eighteenth Century: Exploring Genres* (Aldershot, 2002).

6 Versions of the self

Fox, Christopher, *Locke and Scriblerians: Identity and Consciousness in Early Eighteenth-Century Britain* (Berkeley, 1988).
Martin, Raymond, *Naturalisation of the Soul: Self and Personal Identity in the Eighteenth Century* (London, 2000).
McKeon, Michael, *The Origins of the English Novel, 1600–1740* (Baltimore, 1987).
Mullan, John, *Sentiment and Sociability: The Language of Feeling in the Eighteenth Century* (Oxford, 1988).
Porter, Roy, *Flesh in the Age of Reason* (London, 2003).
Sitter, John, *Literary Loneliness in Mid-Eighteenth-Century England* (Ithaca and London, 1982).
Todd, Dennis, *Imagining Monsters: Miscreations of the Self in Eighteenth-Century England* (Chicago, 1995).

7 Sex and gender

Ballaster, Rosalind, *Seductive Forms: Women's Amatory Fiction, 1684–1740* (Oxford, 1992).
Barash, Carol, *English Women's Poetry, 1649–1714: Politics, Community and Linguistic Authority* (Oxford, 1996).
Barker-Benfield, G. J., *The Culture of Sensibility: Sex and Society in Eighteenth-Century Britain* (Chicago, 1992).
Brant, Clare, and Purkiss, Diane, *Women, Texts and Histories 1575–1760* (London, 1992).
Craft-Fairchild, Catherine, *Masquerade and Gender: Disguise and Female Identity in Eighteenth-Century Fictions by Women* (Pennsylvania, 1993).
Hitchcock, Tim, *English Sexualities, 1750–1800* (Basingstoke, 1997).
Hobby, Elaine, *Virtue of Necessity: English Women's Writing, 1646-1688* (London, 1988).
Ingrassia, Catherine, *Authorship, Commerce, and Gender in Early Eighteenth-Century England: A Culture of Paper Credit* (Cambridge, 1988).

Kemmerer, Kathleen, *A Neutral Being Between the Sexes: Samuel Johnson's Sexual Politics* (Lewisburg, 1998).

McColley, Diane, *Milton's Eve* (Urbana, 1983).

Norton, Rictor, *Mother Clap's Molly House: The Gay Subculture in England, 1700–1830* (London, 1992).

Nussbaum, Felicity, *The Brink of All We Hate: English Satires on Women, 1660–1750* (Lexington, 1984).

Nussbaum, Felicity, *The Autobiographical Subject: Gender and Ideology in Eighteenth-Century England* (Baltimore, 1989).

Pollak, Ellen, *The Poetics of Sexual Myth: Gender and Ideology in the Verse of Swift and Pope* (Chicago, 1985).

Rumbold, Valerie, *Women's Place in Pope's World* (Cambridge, 1989).

Shoemaker, Robert, *Gender in English Society, 1650–1880: the Emergence of Separate Spheres* (London, 1988).

Stone, Lawrence, *The Family, Sex and Marriage in England 1500–1800* (abridged and revised, London, 1979).

Trumbach, Randolph, *Sex and the Gender Revolution: Heterosexuality and the Third Gender in Enlightenment London* (Chicago, 1998).

Vickery, Amanda, *The Gentleman's Daughter: Women's Lives in Georgian England* (New Haven, 1998).

8 Forward into the past

Clery, Emma, *The Rise of Supernatural Fiction, 1762–1800* (Cambridge, 1995).

Erskine-Hill, Howard, *The Augustan Idea in English Literature* (London, 1983).

Groom, Nick, *The Making of Percy's Reliques* (Oxford, 1999).

Groom, Nick, ed., *Thomas Chatterton and Romantic Culture* (Basingstoke, 1999).

Johnston, Arthur, *Enchanted Ground: The Study of Medieval Romance in the Eighteenth Century* (London, 1964).

Levine, Joseph M., *The Battle of the Books: History and Literature in the Augustan Age* (Ithaca, 1991).

Summerson, John, *The Architecture of the Eighteenth Century* (London, 1986).

Weinbrot, Howard, *Augustus Caesar in 'Augustan' England* (Princeton, 1978).

Index